AF600343

THE CATHOLIC UNIVERSITY OF AMERICA
CANON LAW STUDIES
Number 79

# APPEALS

## AN HISTORICAL SYNOPSIS AND COMMENTARY

A DISSERTATION

*Submitted to the Faculty of Canon Law of the Catholic University of America in Partial Fulfillment of the Requirements for the Degree of*

DOCTOR OF CANON LAW

BY

THOMAS ARTHUR CONNOLLY, J.C.L.,
*Priest of the Archdiocese of San Francisco*

THE CATHOLIC UNIVERSITY OF AMERICA
WASHINGTON, D. C.
1932

**Nihil Obstat:**

VALENTINUS T. SCHAAF, O.F.M., J.C.D.,
*Censor Deputatus.*

Washingtonii, D. C., die ii Maii, 1932.

**Imprimatur:**

EDWARDUS J. HANNA, D.D.,
*Archiepiscopus Sancti Francisci.*

Sancti Francisci, die iii Maii, 1932.



Printed by
THE PAULIST PRESS
New York, N. Y.

TO

THE MOST REVEREND

EDWARD JOSEPH HANNA, D.D.

ARCHBISHOP OF SAN FRANCISCO

PROMOTOR OF CLERICAL SCHOLARSHIP AND

CANONICAL DISCIPLINE

*in*

*Reverence and Gratitude*

*"Iudicii finis iustitia est"*

S. Ambros.—*"In Ps. cxviii," 14.*

# TABLE OF CONTENTS

PAGE

FOREWORD ..... xi

PART I

HISTORICAL CONSPECTUS

CHAPTER I. PRELIMINARY DISCUSSION ..... 1

1. NOTION ..... 1

2. DEFINITION ..... 3

3. DIVISION ..... 4

CHAPTER II. APPEALS IN ROMAN LAW ..... 8

ART. I. APPEALS IN EARLY ROMAN LAW ..... 9

ART. II. APPEALS IN IMPERIAL ROMAN LAW ..... 13

§1. Under the pre-Justinian Emperors ..... 13

§2. Under the Emperor Justinian ..... 21

CHAPTER III. APPEALS IN EARLY CANON LAW ..... 25

ART. I. FROM THE BEGINNING TO THE COUNCIL OF SARDICA ..... 25

ART. II. FROM THE COUNCIL OF SARDICA TO THE DECREE OF GRATIAN ..... 30

CHAPTER IV. APPELLATE LEGISLATION FROM THE DECREE OF GRATIAN TO THE COUNCIL OF TRENT 40

ART. I. THE DECREE OF GRATIAN ..... 40

ART. II. THE DECRETALS OF GREGORY IX ..... 43

ART. III. THE *Liber Sextus* OF BONIFACE VIII ..... 46

ART. IV. THE CONSTITUTIONS OF CLEMENT V ..... 47

PAGE

CHAPTER V. APPELLATE LEGISLATION FROM THE COUNCIL OF TRENT TO THE PROMULGATION OF THE CODE ........ 50

ART. I. THE COUNCIL OF TRENT ........ 50

ART. II. THE PAPAL CONSTITUTIONS ........ 52

ART. III. THE ROMAN CONGREGATIONS ........ 54

ART. IV. THE ROMAN TRIBUNALS ........ 57

## PART II

## THE PRESENT LEGISLATION

CHAPTER VI. THE RIGHT OF APPEAL ........ 63

CHAPTER VII. LEGAL RESTRICTIONS ON THE RIGHT OF APPEAL ........ 72

NO APPEAL FROM:

1. Sentence of the Roman Pontiff or of the Apostolic Signatura ........ 72
2. A Sentence of a Judge Delegated with the Clause *"Appellatione Remota"* ........ 73
3. A Sentence that is Invalid ........ 75
4. A Sentence that has become an Adjudged Matter ........ 77
5. A Sentence Pronounced in view of a Decisive Oath ........ 77
6. A Judicial Decree or an Interlocutory Sentence that has not Definitive Force ........ 79
7. A Sentence in a Cause that must be Speedily Defined ........ 81
8. A Sentence Pronounced against a Contumacious Person ........ 82
9. A Sentence Pronounced against a Person Who has Formally Renounced his Right to Appeal ........ 86

PAGE

CHAPTER VIII. THE INTERPOSITION OF AN APPEAL 89

ART. I. THE PROPER TRIBUNAL 90

§1. The Judge *a quo* and the Appellant 91

§2. The Judge *a quo* and the Judge *ad quem* 93

ART. II. THE PROPER TIME 102

§1. The Legal Term for an Appeal 103

§2. Legal Exceptions to the Prescribed Term 107

§3. The Lapse of the Term 110

ART. III. THE PROPER FORM 112

§1. The Oral Appeal 112

§2. The Written Appeal 114

CHAPTER IX. THE EFFECTS OF AN APPEAL 117

ART. I. THE EFFECTS OF AN APPEAL RELATIVE TO THE LITIGANTS 117

§1. The Appellee 118

§2. The Co-appellants 121

ART. II. THE EFFECTS OF AN APPEAL ON THE CAUSE PROPER 125

§1. The Suspensive Effect of an Appeal 126

§2. The Appeal *in devolutivo* 132

CHAPTER X. THE PROSECUTION OF AN APPEAL BEFORE THE ORDINARY COURT OF SECOND INSTANCE 138

ART. I. THE ORDINARY TRIBUNAL OF APPEAL 139

§1. The Question of Competence 140

§2. The Ordinary Appellate Tribunal 141

§3. The Mutual Relation of Tribunals 143

§4. Canonical Regulations for Appellate Courts 144

§5. The Principle:—"*A Delegato Appellatur ad Delegantem*" 145

PAGE

Art. II. The Prescribed Form ........ 153
Art. III. The Legal Term ........ 159
§1. *Tempus Utile Prorogabile* ........ 159
§2. The Legal Interruption of the Term ........ 162
§3. The Lapse of the Term ........ 164

CHAPTER XI. THE APPELLATE PROCESS ........ 167
Art. I. The "Litis Contestatio" ........ 167
Art. II. The "Litis Instantia" or Proceedings Proper ........ 170
§1. The Quashing of the Litis Instantia ........ 170
§2. The Presentation of Evidence in the Appellate Instance ........ 172
§3. Incidental Causes in the Appellate Instance ........ 175
A. Contempt of Court ........ 176
B. The Intervention of a Third Party ........ 177
§4. The *"Discussio Causae"* in the Appellate Instance ........ 181
Art. III. The Sentence and Subsequent Appeal ........ 182
§1. The Appeal from a Sentence Pronounced on Ordinary Appellate Causes ........ 182
§2. The Appeal from a Sentence Pronounced on a Matrimonial Cause in the Second Instance ........ 185
A. The Solemn Process ........ 185
B. The Documentary Process ........ 189
§3. The Determination of Costs ........ 191

BIBLIOGRAPHY ........ 195

## FOREWORD

THE initial chapter of Title XIV of the Fourth Book of the Code of Canon Law forms the subject matter of the present dissertation. This particular section of the Code contains the ordinances and prescriptions governing appeals in contentious (civil) causes and it is used likewise as the general norm for all appeals whether in criminal or matrimonial trials or in causes relative to Holy Orders or the religious state. It may be noted herewith relative to the Fourth Book, that the interpretation and application of the principles of judicial procedure contained therein is not accomplished without great difficulty. Such eminent canonists as De Luca, Bouix, Noval and Vidal bear witness to this fact in the prefaces to their respective works on trials and judgments and it is probably for this reason that relatively few commentators have *ex professo* subjected this section of the Code to any degree of exhaustive treatment. Consequently the interpretation and explanation of this particular part of ecclesiastical legislation has not yet advanced beyond the pioneer stage.

The object of the present dissertation is to give a theoretical and practical survey of the general legislation on appeals as contained in the Code of Canon Law. The subject matter is concerned primarily with a distinct question of judicial procedure and accordingly, there is afforded little opportunity for any speculative discussion of the question as such. However, the latter is not entirely overlooked for, not infrequently, the basis, nature and extent of special fundamental principles of procedure relative to the subject under consideration, will be submitted to a thorough and exhaustive investigation in the course of this work.

A study of this character must necessarily touch upon relevant points or incidental questions of canonical judicial procedure and processual formalities and it is presumed that the reader has some knowledge, however superficial, of these general norms, for it is obviously beyond the purpose and aim of this dissertation to engage in any detailed discussion of such concomitant questions. Where points of this nature are intimately connected with or have a direct bearing upon the subject under consideration, they will be subjected to a more complete examination, but, on the whole, reference will be made rather to standard canonical tracts that discuss *ex professo* the subjects at issue.

The work has been divided into two parts comprising an historical conspectus and a juridical survey of the present legislation. The former consists of a brief outline of the origin and development of this particular legal institution. It is not intended to be a thorough research work of original character for the opportunity of perusing the primary sources and documents is not at hand. The purpose is merely to delineate the historical evolution of this judicial remedy through the centuries preceding the publication of the Code. Special attention has been devoted to the development of appeals in Roman Law for the reason that the Roman Law of the first five centuries of the Christian Era, has long been considered as a suppletory source of Canon Law, particularly with regard to judicial procedure. The second part of the dissertation presents for consideration a juridical commentary and interpretation of the principles of the present law relative to appeals.

The writer wishes to take this occasion to give public expression of his gratitude to the Most Reverend Edward Joseph Hanna, D.D., Archbishop of San Francisco, for the privilege of advanced study, to the members of the Faculty of the School of Canon Law for their assistance in the preparation of this monograph, to Monsignor Philip Bernadini, S.T.D., J.U.D., Dean of the School of Canon Law, for the use of his library, to the librarians of the University Library for their many courtesies and to all who have aided him by their constant, inspiring encouragement and unfailing support.

# PART I

## HISTORICAL CONSPECTUS

## CHAPTER I

## PRELIMINARY DISCUSSION

1. Notion. Human justice is not infallible. It is evident that the Church, though founded by God for the holiest of purposes, was and is composed of members whose actions may be colored by error, ignorance or prejudice, that even in the beginning when there existed "one heart and one soul" among the faithful, it had, and therefore, *a fortiori*, in its later existence will continue to have its *actor* and *reus*, its plaintiff and defendant, its civil suits and criminal accusations. The Holy Ghost assures us that every man may err, "Omnis homo mendax." [1] Accordingly and by the same reasoning, every ecclesiastical judge or superior is liable to error in his actions, judgments and decisions. While a definitive sentence ordinarily settles in a decisive and final manner, the merits of a controverted cause, and as such, is presumed to be right and just and to have been pronounced in accordance with the provisions of the law and in compliance with the demands of strict justice, yet it can happen that the sentence in question may be unjust, considered in itself or with respect to the merits of the cause proper. To guard against the unfortunate results attendant upon any possible miscarriage of justice, the judiciary system of the Church, as of any perfect society, possesses certain legal remedies, the application of which will protect the rights of parties engaged in an action who consider the sentence pronounced against them as unjust. The defendant and the plaintiff as well, must have the right of calling upon a higher authority for protection against any manifest injustice, a right which is found embodied in the following modes of legal redress—appeal (*appellatio*)[2] and complaint of nullity (*querela nullitatis*)[3] which are termed the ordinary remedies and the opposition of a third party (*oppositio tertii*)[4] and the restoration of

[1] Psalm CXV, v. 11.

[2] Canons 1879-1891.

[3] Canons 1892-1897.

[4] Canons 1898-1901.

a cause to its former condition (*restitutio in integrum*)[5] declared to be the extraordinary remedies.[6]

It is with the first of these modes of legal redress that this paper is concerned. Appeal affects an *unjust*, not an invalid sentence. It was instituted to remove a grievance or injury unjustly inflicted, or to correct the injustice, inexperience, want of knowledge or other defect of the judge who pronounced the sentence in the first instance, or finally, to enable the litigant who, either through ignorance or negligence, has failed to establish his case properly in the first instance, to remedy this defect in the second instance, the court of appeal.

The Catholic Church is a perfect society, having in itself, all the means necessary to attain its end,[7] and accordingly, it has ever vindicated its right to be completely free and independent of any human power or authority in the matter of fulfilling the purpose for which it was established. Being a perfect society, it has the right of exacting from its adherents everything that is necessary for the complete fulfillment of its end.[8] To effect this properly, it possesses a threefold power, legislative, judicial and coercive,[9] founded on the proposition that the Church is a *societas inaequalis*, that all its members do not enjoy equal rights, that there are rulers and subjects, superiors and inferiors, governors and governed.[10] The judicial power of the Church, concerned as it is with the appreciation of a particular act or series of acts in relation to a particular law, is exercised in accordance with the institution of a hierarchical order. By divine law, there are two grades of tribunals, the Supreme Pontiff upon whom was conferred the primacy of jurisdiction in the person of St. Peter, and the bishops, inferior and subject to the former, who possess ordinary jurisdiction to govern and judge portions of the Church committed to their care. By ecclesiastical law, however,

[5] Canons 1905-1907.

[6] Vermeersch-Creusen, *Epitome*, III, n. 235; Noval, *De Processibus*, n. 635; Roberti, *De Processibus*, I, n. 460.

[7] Chelodi, *Jus de Personis*, n. 15; Ojetti, *Commentarium*, II, p. 121; Roberti, *De Processibus*, I, n. 35 ff.; Vermeersch-Creusen, *Epitome*, I, n. 1.

[8] Canon 1496; Chelodi, *Jus de Personis*, n. 19.

[9] Wernz-Vidal, *De Processibus*, n. 18; *De Personis*, n. 48; Noval, *De Processibus*, n. 43; Chelodi, *Jus de Personis*, n. 19.

[10] De Meester, *Compendium*, I, n. 147.

there are constituted three grades of tribunals and it is with the latter that this work is primarily concerned for it is the main purpose of the judicial remedy under consideration to eliminate as far as possible the possibility of human error by an authoritative review of sentences and decisions pronounced in the several courts.[11]

2. Definition. To appeal, in the strict sense, is to invoke the aid of a superior judge for the purpose of obtaining redress against an injury or grievance, either already inflicted or about to be inflicted by an inferior judge.[12] It is a legal application made to a higher court on account of an unjust sentence that has been rendered in a particular cause by a lower court. The reason for the appeal is the injustice of the sentence itself and the aim of the appeal is to obtain redress against such a sentence by submitting it to a superior judge so that the latter may revoke or correct it. It is a plea directed to an appellate judge for assistance in the protection of the legal rights of the party in question, which rights have been violated or unduly abridged by the sentence pronounced by the lower tribunal, the court of first instance.[13]

An appeal has the appearance of a complaint made against the inferior judge by reason of the sentence rendered by him on the cause in question and it partakes also of the nature of an accusation made by the appellant against the court of first instance. This, however, is not the principal purpose of an appeal. The primary object is the revision of the impugned sentence for the benefit of the

[11] Roberti, *De Processibus,* I, n. 80; Noval, *De Processibus,* n. 95; Wernz-Vidal, *De Processibus,* n. 67. The foregoing remarks relative to the *Jus Publicum Ecclesiasticum* are made here merely by way of introduction. Cf. Ottaviani, *Institutiones Juris Publici Ecclesiastici,* I, nn. 38, 46 and 145 ff. and Cappello, *Summa Juris Publici Ecclesiastici,* nn. 56, 65 and 180 ff. for a complete treatment of these points.

[12] Schmalzgrueber, lib. II, tit. XXVIII, n. 1.

[13] Wernz-Vidal, *De Processibus,* n. 600, note 6; Vermeersch-Creusen, *Epitome,* III, n. 237; Roberti, *De Processibus,* II, n. 467; Noval, *De Processibus,* n. 638; De Meester, *Compendium,* III, *pars* 2, n. 1601. The concept of appeal as contained in canon 1879, particularly with regard to the element of injustice, is not absolute or exclusive for in canon 1986, the defender of the marriage bond is required to appeal from the first sentence of nullity rendered in a matrimonial cause, regardless of whether or not the sentence appears unjust to him.

aggrieved party and in the interests of justice.[14] The appeal itself does not give rise to a new process. It is rather the continued prosecution of the former process for it involves the same parties and is extended to the entire cause of the preceding instance, unless the sentence was only partially appealed. It can never exceed the limits of the first instance.[15]

3. Division. An appeal is allowed only against an *unjust*, never an invalid sentence; similarly, it is never conceded against a decree, whether judicial or administrative. It may be interposed only in a judicial process.[16] Before the promulgation of the Code, appeals were ordinarily classified as judicial or extrajudicial. The former were concerned with definitive sentences or interlocutory judgments that had the force of a definitive sentence, pronounced by a judge acting in his legal, judicial capacity, at the end of a trial that was conducted according to the accepted norms of judicial procedure.[17] It presupposes a valid sentence in compliance with the law and according to the facts of the cause.[18]

An appeal was said to be extrajudicial when it was interposed against administrative decrees of a superior or a judge. In this case the superior does not act in a strictly judicial capacity nor does his decision take the form of a sentence. This mode of redress was ordinarily used against episcopal decrees of whatever nature and is improperly called an appeal.[19] The Code does not make use of the expression "extrajudicial appeal" but designates this legal remedy simply as "recourse"—*recursus*.[20] Recourse is a plain and informal act and it is usually made directly to the Holy See. It may be used, subject to the prescriptions of the Code, against decrees of an administrative, disciplinary or judicial nature and ordinarily, it has only a devolutive effect.[21]

[14] Schmalzgrueber, lib. II, tit. XXVIII, n. 1; Noval, *De Processibus*, n. 638; Roberti, *De Processibus*, II, n. 467.

[15] Roberti, *De Processibus*, II, n. 462.

[16] Canons 1880, nn. 3, 6; 1601; Noval, *De Processibus*, n. 642.

[17] Lega, *De Judiciis*, I, n. 618; Schmalzgrueber, lib. II, tit. XXVIII, n. 4.

[18] Cocchi, *De Processibus*, n. 222.

[19] Bouix, *De Judiciis*, II, p. 246.

[20] Noval, *De Processibus*, n. 642; Wernz-Vidal, *De Processibus*, n. 600, note 9; Vermeersch-Creusen, *Epitome*, III, n. 237; can. 1601.

[21] Wernz-Vidal, *De Processibus*, n. 600; cf. canons 296, §2; 298; 345; 454;

An appeal is regarded as "just" when it is made for a reasonable or probably reasonable cause. It is admitted and conceded in matters of great and even of less importance if the sentence rendered is valid and there is some foundation for the claim that the judgment pronounced is in some manner unjust.[22] It is termed "frivolous" when it is based on futile or inane reasons, "frustratory" when made merely for the purpose of delaying the just execution of the sentence or of prolonging the final settlement of the trial itself.[23]

Canonists generally admit that any person has a natural right to appeal to a higher authority against injustice. They concede this when appeal is understood or regarded in a general manner, merely as a species of defense or a remedy against a malicious or manifestly unjust judgment of a superior, for a legitimate defense may be denied to none. When, however, appeal properly so called, or judicial, is considered in a strict sense, certainly it is not derived from the natural law. For otherwise, the Supreme Pontiff, in reserving to Himself the decisive and final settlement of special causes that admit no appeal whatever,[24] would be violating the natural law; the same condition would exist in those cases that are occasionally committed by the Pope to delegated judges with the restriction, *appellatione remota;*[25] finally the Code itself[26] prohibits the interposition of an appeal against certain sentences of a particular nature, a restriction that would also infringe upon or transgress the natural law. The right to appeal strictly speaking from an unjust sentence, then, is based not on the natural but on ecclesiastical law for it may be exercised only in accordance with the formalities, prescriptions

513; 1340, §3; 1395, §2; 1428, §3; 2146, §1; 2243, §1 for decrees that can be made only *in devolutivo;* and canons 498; 647, §2, n. 4; 1569, §2; 2287 that permit recourse *in suspensivo.* Cf. also Augustine, *A Commentary,* VII, *appendix* II, p. 485.

[22] Bouix, *De Judiciis,* II, p. 248; Lega, *De Judiciis,* I, n. 631; Wernz-Vidal, *De Processibus,* n. 600.

[23] Vermeersch-Creusen, *Epitome,* III, n. 237; Schmalzgrueber, lib. II, tit. XXVIII, n. 5; Lega, *De Judiciis,* I, n. 631; cf. *A. S. S.,* IV (1869), 382.

[24] Canon 1557, §1.

[25] Canon 1880, n. 2.

[26] Canon 1880.

and provisions determined by the Code, that is to say, positive law.[27]

Finally, the interposition of an appeal may have a devolutive or a suspensive effect on the sentence appealed. An appeal from a definitive sentence or from an interlocutory judgment that has the force of a final sentence, has a devolutive effect when the entire cause that has been appealed, together with all its accessories, passes or devolves from the inferior judge to the appellate tribunal to which the cause has been appealed. The latter, the superior judge henceforth takes cognizance of the cause in question, admits it into his tribunal to pass upon the admissibility or legality of the appeal and if admitted, to decide eventually the issue itself, to affirm, modify or annul the judgment of the lower court: in short, to pass final judgment on the cause itself.[28]

The suspensive effect of an appeal consists in this that the appeal stays the effect of the sentence; the latter cannot be executed and the jurisdiction of the judge in the cause is likewise suspended with regard to the carrying out of the sentence appealed. The legal force of an otherwise valid judgment is suspended, the execution thereof is prevented and the judge of the first instance is hindered from taking any further action in the matter. The entire cause is left *in statu quo,* subject, however, to provisional execution of the sentence under certain circumstances determined by the Code.[29] Moreover, in accordance with the principle, *lite pendente, nihil innovetur,*[30] when the law permits an appeal *in suspensivo,* the acts of the judge of first instance, performed in violation of this principle not only after an appeal has been interposed or while it is

[27] Schmalzgrueber, lib. II, tit. XXVIII, n. 6; Leurenius, lib. II, tit. XXVIII, q. 1006; Bouix, *De Judiciis,* II, p. 247; Lega, *De Judiciis,* I, nn. 619, 620; Peries, *La Procédure Canonique Moderne,* pp. 228-230; Noval, *De Processibus,* n. 639; Wernz-Vidal, *De Processibus,* n. 601.

[28] Lega, *De Judiciis,* I, n. 627; Wernz-Vidal, *De Processibus,* n. 607; Roberti, *De Processibus,* II, n. 477; Vermeersch-Creusen, *Epitome,* III, n. 240; canon 1889.

[29] Lega, *De Judiciis,* I, n. 625; Roberti, *De Processibus,* II, n. 476; Vermeersch-Creusen, *Epitome,* III, n. 240; Noval, *De Processibus,* n. 653; De Meester, *Compendium,* III, *pars* 2, n. 1605; canons 1889, 1917, §2.

[30] Canon 1889, §1.

pending, but also during the ten days allowed for the filing of an appeal, are to be revoked by the appellate judge.[31]

The foregoing brief preliminary notions regarding this legal institution are given here in summary form merely for the purpose of granting the reader a knowledge of appeals sufficiently clear and concise as to enable him to understand rightly the gradual development of the remedy itself. They are not intended to be complete in any manner for they must of necessity be more fully enlarged upon in the second part of this work, the commentary on the present appellate legislation in the Code of Canon Law.

[31] Wernz-Vidal, *De Processibus,* n. 607; Roberti, *De Processibus,* II, n. 476.

## CHAPTER II

## APPEALS IN ROMAN LAW

ROMAN LAW has been called the law of all the world. It did not suffer destruction upon the fall of the Roman State but continued its influence on the law of each nation that was subsequently carved out of the fallen Empire. Its form was changed somewhat to accommodate the varying demands pursuant to its adoption by other nations but substantially, Roman Law as codified by Justinian exerted widespread influence on the legal institutions of other nations. The Church was no exception to this rule. Probably no part of Canon Law is so thoroughly based upon and governed by the principles of Roman Law as the first section of the Fourth Book: *De Judiciis.* The reason for this is evident for Roman Law, due particularly to the influence of the Church on the Christian Emperors, rested on principles of natural justice and equity and the incorporation of the Roman jurisprudence relative to judicial procedure into ecclesiastical codes of law was accomplished without great difficulty. Certain statutes and prescriptions were of necessity changed and modified to harmonize with the divine mission of the Church. This resulted in time in the formation and establishment of a procedural system of law that was by far more perfect than its contributory source.[1] The legal prescriptions relative to appeal were incorporated practically in the same manner as the other principles of judicial procedure.

It is somewhat difficult to classify the development of Roman Law into logical periods for the purpose of tracing the development of any one legal system. For the sake of clearness, the division will follow the order selected by most writers and more or less covered by extant writings and sources, namely, the period of early Roman Law embracing practically the entire Republic and the beginning of

[1] Noval, *De Processibus,* n. 34. Cf. also c. 7, C. II, q. 1; c. 38, C. XI, q. 1; c. 2, C. XXI, q. 6; c. 1, X, *de novi operis nuntiatione,* V, 32; Roberti, *De Processibus,* I, n. 2; Maroto, *Institutiones,* I, n. 380.

the Empire and the period of Imperial Roman Law beginning with the second century of the Christian Era and ending with the promulgation of the Justinian Code and Novels toward the middle of the sixth century. Roman Law as codified under Justinian was not a new system of legal jurisprudence but a collection of doctrines and institutions that had matured in the years preceding the reign of Justinian, the most important development taking place under the celebrated jurists of the classical age, Labeo, Julianus, Gaius, Scaevola, Celsus, Papinianus, Ulpianus and Paulus.[2] The writings and treatises of these jurists form the major part of the *Digest* of Justinian; the *Code* of the latter is a consolidation of the Gregorian, Hermogenian and Theodosian Codes. The later development of Roman Law, such as it was, exercised no great influence on ecclesiastical legislation and consequently there is no advantage to be gained in following its progress through the years to the twelfth century.

## Article I. Appeals in Early Roman Law

The law of the City of Rome had already completed a long course of development under the Monarchy before the few scanty historical writings take up the narrative of the legal activities of its rulers. The history of the early stages of Roman Law is very uncertain and it is the tendency of modern higher criticism to discount to a great extent the supposed historical account of Roman Law given by such writers as Cicero, Livy, Pliny, Sallust and others. The conclusions drawn by these authors are greatly influenced by legends and by a tradition that was not at all times of the most reliable variety. Yet these writings yield a picture of Roman jurisprudence, if such it may be called, in which may be found the germ of the great appellate system of a much later day. Naturally, in this early phase of development, the various judicial formalities accompanying this judicial remedy are not to be found. Solemnity of court procedure was introduced gradually, advancing step by step with the growth and development of the Empire itself. It is likewise to be noted that in the beginning, this appellate institution is concerned

[2] Sohm-Ledlie, *Institutes of Roman Law*, n. 18.

exclusively with criminal causes, a fact or condition of things that persisted almost to the second century A. D. Thereafter, there was no substantial distinction between appeals in criminal causes or in civil actions, although the procedural formalities of either differed somewhat.[3] The appellate system in civil or criminal causes developed during the Imperial epoch along identical lines. Both evolved in a somewhat similar manner.[4]

During the Monarchy or in the regal period of Roman Law, the king was the source of all power and the final arbiter in all criminal causes. The majority of historians are of the opinion that, if not in the beginning, at least after some time, there was an appeal to the people, a *provocatio ad populum*, from any judgment of the king or his delegates involving the life of a citizen. It is mentioned by Cicero[5] and other authors. The privilege was probably restricted to the patrician caste, there being no appeal allowed in the case of plebeians. However, the question here rests on no strong historical foundation. There was no question of appeal during this period, relative to *private law*. Each family was a separate and distinct unit; the administration of all matters was carried out individually in each family. When disputes rose between the heads of families, the State did not interfere. Later, however, the State introduced methods of arbitration for the final and just settlement of such controversies.

*Criminal causes*. In the time of the Republic the tribunals of justice were independent of each other, for the criminal jurisdiction heretofore exercised by the kings, passed to consuls and other magistrates upon whom had been conferred the sovereign power of the people.[6] There was no actual subordination of courts at this time and consequently no opportunity of appealing from a lower to a higher tribunal. Yet, there were remedies, recourse to which could be had by any citizen under condemnation for the commission of a

[3] Strachan-Davidson, *Problems of the Roman Criminal Law*, II, p. 177.

[4] Mommsen, *Strafrecht*, p. 469; Mommsen, *Droit Pénal Romain*, II, p. 155—"L'appel du droit civil et celui du droit criminel ont toujours marché de pair et ont suivi en principe un développement identique." Cf. also Strachan-Davidson, *Problems of the Roman Criminal Law*, II, p. 191.

[5] *De Re Publica*, 2, 31.

[6] Hunter, *An Introduction to Roman Law*, p. 1044.

crime. They were the *provocatio ad populum* mentioned above in connection with the law of Rome under the Monarchy, and the magisterial *veto*. Neither of these is a judicial appeal strictly so-called but each has in it some elements of this institution; the former, in as much as the guilty person has the opportunity of submitting his case to a review and the latter, in so far as the judicial process is delayed and the threatened sentence temporarily averted.

The *provocatio ad populum* was an appeal made by a prisoner from a sentence pronounced by a magistrate to the *Populus Romanus* in the *comitia centuriata* which in turn confirmed or rejected the condemnatory sentence. The first important consequence of the *provocatio* on procedure was that the superior magistrate withdrew from administering ordinary criminal justice.[7] This system of *provocatio* endured from its legal establishment by the *Lex Valeria* to the institution of the permanent criminal courts, the *quaestiones perpetuae* by the *Lex Calpurnia* in 149 B. C. Thereafter, it ceased to be exercised for the reason that the formalities of judicial procedure were being worked out gradually, a process that was advanced greatly by the multiplication of courts. Already in the provinces, this fact was recognized and toward the end of the last century of the Republic, any Roman citizen convicted on a criminal charge in a province, could appeal to Rome from the sentence of the governor of the province. But provincial subjects had no such right and the provincial governor might punish them not only by scourging and imprisonment but even by death without granting them the benefit of an appeal.[8]

The magisterial *veto* seems to have been frequently exercised. In as much as each Roman magistrate had been endowed with the sovereign power of the people, any official act of one magistrate could be frustrated by the *veto*, "I forbid," of another magistrate of equal authority.[9] Any citizen could demand this stopping of the acts of a magistrate and this request was called *appellatio* though it was not strictly an appeal. The right of the *veto* belonged especially to the tribune of the people who could exercise it over all magistrates

[7] Strachan-Davidson, *Problems of the Roman Criminal Law*, I, pp. 127, 153.
[8] Sherman, *Roman Law in the Modern World*, II, n. 885.
[9] *Dig.*, 5, 1, 58.

except dictators. The tribune could veto even the acts of a consul or a praetor. Yet a veto did not amend any judicial act but merely stopped it temporarily.[10] Evidences of the exercise of this prerogative may be found in the works of Cicero.[11]

In *private law* during the early period, there was no appeal strictly so-called, as is evident from the methods of procedure employed. The civil process *in iure* or *in iudicio* permitted no appeal as such; this is true of the period of the *Legis Actio* and of the time of the *Formulary System* which followed. However, the declaration of a magistrate given in the process *in iure* could be annulled by the *intercessio* of a coordinate or a superior authority, that is, by means of a counter order of equal imperative force. One order simply stayed the execution of the other. This was a form of the magisterial *veto* as exercised in civil cases.[12] Sohm [13] considers this fact as one of the most important in the development of the system of appeals in Roman Law. Leage [14] speaks of the *restitutio in integrum,* which will be explained later, in connection with the method of dispensing justice in the Empire and declares that this remedy together with the former procedure paved the way for the new system of appeals that began under the Empire and that was perfected, or rather completed by the time of Marcus Aurelius, whereby a litigant might take his case on appeal from the judge who pronounced the sentence to the praetor who appointed him and from the praetor to the *praefectus urbis* and thence to the Emperor.

There is to be seen, therefore, in this first period of Roman Law, some foundation for the great appellate system that progressed rapidly during the early stages of the Empire. While there was no strictly judicial appeal from one judge or magistrate to another immediately superior, most of the necessary elements in a judicial appeal were gradually being assembled and this fact, together with a better understanding of the administration of justice in general and the concomitant desire to see that it be meted out impartially, aided

[10] Sherman, *Roman Law in the Modern World,* II, n. 885.
[11] *Pro Quinctio,* n. 63; *Pro Tullio,* n. 38.
[12] Costa, *Profilo Storico del Processo Civile Romano,* p. 64.
[13] Sohm-Ledlie, *Institutes of Roman Law,* p. 228.
[14] *Roman Private Law,* p. 378.

in no small degree in the establishment of the correct procedural formalities.

## Article II. Appeals in Imperial Roman Law

The Roman Law of this period has left to posterity a wealth of splendid juristic principles, principles that have exerted a wide influence on the canon and civil law of all ages. Its greatest period of development occurred in the classical age, comprising the second century and the first half of the third during which the great jurists of the time made their outstanding contribution to the development of scientific jurisprudence. However, at best, the appellate system was only gradually evolved and many inaccuracies and much obscure legislation will be noted before the finished product is presented.

### §1. *Under the pre-Justinian Emperors*

The practice of generally appealing to the Emperor who was authorized to withdraw any suit in the Empire from the ordinary courts for the purpose of bringing it before his own tribunal, led during this period to the immediate development of the modern system of appeal under which the courts are ranged in a series of lower and higher instances, the higher court trying the cause over again for the purpose of pronouncing a new sentence on the matter in question.[15] The entire judicial system of the Republic was gradually changed and replaced by a more centralized and consequently more effective form of judicial organization. Upon the advent of the *cognitio extraordinaria* for civil actions in the first days of the Empire, a system which later became the ordinary norm for all court trials, all sentences were appealable, unless otherwise explicitly restricted by law. Under this method of procedure, the two stages of judgment *in iure* and *in iudicio* disappeared and the magistrate or his delegate before whom the cause was introduced, heard and decided the entire affair.[16] The independent magistrates of the Republic were thus displaced by dependent officials. However, some vestiges of the former system are yet to be found in the early stages of the Empire. For the first three centuries, the consuls are con-

[15] Sohm-Ledlie, *Institutes of Roman Law*, p. 228, note 5.
[16] Buckland, *A Text Book of Roman Law*, p. 604.

tinued as magistrates but they are gradually stripped of their power. The number of praetors was considerably enlarged but the *praetor urbanus* and the *preaetor peregrinus* soon lost their original civil and criminal jurisdiction. The tribune of the people continued to exercise his right of *veto* and *intercessio* but only under the superior authority of the Emperor. The provincial governor, as in the time of the Republic remained in control of the provinces. He was still a powerful judicial officer and had jurisdiction both civil and criminal, although the former extended only to persons domiciled in his province.[17]

A brief survey of the newer court officials will give an idea of the system employed and will be of considerable aid in the interpretation of subsequent legislation on the subject of appeals during this period. The city prefect, *praefectus urbis,* was a transformed magistrate of the Republic. In time he acquired the functions of the praetor and became next to the Emperor, the supreme civil and criminal magistrate during the early Empire.[18] His jurisdiction comprised the city of Rome and all adjacent territory to the extent of a hundred miles.[19] An appeal lay from him to the Emperor.[20] During the later Empire, the city prefect was continued in office but his prominence declined in favor of the newer and more important praetorian prefect [21] who gradually became his superior, so that an appeal could be made from the city prefect to the praetorian prefect.

The office of praetorian prefect was created by Augustus. In the beginning he was the aide-de-camp and bodyguard of the Emperor but soon became endowed with civil and criminal jurisdiction. In the third century he superseded the city prefect and for the remainder of the Empire, the praetorian prefecture, next to the Emperor, was the highest court in the land. Three of the greatest Roman jurists were praetorian prefects, Papinian, Paul and Ulpian.[22] All Italy beyond a hundred miles from Rome was subject to the jurisdiction of the praetorian prefect and all appeals both in civil

[17] Sherman, *Roman Law in the Modern World,* II, nn. 888-890.

[18] *Dig.,* 1, 12, 1, §§ 1, 7, 8, 14.

[19] *Dig.,* 1, 12, 1, 4.

[20] *Dig.,* 4, 4, 38; 45, 1, 122, 5.

[21] *Dig.,* 1, 11; *Cod.,* 1, 26, 27; 12, 3.

[22] *Dig.,* 12, 1, 40.

and criminal causes were made from the provincial governors to this official.[23] Although, originally the law made no provision for an appeal from the judgment of the praetorian prefect,[24] in the fourth century it was possible to have such a sentence reviewed by petitioning the Emperor for this purpose. There is some controversy relative to the practise of appealing from the sentences of the praetorian prefect and legislation on the question is obscure and even at times contradictory.[25]

Appointment of other officials was also made during this period. These exercised jurisdiction over civil and criminal causes of a minor or less important nature. The prefect of police in the city of Rome under Augustus, may be mentioned in this connection. An appeal from his decision could be made to the city prefect or even to the Emperor if the matter was important.[26] The prefect of the food supplies, *praefectus annonae,* also possessed civil and criminal jurisdiction and an appeal could be made from his sentence likewise to the city prefect.[27] The *defensores civitatum,* provincial city magistrates of the later Empire, created by Valentinian I in 364 [28] enjoyed petty civil and criminal jurisdiction [29] and appeals from their judgments were heard before the provincial governors.[30] Permanent petty judges, *judices pedanei,* are mentioned in a statute of Diocletian abolishing early formulary procedure [31] and in the later Empire, they were delegated by the Emperor, by the provincial governor or by law to hear petty cases. An appeal could be taken from the sentence of a petty judge to the court of the provincial governor.[32]

With the establishment of the foregoing judicial organization, the groundwork for the ensuing appellate system was laid out with all the essential elements present. All appeals from any part of the

[23] *Dig.,* 12, 1, 40; 22, 1, 3, 3; *Cod.,* 7, 62, 32; 9, 2, 6.

[24] *Dig.,* 1, 11, 1, 1; *Cod. Theod.,* 11, 30, 16; *Cod.,* 7, 62, 19.

[25] See in this connection *Cod.,* 1, 19, 5; 7, 42; 7, 62, 30; 7, 62, 35; *Nov.,* 82, 12.

[26] *Dig.,* 1, 15, 3, §§ 1 and 4; 12, 4, 15; 47, 2, 57 (56), 1; 19, 2, 56; 20, 2, 9.

[27] *Dig.,* 48, 2, 13; 14, 1, 1, 18.

[28] *Cod. Theod.,* 1, 29, 1; *Cod.,* 1, 55.

[29] *Cod. Theod.,* 1, 29, 7; *Cod.,* 1, 55, 1 and 3; *Nov.,* 15, 6.

[30] *Cod.,* 7, 62, 5; 10, 32 (31), 2; *Nov.,* 15, 5.

[31] *Cod.,* 3, 3, 2.

[32] *Cod.,* 2, 7, 25; 3, 3.

Empire and from any inferior judge could be laid before the praetorian prefect or even before the Emperor if they were concerned with important matters, regardless of the standing or the position held by the court of first instance.[33] The Emperor's appellate jurisdiction was, therefore, ample and varied; he could in addition delegate the hearing of an appeal which he could not decide personally, to some inferior judge.[34] Appeals in less important matters in the provinces were heard by the provincial governor. His was the court of appeal from local, city or petty magistrates; from the governor, an appeal could be taken to the city prefect or to the praetorian prefect.[35]

If the case was in any way difficult or involved, the Emperor could give an opinion by rescript at the request of a subordinate judge or even of the litigant himself. The Emperor could therefore act also as the court of first instance in addition to being the court of appeal.[36]

There is a wealth of legislation regarding appeals during this period but it is somewhat difficult to give the correct appellate procedure of any one time or age because the legislation is not in good order, the statutes were issued to take care of emergency conditions and no attempt was made to coordinate and arrange them till much later. Appeals were allowed not only from final judgments but also in many instances from interlocutory sentences.[37] Notice of appeal was given in court vocally by the use of the word "appello" or by applying in writing for dimissorial letters within two or three days from the time that the sentence was communicated to the litigant, two days if the appellant was conducting his own cause, three if as a guardian or a proxy, he was acting for another. The dimissorial letters were called *apostoli;* the pre-Justinian legislation contained

[33] *Cod. Theod.*, 11, 30, constits., 3, 8, 11, 13, 16, 23, 29, 30, 44, 61, 62; 11, 34, 2; *Cod.*, 7, 62, constits., 2, 23, 38; *Nov.*, 23, 3.

[34] *Cod. Theod.*, 11, 30, 16.

[35] *Dig.*, 49, 1, 6; *Cod.*, 7, 62, 29.

[36] *Cod. Theod.*, 11, 29, 1; 11, 30, 55; 9, 21, 2, 3; 9, 40, 10; *Cod.*, 12, 1, 16. This method of referring cases to the Emperor is shown by the titles in the *Code* and the *Digest* which treat of appeals and the former procedure together. *Dig.*, 49, 1, *de appellationibus et relationibus* and *Cod.*, 7, 62, *de appellationibus et consultationibus*.

[37] *Dig.*, 49, 5, 2.

no definite time within which they were to be presented to the judge of the court of appeal.[38] The days on which the judge was not accessible were not counted and if the appellant himself was absent, the term was computed from the time that knowledge of the sentence was communicated to him.[39] Five days were allowed in which to obtain the *apostoli* containing the facts of the cause, the names of the parties and the judge and all other necessary information. Later on in this period, when the time for presenting the dimissorial letters to the judge of the appellate court was determined, failure to submit them within the stated time involved defeat by prescription. If the judge from whose sentence the appeal was made, refuses to allow the appeal, a further appeal may be made on this refusal.[40] Appeals were also allowed from the judgment given in pursuance to a rescript of the Emperor but in this instance, the Emperor was not lightly to be consulted and only if it could be proved that the facts in the cause were not stated accurately.[41] Appeals from sentences imposing pecuniary penalties were also permitted at this time but only if they were severe and burdensome.[42] Appeals that were interposed merely for the purpose of delaying the execution of a just sentence or of obstructing the process of a trial were not to be heard nor admitted.[43]

In the time of Diocletian and probably before, an appeal entailed the rehearing of the entire cause and in addition, new facts could be introduced and new witnesses produced.[44] If an appeal was made successfully and the sentence revised, the reversal of the sentence benefited others associated in the trial even though the latter had not appealed.[45] In criminal trials, an acquittal was not final and the accuser could appeal the cause in order to have the sentence reversed.[46] In the beginning of the third century, it was

[38] *Dig.*, 49, 7.
[39] *Dig.*, 49, 5, 2, 5, 4.
[40] *Dig.*, 49, 5, 5.
[41] *Dig.*, 49, 1, 1; 49, 3, 1.
[42] *Cod. Theod.*, 11, 29, 1.
[43] *Dig.*, 49, 5, 4.
[44] *Dig.*, 49, 1, 13 *pr.*; 49, 1, 17 *pr.*; 49, 5, 1.
[45] *Dig.*, 49, 1, 10, 4.
[46] *Dig.*, 49, 14, 9.

stated that not only the person condemned by a sentence could appeal but also any other interested party could appeal on behalf of the former.[47]

The right of appeal was expressly granted by law, subject to the restrictions determined by the law itself. In the year 340, Constantius declares that "both in civil and criminal causes, in which the fate of a man's life and property is involved, all judges must admit appeals," [48] and the same statement is made a few years later with the threat of a heavy fine for the judge who refuses to obey the edict of the Emperor.[49] Valentinian in 364 imposed similar penalties [50] which were confirmed by Arcadius and Honorius in 399 with the statement "Know all men that from capital punishment and loss of goods, the right of appeal is granted." [51] When an appeal has been interposed against a sentence, the execution of the sentence is suspended or delayed, subject to the restrictions imposed by the law.[52] However, there is some ambiguity in connection with this feature of the suspensive effect of an appeal. The intention of the legislator is not always clearly determined with regard to the sentences that admit an appeal *in suspensivo* and those which must be executed in spite of any appeal. Certainly, the tendency is to delay the execution of the appealed sentence whenever possible, whether in criminal or in civil causes. In criminal causes particularly, an accused man who is condemned and appeals from the condemnatory sentence, must be considered innocent.[53] This same inclination is noticed also in those portions of the *Digest* that treat of criminal trials and judgments and the fate of the criminal himself when he interposes an appeal or when his appeal itself is pending.[54]

The law of the period also contains certain limitations on the right of appeal. For some matters, there was obviously no appeal necessary. The judge of the first instance could order the correction

[47] *Dig.*, 49, 1, 6.
[48] *Cod. Theod.*, 11, 30, 20.
[49] *Cod. Theod.*, 11, 30, 22 and 25.
[50] *Cod. Theod.*, 11, 30, 33.
[51] *Cod. Theod.*, 11, 30, 58.
[52] *Dig.*, 49, 5, 6, 7.
[53] *Dig.*, 49, 7, 1, 3.
[54] *Dig.*, 49, 6, 8; 49, 1, 25; 49, 11, 1; 49, 9, 1.

of all material errors that might appear in the record or himself rectify a sentence that was manifestly invalid. For example, a sentence that was pronounced upon a party to a cause who had died, was invalid;[55] a sentence was likewise defective and invalid if a defendant had been summoned to a trial by a peremptory edict or citation that had actually not been proposed to him or come to his notice,[56] or if a judge denied the existence of rights claimed by one of the parties to the suit and plainly granted to him by the imperial constitutions [57] or, finally, if the judge, in his sentence had ordered the performance of some action that was physically impossible.[58]

In other cases, however, limitations and restrictions of a different nature are observed. As early as the year 220, it was stated that a single appeal was not sufficient to compel the judge of first instance to grant dimissorial letters. The appellant must show that he has pressed his appeal long and earnestly.[59] In 240, the right of appeal is denied to certain notorious criminals who were guilty of treason or sedition [60] and in 317, Constantine refused the benefit of appeal to certain criminals who were convicted of heinous crimes against the State,[61] and particularly if the offender had confessed his crime or certain and clear proofs of his guilt were produced.[62] Constantius and Constans issued similar decrees in 344.[63] In 392, the Emperors Arcadius and Honorius prohibited under heavy penalties the postponement of the execution of judicial sentences under the pretext of appeal.[64] The same Emperors a few years later denied the privilege of appeal to all public debtors.[65] The Emperor Constantius seems to have been particularly severe in denying the benefit of appeal to certain classes of litigants. In 354, he threatened to fine the proconsul of Africa if the latter admitted futile appeals in treasury

[55] *Dig.*, 49, 8, 3.
[56] *Dig.*, 49, 8, 1, 3.
[57] *Dig.*, 49, 8, 1, 2.
[58] *Dig.*, 49, 8, 1, 3.
[59] *Dig.*, 49, 6, 2.
[60] *Dig.*, 49, 1, 16.
[61] *Cod. Theod.*, 9, 10, 1; 9, 22, 1; 9, 24, 1, 3.
[62] *Cod. Theod.*, 9, 40, 1; 11, 36, 1.
[63] *Cod. Theod.*, 9, 40, 4; 11, 36, 7.
[64] *Cod. Theod.*, 9, 40, 15.
[65] *Cod. Theod.*, 11, 36, 32.

cases [66] and in the following year, he forbade all such appeals.[67] Still later, he issued more rigorous prescriptions and it was somewhat difficult for the judges to ascertain just when to deny and when to allow an appeal. The Theodosian Code is replete with cases where perplexed judges and officials did not know how to interpret the will of the Emperors as outlined in their respective decrees,[68] or rescripts.[69]

The impression received after reading the Theodosian Code is that what a judge might or might not be allowed to do, depended to a great extent on his influence at the Emperor's court. The contradictory decrees and rescripts found in this particular body of legislation cause problems that puzzle even the most erudite students of Roman Law. However, the fact that appellate legislation was not well ordered or well defined during this period does not detract from the evidence of the development of the institution of appeal in the Roman Law of this era. A complete system of courts has been established wherein appeals are tried, admitted or rejected. The appeal must be made ordinarily to the tribunal that is immediately superior to the court of first instance. While the appeal is pending, it ordinarily has a certain suspensive effect that is not as yet well determined. The entire cause is retried, new evidence and new witnesses may be produced. The time allowed for the placing and the prosecution of an appeal is determined and during this term, nothing must be added to the case by the judge or by either party except as provided by law. Legislation defines who shall and who shall not have the benefit of an appeal. In short, every possible convenience is set up to assure a just sentence on every controverted cause whether civil or criminal, the latter occupying by far the more important position.

It should be remembered that at this time the Roman Empire was rent by civil war and disturbed by barbarian invasions and that the Emperors could spare little attention from the defense of their thrones and the necessity of meeting the demands of the exchequer

[66] *Cod. Theod.*, 11, 36, 10.
[67] *Cod. Theod.*, 11, 36, 12.
[68] *Cod. Theod.*, 11, 36, 4; 11, 36, 14; 9, 10, 1.
[69] *Cod. Theod.*, 1, 2, 2; 13, 10, 8; 12, 1, 36; 10, 10, 15; 11, 30, 6.

to be greatly interested in the juridical formalities of court procedure. This accounts in some measure for the evident contradiction seen in the imperial decrees and constitutions. Nevertheless, the development of the institution of appeal took place almost entirely during this period and the codification of the existing legislation by Justinian while it was a necessary and valuable contribution to Roman Law, was for the most part merely a reordering and revision of the enactments of his predecessors.

### §2. *Under the Emperor Justinian*

The codification of the existing legislation regarding court procedure and the clarification of the judicial formalities connected with trials, accomplished by Justinian, resulted in a definite and concise code of law, a code that was easily understood and readily interpreted. Abundant provision was made in this body of laws for the carrying of a cause by appeal from an inferior court to a superior tribunal.[70] An appeal to a superior judge was generally admitted against any definitive sentence.[71] In the matter of appeal from an interlocutory sentence, however, a change is noted from the preceding legislation. In the early Empire, such sentences were appealable but later, certain restrictions had been placed on them.[72] Under Justinian, they were prohibited.[73] The court of second instance either confirmed the decision, in which case the appellant was held liable for costs to the court and to the appellee, or revised it; it was not remitted for judgment to the inferior court.[74] Notice of an appeal was to be given verbally, "I appeal," as before, or in writing within ten days from receiving the knowledge of the sentence.[75] The appeal must be made *gradatim* through the regular channels and not from minor judges or tribunals to the highest courts

[70] Hunter, *Introduction to Roman Law,* pp. 71, 72, 1044-1048; Moyle, *Institutes of Justinian,* I, p. 665.

[71] *Cod.,* 7, 62, 3; cf. Vidal, *Institutiones Juris Civilis Romani,* n. 191.

[72] *Cod. Theod.,* 11, 36, 18.

[73] *Cod.,* 7, 62, 36; 7, 45, 16; cf. canon 1880, n. 6.

[74] Buckland, *A Text Book of Roman Law,* p. 665; cf. canon 1891, §1.

[75] *Nov.,* 23, *pr.,* 1; 119, 5; 123, 21. Cf. *Dig.,* 49, 1, 3 and 4, and canon 1881.

in the land.[76] The appellant was also obliged to give security for costs, which were fixed by the court.[77]

When an appeal was not interposed at the time that the sentence was pronounced, the proceedings were as follows. The appellant drafted a written petition of appeal, containing the names of all the parties to the suit and of the judge, the judgment rendered and the reasons for the appeal. Those interested in the appeal were to swear that the petition contained no evidence of fraud or deceit.[78] The petition of appeal, the *libellus appellatorius,* was given to the judge who pronounced the sentence and he could not ordinarily refuse to allow the appeal unless it was based on futile or unreasonable grounds or was interposed against a sentence that was not appealable by law.[79] If it so happened that a judge refused on insufficient or improper grounds to permit the appeal, his action was punishable by fine [80] and the aggrieved party could appeal from such an unwarranted refusal directly to the appellate court.[81] If the judge denied the appeal for sound and legal reasons, a written copy of the latter was to be given to the appellant.[82] The next step in the proceedings was the transmission of the cause to the appellate court. The *litterae dimissoriae* were applied for [83] and within thirty days, the entire record of the case was to be sent to the superior court.[84] Mutilation or suppression of any part of the court record made the judge of first instance liable to certain penalties.[85] The appellant must prosecute his appeal within a certain space of time, which never exceeded six months, or forfeit his right to appeal.[86] The effect of the appeal was ordinarily to suspend the judgment or sentence until the appeal was decided and a new sentence pronounced,

[76] *Nov.*, 23, 3. On the principle, "*par in parem non habet imperium,*" appeals to judges of equal power or jurisdiction were also forbidden, *Nov.*, 23, 4.

[77] *Cod.*, 7, 62, 6, 4.

[78] *Nov.*, 124, 1; *Dig.*, 49, 1, 1, 4; 49, 1, 13, 1; 49, 1, 3, 3. Cf. canon 1882, §2.

[79] *Cod.*, 7, 65, 8.

[80] *Cod.*, 7, 62, 22; 7, 62, 31.

[81] *Dig.*, 49, 5, 5, *pr.*

[82] *Dig.*, 49, 5, 6; 49, 1, 25.

[83] *Dig.*, 49, 6, *un.*

[84] *Cod.*, 7, 62, 24. An earlier statute in the *Theodosian Code,* 11, 30, 8, had allowed only twenty days.

[85] *Cod.*, 7, 62, 15.

[86] *Cod.*, 7, 63, 5, *pr.; Nov.*, 119, 4; 126, 2.

and during this term, the principle "*appellatione interposita, nihil innovari*," was observed and the judge of first instance could do nothing to hinder the appeal or weaken the case proper.[87] In its review of the cause, the appellate tribunal could receive new evidence or listen to new arguments which were not presented to the court of first instance. It had the power of reversing as well as confirming the sentence of the lower court,[88] but the superior tribunal was not to remand the cause to the inferior court for a new trial.[89]

The appealed cause was to be settled decisively within one year from the time it reached the appellate court. If any reasonable interruption occurred during this period, another year was allowed; but if the case was not decided within that time, it generally became a *res iudicata* and the sentence was ordered to be executed.[90] In one and the same cause, there could only be two appeals or, in other words, the cause could be tried only before three grades of jurisdiction.[91]

Justinian abolished the practice of having causes referred to the Emperor for the purpose of obtaining a decision by rescript. The Emperor gradually retires from active participation in the judicial proceedings of the Empire and his position is taken by the all powerful praetorian prefect. Justinian made provision, however, for the review of the sentences of the praetorian prefect by the Emperor on the receipt of a petition to that effect.[92]

In this period, there is noticed also the distinction between appeals and other remedies or forms of legal redress. Among the latter were the *Restitutio in integrum* and the *Libellus supplex ad Principem*. The former was usually allowed against a sentence validly pronounced in regular court procedure but based on false documents or on a judicial oath that was falsely sworn.[93] The *Libellus Supplex* was the ordinary method employed to have a sentence of the praetorian prefect reviewed by the Emperor. It did not have a

[87] *Cod.*, 7, 62, 3; *Dig.*, 49, 7, 1.
[88] *Cod.*, 7, 62, 6, 1; 7, 63, 4.
[89] *Cod.*, 7, 62, 6, *pr.*
[90] *Nov.*, 49, *pr.*, 1; 93, 1.
[91] *Cod.*, 7, 70, *un.*
[92] *Nov.*, 125; 113, 1; 82, 12.
[93] *Cod.*, 7, 58; *Dig.*, 12, 2, 31; 42, 1, 33.

suspensive effect, except when certain conditions determined by law were present.[94]

A perusal of the legislation in the Code of Canon Law relative to appeals will demonstrate clearly the extent to which this legal institution has developed since the time of Justinian. It will be seen readily that most of the important elements of a judicial appeal that appear in the Code are to be found in the Justinian legislation. The appeal is interposed orally or in writing before the judge who pronounced the sentence on the cause in question. Ten days from the time that notice of the sentence was received, are allowed within which notice of appeal must be given. On receiving such notification, the judge of the first court is to forward the acts of the cause to the appellate tribunal and that within a certain determined space of time; the inferior judge is prevented by law from acting further on the cause. The appellant is given a certain term within which he must prosecute his appeal and the latter must be finally and decisively settled within one or at the most, two years from the time it was received into the superior court. The appeal ordinarily has a suspensive effect. The appellate process is a continuation of the former, during which the entire cause is reviewed by the higher tribunal and at the conclusion of this examination, the superior judge confirms, revises or revokes the sentence of the lower court. Practically all of the essential elements of a judicial appeal in ecclesiastical law are to be found in the Justinian legislation; some differences are also to be noted, but they are for the most part concerned with features peculiar to ecclesiastical needs and requirements.

[94] *Cod.*, 7, 62, *constits.* 19, 35, 39; 7, 70, *un; Nov.*, 119. 5.

# CHAPTER III

## APPEALS IN EARLY CANON LAW

Ecclesiastical legislation in the early ages of the Church was somewhat incomplete and fragmentary. The laws were made as circumstances demanded without any formal system or preconceived plan. There existed a certain uniformity of practise, based on the prescriptions of the divine law but as long as the period of persecution endured, the written canon law necessarily remained very meagre and unity of legislation in purely disciplinary matters was not possible. The tendency to unification and centralization was, however, apparent even in those early days and it became more manifest as the Church increased in numbers and spread in extent.

A history of the institution which is to be treated here, will not be found in well formulated juridical principles. Its development must be gleaned from facts which will demonstrate that this judicial remedy is a legal instrument of long standing in ecclesiastical circles. In this regard, the letters addressed to and received from the various pontiffs, the legislative enactments of councils and synods, the written treatises of the early Fathers and Doctors, all serve to produce sufficient information to prove conclusively that many of the Church's subjects availed themselves even in this early age of the right of appeal against grievances of a judicial character.

### Article I. From the Beginning to the Council of Sardica

Since in all governments, there is a tribunal of appeal whose decision and judgment is final, similarly from the very institution of the Church, appeal from the judgment of the bishop to that of the Supreme Pontiff was an accepted practise and principle. By it, the sentence of the inferior judge was confirmed when found conformable to justice and law; or if otherwise, reversed and corrected. That this right existed and was recognized from the very beginning, has been denied by many groups from the time of the Eusebians to the period of the Gallican controversy. The demonstration and proof of the possession of this right in support of the primacy of jurisdiction enjoyed by the Pope, lies in the field of dogmatic theology.[1] It is the purpose of this work to consider the facts of the case from the juridical standpoint exclusively.

The first evidence of an appeal to the Pope may be found in the first epistle of St. Clement to the Corinthians, written in the year 97. It is difficult to make out whether this appeal was in many manner judicial in character. The Corinthians rebelled against two of their sacerdotal leaders and ejected them from office. A statement to this effect seems to have been sent to the Pope who after some time, replied to the Corinthians, rebuking them for their sedition and rebellion and restoring the two priests by a formal sentence to their previous positions.[2] There is some controversy and dispute over the question as to whether or not St. Clement had been appealed to by the Corinthians to regulate their ecclesiastical affairs, but regardless of this, the general tone of the letter and the manner in which it was received by the Corinthians demonstrate that even in this early period, the Church at Rome felt itself in possession of superior, exceptional authority which it did not cease to claim later.

The next example of an appeal to the Roman See was that of the priest Marcion of Pontus, who, having committed a grave crime, was condemned by his father, the Bishop of Synope, in the year 141. According to St. Epiphanius,[3] Marcion then fled to Rome where he sought redress at the hands of the clergy of that city, since the See had been left vacant by the death of Pope Hyginus. The former refused to lift the sentence of condemnation, not because they were not competent to do so but for the reason that they considered the sentence as justly pronounced.[4] This was not strictly a judicial process but it does contain some of the elements of the judicial remedy under consideration. For there was a condemnation, an appeal for redress against a grievance and a hearing granted to the appel-

[1] Cf. Tanquerey, *Synopsis Theologiae Dogmaticae Fundamentalis,* I, 439 ff., and approved authors therein noted.

[2] Letter of St. Clement to the Corinthians—*MPG.*, I, 202.

[3] *Adversus Haereses,* XIII—*MPG.,* XLI, 695.

[4] Devoti, *Jus Canonicum Universum,* III, *Appendix,* V, n. 1.

lant. The fact that the sentence was not reversed, does not detract from the historical value of the case in question.

St. Cyprian records the case of one Privatus, Bishop of Lambesita, who, on being condemned in the year 250 by a council of ninety bishops, appealed to Rome for vindication. The bearer of his appeal, Futurus, arrived at Rome after the death of Pope Fabian and presented his appeal to the Roman clergy. The latter had been warned by a letter from St. Cyprian of the true state of the case and accordingly they refused to reverse the sentence. However, the appeal was heard and recognized; and the African synod had made no attempt to deny the right of Privatus to appeal to Rome.[5]

A few years later, Felicissimus, a heretic, who with Privatus and three other partisans of the Novatian schism had elected Fortunatus as their Bishop and had been condemned by a synod of bishops under the direction of St. Cyprian, appealed to Pope Cornelius for a revocation of the sentence of condemnation. Cyprian sent a letter to the Pope in which he criticised the audacity of these men in appealing to the Church at Rome for redress against a sentence that was based on such clear and indisputable proofs. The letter informed the Pope of all the facts of the case. Cyprian does not deny the right of these men to appeal but objects to the appeal to Rome on the grounds that the appeal should be placed where the witnesses, accusers and other parties to the trial could be present and able to testify for or against the accused.[6]

In the year 255, Pope St. Stephen writes, in reply to a letter from St. Cyprian urging the condemnation of Marcianus, Bishop of Arles, who had become a partisan of the Novatian schism, that trials should be held in the various provinces and the matter terminated there unless an appeal is made to the Holy See.[7] This is but another indication of the fact that the right to appeal from a sentence brought by a synod was recognized by the Pope and was granted to all.

The Spanish Bishops Basilides and Martialis, who had been condemned and deposed by a synod in 254, appealed to Pope St.

[5] St. Cyprian, *Ep.* LV—*MPL.*, IV, 348; cf. also *MPL.*, III, 810.

[6] St. Cyprian, *Ep.* LIX—*MPL.*, III, 795; cf. *MPL.*, IV, 348, and Devoti, *Jus Canonicum Universum*, III, *Appendix*, V, n. 3.

[7] St. Stephen, *Ep.*—*MPL.*, III, 1005.

Stephen to be restored to their sees. Their appeal was recognized and heard by the Pope who reinstated them. However, the objections of their subjects were so violent that in the quarrel that followed, St. Cyprian was sought by the Bishops Sabinus and Felix who had been deposed on the return of Basilides and Martialis. Cyprian declared that the reinstatement of Basilides was invalid because it had been obtained by fraudulent methods. However, apart from this, the appeal was recognized by Cyprian as legitimate, even though he declared the reversal of the sentence to be invalid.[8]

The first introduction of appellate legislation into the general law of the Church occurred in the first ecumenical council held at Nicaea in the year 325. The fifth canon of this council decrees that a provincial synod shall be held twice each year, before the season of Lent and in the Fall of the year and it shall be composed of all the bishops of the province. The synod shall have for its purpose to see that the sentences of excommunication and similar penalties have been justly rendered and for some determined disobedience.[9] In addition, bishops are forbidden to receive persons excommunicated by another bishop. The provincial council or synod seems to have the right of annulling the sentence of the bishop if it sees fit to do so, reviewing in the second instance the sentence of the bishop. Canon 4 of the same council is concerned with the reordering of the hierarchy and declares that each civil province shall be an ecclesiastical province and the latter shall be governed by a metropolitan. Canon 6 speaks of a higher order of the hierarchy, the patriarch and gives additional rights to the Patriarchs of Alexandria and of Antioch.[10] The groundwork for the future appellate system of the Church in which the metropolitan and patriarch occupied prominent positions, is being laid gradually.

In a synod held at Antioch in 341, it was decreed that anyone who has been excommunicated by his bishop, shall not be received by another until a synod shall be held and he appears before it to defend himself. He must succeed in convincing the synod of his innocence and in obtaining a new sentence absolving him of guilt in the matter. Canon 12 of the same synod prohibits a deacon, a

[8] St. Cyprian, *Ep.* LXVIII—*MPL.*, III, 1021; cf. *MPL.*, IV, 400.
[9] Mansi, *Sacrorum Conciliorum Nova et Amplissima Collectio*, II, 679.
[10] Mansi, II, 697.

priest or a bishop deposed by a synod, from appealing to the Emperor. The guilty person should lay his case before a higher synod and a larger assembly of bishops. The fifteenth canon declares that if a bishop has been tried by all the bishops of a province and all have unanimously rendered a sentence against him, he shall not have the benefit of an appeal.[11] There is no mention made here of the suspensive effect of an appeal but the appeal itself is recognized as a matter of right under certain conditions and unless it contravenes the existing law. There is found, moreover, in the legislation affecting the hierarchy, an attempt to regulate the jurisdiction of the respective prelates which in later years will be of some assistance in the determination of the different instances for appeals.

In connection with this synod of Antioch, the case of St. Athanasius and other bishops is worthy of note. St. Athanasius, Bishop of Alexandria, Marcellus, Bishop of Ancyra, Paul, Bishop of Constantinople and Asclepas of Gaza, all had been banished from their respective sees by the Eusebians, Athanasiuus being deposed by the synod of Antioch. These bishops appealed to Rome to Pope Julius I who in turn convoked a synod at Rome in the same year.[12] This synod, consisting of some fifty bishops, examined the appeals of the deposed eastern bishops and with Pope Julius, upheld the appeals from the synod. Whereupon the Pope reinstated them and gave them letters restoring each one to his own see.[13]

It will have been noticed that during this period preceding the Council of Sardica, the practice of appealing to the Pope was generally accepted by all. Rome is the court of last appeal where redress may be sought not only against episcopal sentences but also against synodal judgments. The provincial synod is declared to be the court of second instance for appeals from the sentence of excommunication rendered by the bishop. All the formalities of judicial procedure are not observed; in fact these may only be conjectured for the accounts of the councils and synods furnish no information with respect to this particular feature. While the evolution

[11] Mansi, II, 1311, 1314.

[12] Socrates, *Historia Ecclesiastica,* lib. II, cap. XV—*MPG.,* LXVII, 211; lib. II, cap. XXIII—*MPG.,* LXVII, 255. Cf. also Sozomen, *Historia Ecclesiastica,* lib. III, cap. VIII—*MPG.,* LXVII, 1051.

[13] Mansi, II, 1351; cf. also II, 1186, and *MPL.,* VIII, 916.

of the institution of appeal is only beginning, some of the principal elements of this judicial remedy are present from the very start and the foundation is slowly being laid for the appellate system, the development of which will become more clearly outlined during subsequent centuries.

### Article II. From the Council of Sardica to the Decree of Gratian

The Council of Sardica was convoked on the order of the Emperors Constans and Constantius in the year 344 to settle the bitter feud between the Eusebians and Athanasius and the latter's followers which was dividing the Eastern Church. After confirming the sentence rendered by the Pope in the synod held at Rome in 341, the Council passed several enactments regulating the procedure to be followed in making appeals to Rome. It was not the intention of the Council thereby to grant the Bishop of Rome a privilege that he did not yet possess, the privilege of receiving appeals from any part of the Christian world. The Council recognized this as a right, and as a necessary consequence of the Primacy, belonging to the Pope by divine institution and often exercised *de facto* before the Council of Sardica. But in view of the recent reprehensible methods employed by the Eusebians against the bishops who had appealed to Rome, the Council intended to express solemnly the Pope's right to receive appeals and to prescribe the line of conduct to be observed whenever cause for such appeals should arise.

Canon 3 of the Council states that if a bishop shall be deposed by the bishops of his province, he may personally appeal to Rome directly or through the judges who had condemned him. The Holy See will decide whether or not the appeal is to be heard. If it is not admitted, the sentence of the first court is to be confirmed; if the appeal stands, Rome shall appoint a court of second instance to hear the appeal and review the case, and this court shall be composed of the bishops of the neighboring province. Canon 5 directs that these bishops thoroughly investigate the affairs and give sentence strictly in accordance with the truth. The Pope, at the request of the appellant, may send judges of his own to preside over the court of second instance. Canon 4 declares that if a bishop who has been deposed desires to appeal his case to Rome, no other bishop shall be appointed to his see until the Bishop of Rome shall have adjudged the appeal and pronounced sentence on the cause in question. This is the first evidence of the suspensive effect of an appeal in ecclesiastical legislation.[14]

Febronius,[15] Van Espen[16] and other Gallicans engaged in a lengthy controversy with the "Curialists" over the canons of this synod, declaring that the rights contained in these canons were newly given to the Pope, that he did not possess them previously; that, moreover, there is no real judicial appeal mentioned in this synod for the reason that the court of appeal is composed of the same bishops as the court of first instance. However, without entering into this dispute, it is plainly evident that appeals were made to Rome before this Council was convoked; with regard to the second objection, a perusal of the canons will show that the personnel of the court of second instance directly excludes the judges of the lower tribunal. The entire question is thoroughly treated by Devoti.[17] The legislative enactments of this Council are concerned directly with judicial appeals. Most of the features of an appeal are present, the first court, a judicial sentence, the second instance, superior to and different from the preceding tribunal and a suspensive effect that is real, prohibiting the judges of the first instance from executing the sentence rendered on the case until the appeal is decided one way or the other.

Canon 14 states that a priest or deacon who has been excommunicated by his own bishop, may have recourse to the neighboring bishop or metropolitan for the purpose of having his case thoroughly investigated and the sentence passed on him confirmed or rejected. The bishop who pronounced the sentence in the first instance, shall not place any obstacle in the way of such recourse.

[14] Mansi, III, 23 ff.; cf. also Hardouin, *Conciliorum Collectio Regia Maxima,* I, 637 ff.

[15] *De Statu Ecclesiae et Legitima Potestate Romani Pontificis,* cap. II, 4, pp. 83-85; cap. II, 10, p. 113 ff.

[16] *Jus Ecclesiasticum Universum, pars* III, tit. V, cap. II, n. 1 ff.

[17] *Jus Canonicum Universum,* III, *Appendix,* IV and V; cf. also Kearney, *The Principles of Delegation,* pp. 23-24; Zaccaria, *Anti-Febronius,* II, 303, and III, 287.

The sentence, however, is to be executed for the suspensive effect of the recourse is explicitly denied here.[18]

There is continued evidence of the use of appeal in the years that follow. In 357, Eusthatius, Bishop of Sebaste, who had been deposed by the Arian synod of Melitene, appealed to Pope Liberius who revoked the condemnatory sentence and restored the bishop to his see.[19] In the year 374, Peter, Patriarch of Alexandria, was driven from his see by the Arians and he forthwith appealed to Pope Damasus who reinstated him after excommunicating the Arian usurper Apollinaris and his immediate followers.[20] The same Pope, a few years later in 381, refused to receive the appeal of Priscillian, one of three Spanish bishops condemned for heresy by the national council of Saragossa. The appeal was denied on the grounds that no evidence of injustice was apparent and accordingly, the sentence pronounced by the council remained in force.[21]

Another appeal of great moment was that lodged by St. John Chrysostom in 404. He had incurred the hatred of the Empress Eudoxia by preaching against her licentious manner of living and she in return had prevailed upon her husband, the Emperor Arcadius, to have John condemned at the schismatical synod of Chalcedon and deposed. St. John then appealed to Pope Innocent I [22] who pronounced that the sentence rendered against him was null and of no effect and that a new inquiry would take place at Rome. However, despite the Pope's intervention, St. John was again exiled through the powerful influence of the Empress. Regardless of the practical effect of this appeal, the latter was strictly judicial in character, made after a trial and for the purpose of having the sentence in question rescinded. The Emperor Honorius bears witness to this fact in a letter written to his brother Arcadius.[23]

A series of synods was held in Africa during this period, which effected some change in the appellate procedure in that country. A

[18] Mansi, II, 28; this canon is recorded as 17 in Mansi. Cf. also Thomassinus, *Vetus et Nova Ecclesiae Disciplina, pars* II, lib. I, *cap*. 15, n. 8.

[19] St. Basil, *Ep*. 263—*MPG*., XXXII, 978.

[20] Mansi, III, 485.

[21] *Ep. Damasi—MPL*., XIII, 232, 248; cf. also *Corpus Scriptorum Ecclesiasticorum Latinorum*, XVIII, 34.

[22] St. John, *Ad Innoc.—MPG*., LII, 530.

[23] *Ep. Honorii—MPG*., LII, 539, 540.

council convoked in Carthage in 390 decreed that a priest who has been excommunicated or punished by his superior, may appeal to the neighboring bishops who are empowered to hear his case and reconcile him again to his bishop if the facts of the case warrant such a step.[24] Another synod held at Carthage in 397 declared that if an appeal is made from one ecclesiastical court to another and higher tribunal, the appeal in no case shall be considered as a reflection on the integrity of the judges of the previous instance, unless it can be shown that they were deliberately unjust in their actions.[25] Canon 66 of the Council of Carthage, held in 398, stated that any priest or deacon who considered the sentence pronounced against him as unjust, could appeal to a synod for redress.[26] The eleventh Carthaginian synod celebrated in 407 decreed that in all cases of appeal where the judges of the second instance were selected with the consent of the appellant, there could be no further appeal from their decision.[27]

The case of the heretic Caelestius is a particularly involved question, but it is an example of an appeal that was the occasion of clarifying certain obscure features of this legal remedy. The synod of Carthage held in 416 condemned Pelagius and his disciple Caelestius and notice of the condemnation was sent to Pope Innocent I by St. Augustine and other bishops present at the synod.[28] Caelestius appealed to the Pope to have the sentence revoked but did not prosecute the appeal and in the following year, the sentence of condemnation was confirmed by Pope Innocent. The successor of Innocent, Pope Zozimus, a few years later admitted the appeals of both Pelagius and Caelestius and granted them a rehearing. In two letters written to the African bishops, he declares that apparently both heretics have made a retractation of their errors and that consequently he feels moved to reinstate them.[29] Whereupon, the African bishops to the number of 214, assembled in a general synod and wrote to Pope Zozimus urging him not absolve the heretics on a

[24] Mansi, III, 695; Hardouin, I, 953.
[25] Mansi, III, 921.
[26] Mansi, III, 956; Hardouin, I, 983.
[27] Mansi, III, 802, 1163; Hardouin, I, 919.
[28] St. August., *Ep.* CLXXV—*MPL.*, XXXIII, 758; Mansi, IV, 332.
[29] *Ep. Zozimi*—*MPL.*, XLV, 1719, 1721.

vague promise of submission to the Apostolic See.[30] The Pope thereupon decided to reexamine the case but Caelestius refused to appear and the former sentence of condemnation was confirmed by the Pope in 418.[31] This plenary synod decreed in addition that all priests, deacons or inferior clerics who feel agrieved at a sentence pronounced against them by their bishops, may appeal to the neighboring bishop who shall settle the dispute by confirming or revoking the sentence in question. If any of these desires to appeal further, such appeal must be placed only with primates or with provincial synods. Whosoever appeals to a court across the sea, that is, to Rome, shall not again be received into communion by any bishop in Africa.[32] This enactment caused no end of discussion and controversy but it is evident that the primary purpose of it was to prevent the interposition of useless and futile appeals before the Holy See merely with the idea of retarding the execution of just and lawful punishments. It is entirely in harmony with the principles of St. Cyprian with regard to the appeals of minor clerics. At no time, did the Church of Africa deny the Pope's right to receive appeals from that country; on the contrary, that right was recognized and respected.[33]

The appeals of the priest Apiarius, form the basis of the so-called African Controversy of the years 418-423. The question is treated in all its various aspects in works, historical or canonical, of authors on both sides of the controversy. Obviously, the question can only be discussed here in so far as it touches upon the subject under consideration. It is sufficient for the purposes of this work to state that Apiarius was condemned by his bishop and immediately appealed to Pope Boniface who examined the case and reinstated him. In order to have his sentence enforced and to settle in a becoming manner the procedure required for the placing of appeals before the Holy See, the Pope sent three legates to Africa under the

[30] *Paulini Libellus—MPL.*, XLV, 1724.

[31] Marius Mercator, *Commonitorium de Caelestio—MPL.*, XLVIII, 67.

[32] Mansi, III, 822; Hardouin, I, 934; Thomassinus, *Vetus et Nova Ecclesiae Disciplina, pars* II, lib. I, cap. XV, nn. 13, 14.

[33] For a clear and more complete exposition of the case of Pelagius and Caelestius and their respective appeals to the Holy See, cf. Chapman, "The Holy See and Pelagianism," *Dublin Review*, CXX (1897), 88; CXXI (1897), 99.

leadership of Faustinus, Bishop of Potenza. In the African general synod of 419, the priest Apiarius was received into the communion of the African clergy.[34] A few years later, he again fell from grace and was once more excommunicated. Again he sought to have his sentence revoked, this time before Pope Celestine. The Pope reinstated him and sent Faustinus once more to Africa to have the entire case reexamined by a synod of bishops. In the course of the synodal deliberations, Apiarius confessed to all the evil deeds of which he had been accused and remained under the sentence of excommunication that had previously been pronounced against him.[35]

Canon 17 of this synod prohibiting appeals to Rome on the part of priests and inferior clerics, and the strong, decisive tone of the letters sent to Pope Boniface and Pope Celestine, lead Protestant and Gallican writers to believe that the African Church rejected the Pope's supreme authority as well as his right to receive appeals and in addition, to intervene in all affairs pertaining to the government of their church. However, there is nothing in the documents to indicate this state of mind on the part of the African bishops. On the contrary, the canons and enactments of the councils and synods contain repeated expressions of loyalty and reverence for the Pope even though at times they contain complaints of unfair treatment on the part of the Roman See or point out the neglect of the latter toward the African canons. It must be admitted that the actions of the two Popes somewhat embarrassed the Church of Africa when consideration is given to the intense respect that these bishops held for their own ecclesiastical institutions and especially for their canons. In addition, the choice of the overbearing Faustinus as the Popes' delegate was an unfortunate one and this alone served to prejudice the bishops and increase their opposition to what they considered the undue interference of the Holy See. However, when the entire matter is summed up, the conclusion can only be that, although the African bishops resented the Popes' interference and op-

[34] Mansi, III, 831; Hardouin, I, 939.

[35] The facts of the second appeal are related in the celebrated letter *Optaremus* sent to Pope Celestine by the bishops of Africa assembled in a synod in 424,—Mansi, III, 839; Hardouin, I, 947; Thomassinus, *Vetus et Nova Ecclesiae Disciplina, pars* II, lib. I, cap. XV, n. 17; Devoti, *Jus Canonicum Universum*, III, *Appendix*, V, nn. 17, 26 ff.; Chapman, "Apiarius," *Dublin Review*, CXXIX (1901), 98.

posed the filing of appeals directly to Rome on the part of priests and minor clerics, yet at no time, did they reject the Pope's supreme authority or deny his right of exercising complete jurisdiction over the whole Church and incidentally of receiving any and all appeals submitted to him. They had subscribed to the letter *"Quamvis Patrum Traditio"* written by Pope Zozimus in 418 to Aurelius and others gathered in a synod at Carthage, wherein the Pope had claimed that the Apostolic See, having from the very beginning the care and guidance of all the churches, had the right of receiving appeals from all the Christian world, that the sentence of the Pope is final and that it cannot be retracted or reversed by any other authority.[36]

In partial support of this, the appeal of Anthony, Bishop of Fussala, may be mentioned. This bishop had been removed from his the episcopate. He immediately appealed to Pope Boniface I and see by St. Augustine in 423 without however being deposed from the Pope restored him to his see on the condition that the charges brought against him were false and the facts related in his libellus were true. But Anthony attempted to regain possession of his see with the aid of the civil power, which Augustine reported to the Pope and declared at the same time that the facts related by Anthony in his libellus were false. The great Doctor did not deny Anthony's right to appeal to the Pope but merely sought to state the facts of the case as they stood. In addition, he quotes three cases of appeals of a recent date, made by African bishops which the Pope had settled as he himself had done.[37]

There are numerous other cases of appeals during this period that merit some consideration and attention. In 433, Eutherius, the Metropolitan of Tyane, and Helladius, Metropolitan of Tarsus, condemned by the General Council of Ephesus in 431 as tainted with the heresy of Nestorius, appealed to Pope Sixtus III who ordered them reinstated on the condition that they would anathematize Nes-

[36] Ep. *"Quamvis Patrum Traditio,"* 21 March, 418—*Fontes*, n. 21; Mansi, IV, 366. This same claim was repeated a few years later by Pope Boniface I in the letter *"Retro Majoribus Tuis,"* written to Rufus, Bishop of Thessaly, 11 March, 422—*Fontes*, n. 22. Added confirmation is found in the letter written to the bishops of Dardania in 495 by Pope Gelasius, Ep. XIII—*Corpus Script. Eccles. Latin.*, XXXV, 378.

[37] Ep. August., CCIX—*MPL.*, XXXIII, 953.

torius and his doctrines.[38] In a synod held at Constantinople, Eutyches was condemned for promoting heresy. In the same year 448, he appealed to Pope Leo I but the latter on the advice of Flavian, Bishop of Constantinople, confirmed the sentence pronounced against him.[39] In the pseudo-synod of Ephesus, held in the following year, Flavian and Theodoret, Bishop of Cyrus, were condemned and both appealed to Pope Leo who restored them to their respective sees.[40]

During the remainder of this period of the *jus antiquum*, the legislation relative to appeals is found principally in the various enactments of provincial councils and synods. These laws are not stated in the clearest terms, nor do the legislators attempt to systematize the existing legislation of the subject. One point seems to be clearly established to the effect that in the case of a dispute between a cleric and his bishop, the former must not take his appeal to the Emperor nor to any secular judge. Thus decreed the Council of Chalcedon in 451.[41] According to canon 9 of this same council, the provincial synod still appears to be the court of second instance in the question of appeals from episcopal sentences. Under certain circumstances, canon 17 decrees that an appeal may be taken from the metropolitan to the primate, particularly if the former is in any way concerned in the case.[42] The synod is declared to be the ordinary court of appeal also by enactments of the synod of Viseu in Gaul, held in 442,[43] the synod of Orleans, 538,[44] and the synod of Rheims, 624.[45]

Prior to this time, however, in scattered instances, the metropolitan had been named in synodal decrees as the court of appeal for

[38] Ep. Sixti III—*MPL.*, L, 593.

[39] Mansi, V, 1014, 1323; cf. also *MPL.*, LIV., 717.

[40] Ep. Leonis XXIII—*MPL.*, LIV, 731; Ep. LII *ad Leon.*—*MPL.*, LIV, 849, 851. Cf. also *Pasch. Quesnelli Dissertatio Septima de Causa Eutychis*, and *Balleriniorum Observationes*—*MPL.*, LV, 646, 663; *Pasch. Ques. Dissert. Octava de Causa Flaviani*, and *Ballerin. Observat.*—*MPL.*, LV, 670, 685, 702, 726; *idem, Dissert. Decima de Causa Theodoreti*, and *Ballerin. Observat.*—*MPL.*, LV, 739, 753.

[41] Mansi, VII, 362; Hardouin, II, 606.

[42] Mansi, VII, 366; Hardouin, II, 608.

[43] Can. 5—Mansi, VI, 454.

[44] Can. 20—Mansi, IX, 17.

[45] Can. 5—Mansi, X, 594.

all disputes between bishops and their priests or clerics. The fifth synod of Orleans, held in 549, permits this course of action.[46] Similar decrees were passed by the third council of Toledo in 589,[47] in a synod held in the same city in 638 [48] and in the council of Frankfort in 794.[49]

These decrees had only local force for their respective provinces but they nevertheless show a gradual development in appellate procedure in as much as the knowledge that criminal as well as civil causes could be decided more expeditiously by a metropolitan than by a synod of bishops, prompted the ecclesiastical authorities to simplify the process of appealing from one court to another. The Eighth Ecumenical Council, assembled at Constantinople in 868 made this procedure the rule for the entire Church, that any priest or deacon who regarded the sentence passed against him as unjust, could appeal to the metropolitan and denounce his sentence to the latter. Bishops likewise were to appeal to the metropolitan unless they suspected him for some reason or other, in which case, the appeal could be placed before the patriarch.[50]

The period of ecclesiastical legislation that has just been considered, bears witness to a certain amount of development in canonical appellate procedure. The progress has not been rapid, nor has it been made along well defined lines, but the main elements of an appeal may be recognized as well as some of the concomitant formalities. The legal niceties of judicial procedure, however, are noticeably lacking. But these will naturally be established in the course of time, once the underlying structure of the appellate system is formed. An appeal, at the end of this period, is granted to all the faithful and the clergy, although the law is much more concerned with the latter class. In the beginning the appeal was ordinarily made from the bishop's court to the provincial synod which had the power of confirming or revoking the sentence appealed; later, it is enacted that the appeal is to be prosecuted before the court

[46] Can. 17—Mansi, IX, 133.

[47] Can. 20—Mansi, IX, 998.

[48] Cap. 12—Mansi, XI, 1074.

[49] Can. 6—Hardouin, IV, 905.

[50] Reg. 26—Hardouin, V, 911; cf. *Thomassinus, Vetus et Nova Ecclesiae Disciplina, pars* II, lib. I, cap. XVII, n. 4.

of the metropolitan who, likewise, can reexamine the cause and confirm or reverse the sentence. The suspensive effect of an appeal may also be noted but this feature is not always clearly stated nor is there any well determined legislation sufficiently plain and clear to indicate that every appeal has a suspensive effect. Very probably, appeals from sentences pronounced against certain heinous crimes, were not *in suspensivo*.[51] The court of last appeal is the Holy See and the sentence of the Pope is regarded as final and decisive in all respects. All have the right to appeal to him with the knowledge and assurance that justice will be meted out and that a cause once decided, cannot be changed or reversed by any other tribunal. Pope St. Leo IX repeated this claim once more in a letter to Michael, Bishop of Constantinople, in 1053.[52]

[51] Thomassinus, *Vetus et Nova Ecclesiae Disciplina, pars* II, lib. I, cap. XVII, n. 2.

[52] Ep. "*In Terra Pax Hominibus,*" 2 Sept., 1053, §11, §32—*Fontes*, n. 27; Mansi, XIX, 641, 653.

# CHAPTER IV

## APPELLATE LEGISLATION FROM THE DECREE OF GRATIAN TO THE COUNCIL OF TRENT

It is during this period from about the middle of the twelfth century to the middle of the sixteenth, that the development of canonical jurisprudence made its greatest strides. It is the period of the *jus novum*. The first two centuries of this era in particular, form the golden age of canon law, during which the gradual development of the Church's legal institutions along well defined lines is to be seen, a development that received a decided impetus with the advent of the printing press in the middle of the fifteenth century. This invention made legal texts more accessible to students. The canonists learned from the humanists to clothe their teachings and jurisprudence in more attractive garb, the former subtle and useless discussions were gradually eliminated and greater attention was given to historical and critical investigation. More reliable editions were published and spurious texts which had found their way even into the *Corpus Juris* were discarded.

Although this period witnessed a pronounced development in canonical legislation in general, the appellate system did not follow the regular trend or growth. There was in this case, no gradual progress but rather an undated and wholesale acceptance of the institution of appeal and the regulations concerning it from Justinian Law. This incorporation took place in the Decree of Gratian where the entire appellate procedure as perfected by the Emperor Justinian may be found. From this point of view the canonical institution of appeal reached its highest degree of development long before many of the other procedural laws of the Church began their course of progressive evolution.

### Article I. The Decree of Gratian

The Decree of Gratian never received official approbation. Although it enjoyed great authority, it always remained a private compilation of law. Its authority was that of the sources of its canons and those parts of it that were taken from the pseudo-Isidorian Decretal, are unworthy for the most part of historical faith.[1] However, it cannot be denied that the Decree exerted a great amount of influence during that period before the Decretals of Gregory IX were promulgated. Its use as a text book in universities and schools of law served in great measure to promote this influence; the general respect with which it was regarded and the effect of custom relative to the observance of many of its enactments contributed in no small degree to the authority it exercised over the development of ecclesiastical legislation of the time.[2]

Provision is made by the Decree for the interposition of an appeal against any judicial sentence pronounced by an ecclesiastical judge and the further prosecution of that appeal before a higher and superior tribunal. The right of appeal is denied to no one, even in criminal causes.[3] The Holy See possesses supreme jurisdiction and accordingly can judge all men and this judgment can be retracted by no other authority. The sacred canons grant the faculty of appealing to Rome to all men but declare at the same time that there can be no appeal from the Roman See, not even to a general council or synod because neither has authority over the Holy See.[4]

An appeal may be made *viva voce* [5] or it may be made in writing within ten days from the time that the sentence was pronounced. It may be presented by the appellant personally or through a proxy.[6] Dimissorial letters or *apostoli* are then given by the judge of the first instance and while the appeal is pending, this judge is obliged to refrain from participating further in the appealed cause.[7] There is in addition a certain suspensive effect mentioned in connection with particular penalties but this feature is not fully determined.[8]

One year is allowed for the prosecution of an appeal but if,

[1] *Praefatio Novi Codicis Iuris Canonici.*

[2] Cf. Lijdsman, *Introductio in Jus Canonicum*, II, n. 115; Maroto, *Institutiones Iuris Canonici*, I, n. 72.

[3] Cc. 1, 6, 7, 8, 9, 10, 16, 17, 20, 21, 22, C. II, q. 6.

[4] C. 10, 16, 17, C. IX, q. 3.

[5] C. 41, C. II, q. 6.

[6] C. 28, C. II, q. 6.

[7] C. 31, C. II, q. 6.

[8] C. 3, C. III, q. 6; c. 12, C. II, q. 1; c. 2, C. II, q. 6.

within this period of time, the appellant is prevented from acting by any reasonable cause, an extra year may be granted for the purpose of completing the appellate proceedings. If this further term expires without any attempt being made to end the appeal, the sentence is to be executed for the cause has become a *res judicata*.[9]

The forty-first canon or chapter of the second cause summarizes the *Code* of Justinian relative to appellate procedure. Gratian declares, quoting from this source, that no appeal is necessary from sentences that are of their very nature invalid, such as, sentences that contain neither condemnation nor acquittal, sentences pronounced against minors or litigants who have died, sentences brought by judges who are manifestly corrupt or who have overstepped their legal boundaries. Appeals are not to be admitted when placed by those who are contumacious or who have committed and confessed certain crimes of a very grave nature or who have been convicted of such crimes by irrefutable arguments. When many are condemned by a sentence and but one party appeals from that sentence, if the appeal is successful, the benefits therefrom are communicated to the others engaged in the same action. The judge whose sentence has been appealed must within thirty days send the acts of the case to the superior tribunal.[10]

The majority of these regulations governing appellate procedure have been taken from Roman Law and the influence exercised by them as they were incorporated in the Decree of Gratian, becomes more manifest during the subsequent years. They rapidly became the ordinary norm according to which appeals were made and prosecuted and although they were borrowed from Roman Law, a new spirit was infused into them and in the course of time, they receive their binding force from ecclesiastical authority.

Two general councils were held during this period but since most of the decrees and enactments of these councils were included in the

[9] C. 41, C. II, q. 6.

[10] C. 41, C. II, q. 6. This section of the Decree of Gratian incorporates the prescriptions of Roman Law as contained in the Justinian *Code,* 7, 62; 7, 63; 7, 64; 7, 65; 7, 68; 7, 69; 7, 45, and *Nov.*, 23. The ordinances of the *Digest* relative to appeal appear in the Decree of Gratian as follows: C. 28, C. II, q. 6 from *Dig.*, 49, 1, 3 and 4; c. 29, C. II, q. 6 from *Dig.*, 49, 4, 5; c. 30, C. II, q. 6 from *Dig.*, 49, 5, 1; c. 31, C. II, q. 6 from *Dig.*, 49, 6, 1.

Decretals of Gregory IX, they will be considered under that heading.[11]

## Article II. The Decretals of Gregory IX

The Decretals of Gregory IX incorporated the regulations of Roman Law governing appeals and applied them to ecclesiastical appellate procedure. The twenty-eighth title of the second book of the Decretals corresponds to that of the forty-ninth book of the Digest and the subject and matter of appeals is practically the same in both laws, the only difference being a matter of detail, due to the particular needs and requirements peculiar to ecclesiastical legislation.

An appeal is declared to be a remedy for the unjustly oppressed and a legitimate defense of innocence; it is not to be used or tolerated as a defense of iniquity. Judges are advised to take cognizance of this when investigating the merits of an appeal. Appeals that are made for the purpose of delaying the execution of a just sentence, are not to be admitted.[12] Appeals may be interposed even in unimportant matters but if the appeal is not prosecuted, the sentence shall stand. An appeal may be made at any time during the trial except where the law prohibits such appeal.[13] Those who have been excommunicated may avail themselves of this form of defense and appeal from the condemnatory sentence if the latter is not considered to be just.[14] To prevent abuses on the part of delegated judges, Innocent III decreed that when a judge is delegated by the Pope to hear a cause and subdelegates his authority *in totum,* an appeal from the sentence of the subdelegated judge is to be made to the Pope and not to the delegated judge.[15]

Certain restrictions are placed on the right to appeal, the most important being the case where the clause "*appellatione remota*" appears. When a cause is remitted for judgment with this injunction

[11] III Lateran Council convened in 1179 under Pope Alexander III—Mansi, XXII, 313; IV Lateran Council convoked by Pope Innocent III in 1215—Mansi, XXII, 990.

[12] C. 38, X, *de appellationibus, recusationibus et relationibus,* II, 28.

[13] Cc. 11, 12, X, *de appellationibus, recusationibus et relationibus,* II, 28.

[14] C. 5, X, *de exceptionibus,* II, 25.

[15] C. 27, X, *de officio et potestate delegati judicis,* I, 29.

stated in a simple and unqualified manner, the prohibition extends to all parts of the cause in question.[16] When, however, the clause is inserted in the middle of a letter of delegation, it prohibits appeal from what precedes, not from what follows unless the same clause is found also at the end of the letter. This clause refers to all appeals not merely to frustratory or dilatory appeals.[17] In addition, no appeal is allowed from a sentence that has become a *res iudicata* [18] or when evidence of fraud or deceit is discovered in the appeal itself or in the manner of placing it.[19] Those who are guilty of notorious or heinous crimes are denied the remedy of appeal if their guilt is most clearly evident.[20] The appeal of a contumacious party is not to be admitted by the judge [21] and moreover, an appeal is denied if the purpose of it is to impede or hinder bishops or those in authority from correcting abuses or reforming the morals of their subjects, unless the appellant can show that the bishop has become oppressive in his zeal.[22] Finally, it is decreed that those who are evidently guilty of usury are not to have the advantage of an appeal if this remedy is used merely for the purpose of preventing or delaying restitution.[23]

Appeals may be made orally [24] or in writing within ten days after notice of the sentence has been received.[25] The appeal is to be presented to the judge who pronounced the sentence on the cause in question, with the reasons or motives which prompt it. A reasonable cause is required for the validity of the appeal.[26] The judge from whose sentence the appeal is taken, is then to determine the time within which the appeal is to be prosecuted before the appellate court. The law allows one year ordinarily for the prosecution of an appeal before the tribunal of second instance but in exceptional cir-

[16] C. 41, X, *de appellationibus, recusationibus et relationibus,* II, 28.
[17] Cc. 53, 71, X, *de appellationibus, recusationibus et relationibus,* II, 28.
[18] C. 4, X, *de appellationibus, recusationibus et relationibus,* II, 28.
[19] C. 15, X, *de appellationibus, recusationibus et relationibus,* II, 28.
[20] C. 5, X, *de appellationibus, recusationibus et relationibus,* II, 28.
[21] C. 8, X, *de officio iudicis ordinarii,* I, 31.
[22] C. 13, X, *de officio iudicis ordinarii,* I, 31.
[23] C. 11, X, *de usuris,* V, 19.
[24] C. 34, X, *de appellationibus, recusationibus et relationibus,* II, 28.
[25] C. 15, X, *de sententia et re iudicata,* II, 27.
[26] Cc. 59, 61, X, *de appellationibus, recusationibus et relationibus,* II, 28.

cumstances or for sufficient reasons, two years may be granted by the judge.[27] The appellant is required by law to bring his appeal to the superior tribunal within the term allotted by the judge of first instance;[28] if he neglects to do this, the sentence becomes a *res iudicata* and is to be executed.[29] However, if the appeal had been taken from an interlocutory sentence, the judge of first instance retains his jurisdiction over the appellant and proceeds with the cause.[30] This feature is a departure from the Roman Law on appeals from interlocutory sentences. The latter had been abolished by Justinian for the reason that they were the source of great abuses on the part of unscrupulous litigants who used this remedy to obstruct the proceedings of a judicial trial.[31] The party who interposes an appeal and neglects or refuses to prosecute it is held liable for all the expenses involved in the placing of the appeal.[32]

Appeals that are legitimately interposed and admitted by the appellate tribunal, benefit all parties concerned in the cause, the *actor* as well as the *reus* [33] and where several litigants have been condemned jointly by the same sentence, an appeal placed by one of the aggrieved parties, communicates its beneficial effects to the others.[34]

The law attributes a suspensive effect ordinarily to an appeal whether the latter is made to the Holy See or to the ordinary appellate tribunal. The execution of the sentence is delayed pending the investigation into the merits of the appeal or the new trial of the cause in the superior court.[35] Consequently, sentences of excommunication or the infliction of other penalties have no binding power if made after an appeal has been interposed against them.[36] While an appeal is pending, moreover, the law declares that all acts of the

[27] Cc. 5, 57, 61, X, *de appellationibus, recusationibus et relationibus*, II, 28.
[28] Cc. 13, 14, 44, X, *de appellationibus, recusationibus et relationibus*, II, 28.
[29] Cc. 2, 5, 28, X, *de appellationibus, recusationibus et relationibus*, II, 28.
[30] Cc. 33, 61, X, *de appellationibus, recusationibus et relationibus*, II, 28.
[31] Cf. *Cod.*, 7, 62, 36; 7, 45, 16.
[32] Cc. 26, 44, X, *de appellationibus, recusationibus et relationibus*, II, 28.
[33] C. 57, X, *de appellationibus, recusationibus et relationibus*, II, 28.
[34] C. 72, X, *de appellationibus, recusationibus et relationibus*, II, 28.
[35] C. 19, X, *de iureiurando*, II, 24; c. 28, X, *de officio et potestate iudicis delegati*, I, 29; c. 16, X, *de appellationibus, recusationibus et relationibus*, II, 28.
[36] Cc. 52, 55, X, *de appellationibus, recusationibus et relationibus*, II, 28.

judge of first instance, performed for the purpose of changing or otherwise altering the cause in which the appeal is made or which may be prejudicial to the legal rights of the appellant, are to be revoked by the judge of the superior tribunal, in accordance with the principle *"lite pendente, nihil innovetur."* [37]

Finally, provision is made for the admittance of new witnesses and the introduction of new proofs and evidence into the appellate process subject to the prescriptions of the law and if the necessary precautions against fraud and the danger of perjured testimony have been taken.[38]

## Article III. The *Liber Sextus* of Boniface VIII

The *Liber Sextus* of Boniface VIII contains a few important developments regarding the procedural formalities relative to the registration of an appeal. Few changes in the existing appellate legislation were made but certain regulations were more clearly and exactly defined. Appeals that were made *per saltum,* from the archdeacon to the metropolitan, omitting the tribunal of the bishop, were declared to be invalid. Likewise, appeals that were taken from the sentence of the *officialis* of the bishop to the bishop himself, were decreed to be invalid, since, logically, the bishop and his *officialis* form one tribunal. Appeals are to be made from an inferior court to the next hierarchically superior instance.[39]

Similarly, they were to be interposed within ten days from the time that notice of the sentence was received [40] but it is insisted that all appeals must be made in writing, stating at the same time the reasons for the appeal. The reasons must be true and sworn to. The written petition must also request that the judge of the first instance grant the *apostoli.* It may be submitted by the appellant personally or by proxy if necessary but if any of the prescribed for-

[37] C. 19, X, *de iudiciis,* II, 1; c. 10, X, *de restitutione spoliatorum,* II, 13; c. 10, X, *de exceptionibus,* II, 25; c. 49, X, *de appellationibus, recusationibus et relationibus,* II, 28.

[38] C. 15, X, *de probationibus,* II, 19; cc. 17, 46, X, *de testibus et attestationibus,* II, 20.

[39] C. 3, *de appellationibus,* II, 15, in VI°; c. 2, *de consuetudine,* I, 4, in VI°.

[40] Cc. 3, 7, *de appellationibus,* II, 15, in VI°.

malities are lacking, the judge is to regard the appeal as having been deserted. Whereupon the sentence shall be ordered executed or, in case of an appeal from an interlocutory sentence, the appellant shall return to the jurisdiction of the original judge.[41] It is required that the *litterae dimissoriae* or *apostoli* be presented to the judge of the appellate court within thirty days[42] and the judge of the inferior instance is obliged to grant these letters to the appellant. If he refuses to fulfill this obligation and proceeds with the trial, all the subsequent acts are null and void.[43] The principle, "*lite pendente, nihil innovetur,*" is insisted on here also with the result that all the acts of the judge of first instance that are performed not only after the appeal has been interposed but also during the time following the pronouncement of the sentence and before the placing of the appeal proper, are to be revoked by the superior tribunal.[44] Finally, in accordance with the principle, "*is qui in iure succedit alterius, eo iure, quo ille, uti debebit,*" Boniface VIII granted the heir or successor of the appellant the right of continuing the prosecution of the appeal on condition that all the necessary formalities had been complied with and the cause had not become a *res iudicata*.[45]

## Article IV. The Constitutions of Clement V

In the Constitutions of Clement V, the so-called *Clementinae*, certain changes may be noted with regard to appellate procedure. If the cause has been heard in first instance before a collegiate tribunal and the sentence of the latter has been appealed, the appeal need only be filed with one of the judges, although notice of it together with all the facts concerning it, is to be given to the other judges.[46]

It is further decreed that the appellant should seek the *apostoli* in due time. It is sufficient if a petition is made for them at the time that the appeal is filed. If the judge sets a certain time for the

[41] Cc. 1, 4, 10, *de appellationibus*, II, 15, in VI°.
[42] C. 6, *de appellationibus*, II, 15, in VI°.
[43] Cc. 4, 6, *de appellationibus*, II, 15, in VI°.
[44] C. 7, *de appellationibus*, II, 15, in VI°.
[45] *Regula* 46, *R. J.*, in VI°.
[46] C. 1, *de appellationibus*, II, 12, in Clem.

granting of the *litterae dimissoriae* and the appellant does not appear in court to receive them, he shall be thought to have abandoned his appeal. On the other hand, the appellant is granted the right of prosecuting his appeal if the judge neglects to grant the *apostoli* on the determined date.[47] Prosecution of an appeal may be deferred by a compromise or with the expressed consent of the interested parties, in which case, the term for the prosecution of the appeal will be reckoned only from the day that the compromise has been ended or the agreement cancelled.[48] Finally, it is declared that an appeal from an interlocutory sentence must be restricted to that particular point to which objection was made. It cannot be extended to other questions or other parts of the cause which had not been appealed.[49]

Further legislation on the question of appeals during this period is to be found in a few constitutions of the Popes. Clement VI in a letter written in 1351 defines certain points that are to be believed and professed in regard to the plenitude of power possessed by the Pope. The Supreme Pontiff enjoys a primacy of jurisdiction over the entire world, as the lawful successor of St. Peter. He has the power of judging all men and similarly, of delegating judges for the hearing of all causes. There can be no appeal from his sentence of judgment to any other judge.[50] This claim was confirmed and a severe sanction was added to it for all who presumed to appeal to a future general council from a sentence of the Pope, by Pope Pius II in 1459.[51] Pope Julius II repeated and confirmed the claim and the penalty in 1509.[52] Leo X in the constitution *"Regimini Universalis,"* confirmed the decrees of the Fifth Lateran Council held in 1511 and declared in addition that all causes which tend to disturb the ecclesiastical order, are to be concluded as soon as possible by the court of first instance. He stated, further, that no appeal was to be admitted before a definitive sentence had been pronounced; likewise, no appeal was to be accepted from an interlocutory sen-

[47] C. 2, *de appellationibus,* II, 12, in Clem.
[48] C. 4, *de appellationibus,* II, 12, in Clem.
[49] C. 5, *de appellationibus,* II, 12, in Clem.
[50] Ep. *"Super Quibusdam,"* 29 Sept. 1351—*Fontes,* n. 42.
[51] Const. *"Exsecrabilis,"* 18 Jan. 1459—*Fontes,* n. 55.
[52] Const. *"Suscepti Regiminis,"* 1 Jul. 1509—*Fontes,* n. 64.

tence unless the latter had definitive force or the grievance caused by it could be corrected by a definitive sentence.[53] This constitution is the first definite ecclesiastical legislation on interlocutory sentences and is an important development in the history of appeals. It restores the discipline of Roman Law with regard to sentences of this type and appeal from them. The Church law of the period had permitted appeals from such sentences and this practice gave rise to a number of abuses that involved the defeat of the ends of justice by needlessly delaying the execution of a just sentence.

At the end of this period preceding the Council of Trent, the Church was in possession of a complete system of law governing appellate procedure, the most perfect then in existence and one never surpassed for prudence, moderation, absolute fairness and sound practical judgment. It remained for the Council of Trent to clarify and unify certain portions of this legislation to make it more effective and exact.

[53] Const. "*Regimini Universalis,*" 4 Mai 1515—*Fontes*, n. 66.

# CHAPTER V

## APPELLATE LEGISLATION FROM THE COUNCIL OF TRENT TO THE PROMULGATION OF THE CODE OF CANON LAW

THIS period of Canon Law, the *jus novissimum,* did not make any appreciable contribution to the development of the institution of appeal. By this time, the appellate procedure was defined practically as it is today and the various elements of this judicial remedy had been recognized and its provisions observed for many years prior to the Council of Trent. However, the Council reordered and revised certain parts of the existing legislation for the purpose of facilitating appellate procedure for those who used this method of defense legitimately and of rendering it more difficult for defendants who employed it as a subterfuge for delaying court proceedings or averting the immediate execution of a just sentence. These regulations were confirmed for the most part by the papal constitutions and the decrees of the Sacred Congregations that were issued later in this period.

### ARTICLE I. THE COUNCIL OF TRENT

The Council of Trent, while it restricts itself largely to the repetition of the provisions of the existing law as contained in the *Corpus Juris Canonici,* adds a few salutary regulations that tend to make the legislation in the latter body of law, more binding in character. It decreed that the form and tenor of the sacred constitutions is binding on all apostolic legates and nuncios, patriarchs, primates and metropolitans in every case of appeal interposed before them or when they are called upon to decide on the admission of an appeal into a higher instance or to grant inhibitions after an appeal has been made. The canon declared that this procedure was to be observed despite any custom, even immemorial, or privilege to the contrary and that, under the penalty of nullity *ipso iure* and extending to all the inhibitions, proceedings and consequences thereof. Reference is made to the constitution "*Romana*" of Innocent IV.[1]

The courts of inferior prelates for matrimonial and criminal causes are abolished and the first instance is declared to be the court of the local ordinary. Exception is made relative to those causes which pursuant to the appointments of the sacred canons are to be tried before the Holy See or which the Roman Pontiff shall for an urgent and reasonable cause avocate for his own hearing by a special rescript over the signature of the Pope himself. All causes should be terminated within two years from the time that the suit was instituted.[2]

When the law permits the interposition of an appeal from the sentence of a bishop or the latter's vicar general, the appeal must be taken to the metropolitan of the province who shall judge the appeal. If he be under suspicion for some reason, or if he be distant more than two days' journey, or if it be from him that the appeal is made, the cause shall be submitted to one of the neighboring bishops but not to an inferior judge.[3]

The council further decreed that in causes relative to episcopal visitations and the correction of morals, or in questions of competency or incompetency and also in criminal causes, there shall be no appeal from an interlocutory sentence before a definitive sentence has been pronounced on the cause in question. Exceptions are allowed to this regulation if the grievance cannot be repaired by the subsequent definitive sentence or if the latter by law admits of no appeal. In such cases, the statutes of the sacred canons are to be observed.[4] Moreover, a sentence pronounced by the bishop during a visitation or for the correction of morals cannot be appealed if the purpose of the appeal is to delay needlessly the execution of that sentence. Under no circumstances can the execution of the sentence be suspended. This is rather a rigorous regulation, seemingly enacted for emergency purposes as will be disclosed by a perusal of papal documents issued during subsequent years.[5]

[1] Conc. Trident., sess. XXII, *de ref.*, c. 7; c. 3, *de appell.*, II, 15, in VI°.
[2] Conc. Trident., sess. XXIV, *de ref.*, c. 20.
[3] Conc. Trident., sess. XIII, *de ref.*, c. 2.
[4] Conc. Trident., sess. XIII, *de ref.*, c. 1.
[5] Conc. Trident., sess XXIV, *de ref.*, c. 10.

In a criminal cause, the appellant is ordered to present the *acta causae* of the first instance to the appellate judge and the latter is forbidden to proceed until he has inspected these acts. The judge of the lower court is obliged to furnish the *acta* to the appellant within thirty days. Special stress is laid on this feature of appellate procedure.[6]

The foregoing regulations, together with those contained in the *Corpus Juris Canonici,* complete the appellate system that is in the possession of the Church by the end of the sixteenth century. The ordinances and decrees issued by the Popes and the Roman Congregations during subsequent years, are ordinarily for the purpose of interpreting the existing legislation or extending its provisions to cases or conditions that had their own peculiar needs and requirements.

### Article II. The Papal Constitutions

The first papal constitution relative to appellate procedure was published by Pope Pius IV in 1560 during the period following the suspension of the Council in 1552. It was intended to confirm the constitution *"Regimini Universalis,"* issued by Pope Leo X in 1515 to the effect that an appeal from an interlocutory sentence may not be admitted or received by any judge.[7]

The encyclical *"Cum Illud"* [8] which was issued by Pope Benedict XIV in 1742, applies the regulations governing appellate procedure to causes relative to the filling of vacancies in parish churches and permits the benefit of appeal to those who regard themselves as better adapted for the position in question, against one less fit who has been selected by the bishop. This is an example of the extrajudicial appeal of the pre-Code discipline; the present legislation considers this proceeding as recourse, *recursus.*

The most noteworthy constitutions of this Pope, with regard to appeals, are the *"Dei Miseratione"* and the *"Ad Militantis,"* issued in 1741 and 1742 respectively. The constitution *"Dei Miseratione"*[9] dealt with the formalities to be observed in processes affecting the

[6] Conc. Trident., sess. XIII, *de ref.*, c. 3.

[7] Pius IV, const. *"De Salute Gregis,"* 4 Sept. 1560, n. 6—*Fontes,* n. 98.

[8] *Documentum IV, Appendix Codicis Iuris Canonici.*

[9] Bened. XIV, const. *"Dei Miseratione,"* 30 Nov. 1741—*Fontes,* n. 318.

matrimonial bond. The hasty decisions by which some tribunals adjudged a marriage to be invalid and permitted the parties to enter new unions was a problem that faced the Pope.[10] This document stabilized matrimonial procedure and became the basis of the present judicial system for matrimonial causes. It repeated the provisions of the Council of Trent denying competency in matrimonial causes to prelates inferior in rank to the bishop and introduced a new figure in matrimonial trials, the defender of the marriage bond, *defensor vinculi*.[11] His presence was required in all causes concerning the bond of marriage and he was obliged by law to appeal a sentence in the first instance decreeing the nullity of a marriage.[12] After a second sentence had been passed declaring for the nullity of the marriage in question, he could appeal if he were not satisfied with the verdict, or he could refrain from any further action in the case. It was left strictly to his conscience whether or not he should appeal.[13] It is declared again that matrimonial causes never become *res iudicatae* and the parties engaged in the action could contract new marriages only after two conformable sentences decreeing nullity and the lapse of the term allowed by law for the interposition of an appeal.[14] The proper court of second instance was the tribunal of the metropolitan, the papal nuncio, the neighboring bishop or a delegated judge.[15] The Holy See might be the tribunal of the first, second or third instance. Procedure governing appeals in causes that are sent to Rome, is also determined in this constitution and the Pope declared the Congregation of Cardinals for the Interpretation and Execution of the Decrees of the Council of Trent (the Sacred Congregation of the Council) and the Auditory of the Sacred Palace (the Rota) competent to receive and pass on appeals of this nature.[16]

[10] Cf. Bened. XIV, encycl. "*Matrimonii,*" 11 Apr. 1741—*Fontes,* n. 307; encycl. "*Quamvis paternae,*" 26 Aug. 1741—*Fontes,* n. 315; *De Synodo Dioecesana,* lib. IV, cap. 5, n. 6.

[11] "*Dei Miseratione,*" n. 5. It is claimed by some authors that this official had been recognized already in the thirteenth century. Cf. Hostiensis (Henry Cardinal de Segusia), *Summa Aurea,* IV, p. 322.

[12] "*Dei Miseratione,*" n. 8.

[13] "*Dei Miseratione,*" n. 11.

[14] "*Dei Miseratione,*" n. 14.

[15] "*Dei Miseratione,*" n. 10.

[16] "*Dei Miseratione,*" n. 13.

Similar provisions were enacted a few years later by the same Pope for causes concerning Sacred Orders.[17]

The constitution *"Ad Militantis"* [18] was concerned with the enforcement of the decrees of the Council of Trent and outlined at the same time certain restrictions with regard to appeals. It contained and confirmed the provisions of the Council of Trent and the decree issued by Clement VIII through the Sacred Congregation of Bishops and Regulars in 1600,[19] and in addition, placed certain rigorous limitations on appeals *in suspensivo,* enumerating those causes in which an appeal could not suspend the execution of a sentence.[20] There is some ambiguity with regard to the usage of the term *appellatio,* the word being used indiscriminately for judicial, administrative or disciplinary causes. Provision is made, however, for what is called an extra-judicial recourse which is to be had directly to the Holy See *in devolutivo* only, when no appeal was allowed.[21]

## Article III. The Roman Congregations

The regulations issued by different popes through the medium of the Roman Congregations, are concerned for the most part with the interpretation and application of appellate legislation in particular instances or under peculiar circumstances. The decrees have an official character and are authoritative for the special cases for which they were issued, with the result that in time, they became the norm by which the law was applied. The rescripts issued by the Sacred Congregation of the Council during this period had for their purpose the explanation and adaptation of the Tridentine regulations and there are noted among these a few that treat of appellate procedure.

Various ordinances of the Council of Trent relative to delegated judges gave rise to certain doubts regarding the tribunals of appeal. Accordingly, a rescript of the year 1588 declares that an appeal from the sentence of an ordinary who acts as a judge by virtue of papal delegation, is to be made to the metropolitan or ordinary court of

[17] Bened. XIV, const. *"Si Datam,"* 4 Mart. 1748—*Fontes,* n. 385.
[18] Bened. XIV, const. *"Ad Militantis,"* 30 Mart. 1742—*Fontes,* n. 326.
[19] *"Ad Militantis,"* §4, §21, §42, §43 ff.
[20] *"Ad Militantis,"* §5 to §37.
[21] *"Ad Militantis,"* §38.

second instance and not to the Holy See.[22] A rescript of 1592 declares that when it is evident that the judge of the lower court is contumacious in refusing to give the appellant the *acta* of the trial, the appellate judge is empowered to declare these acts null and void.[23] A rescript issued in 1635 decrees that no appeal even from a definitive sentence, is to be received from a contumacious appellant if the latter persists in his contumacy or contempt for the court.[24] In 1700, the Congregation declared in response to certain doubts proposed by the bishops of Sardinia, that an appeal was to be admitted only if it were made by a public document drawn up in accordance with the prescriptions of the law, interposed in those causes appealable by law and against definitive sentences alone, or judgments that had definitive force or a grievance that could not be corrected by a definitive sentence; it declared, moreover, that where an appeal *in suspensivo* was granted by law, it was to be allowed by the judge, that appeals are not to be made *per saltum* but to the next judge hierarchically superior or determined by law as the ordinary court of appeals and that, finally, appeals that were filed for the purpose of preventing the execution of the decrees of the Council of Trent relative to necessary reforms, were not to be admitted.[25] The Sacred Council in 1750 denied appellate jurisdiction of whatever kind to the notary of the diocesan curia[26] and in 1823 declared that the vicar general and his ordinary formed one tribunal and consequently, an appeal from the judgment of the vicar general was to be taken, not to his ordinary, but to the metropolitan.[27] Many rescripts were issued during this period that were concerned primarily with extrajudicial appeals. The word "appeal" is employed but it refers rather to the recourse, *"recursus,"* of administrative or disciplinary procedure.[28]

[22] S. C. C., Tarraconen., a. 1588; S. C. C., Zamoren., a. 1589; S. C. C., Januen., a. 1597—Richter, *Canones et Decreta Concilii Tridentini*, p. 166.

[23] S. C. C., *Comen.*, 5 April 1592—*Fontes*, n. 2240.

[24] S. C. C., *Arianen.*, 28 April 1635—*Fontes*, n. 2575.

[25] S. C. C., *Sardiniae*, 3, 24 April, 15 May 1700—*Fontes*, n. 2977.

[26] S. C. C., *Ravennat. seu Faventina*, 18 April 1750—*Thes. Resolut. S. C. C.*, XIV, 109.

[27] S. C. C., *Ostunen.*, 12 Jul. 1823—*Thes. Resolut. S. C. C.*, LXXXIII, 168.

[28] Cf. S. C. C., *Feretrana*, 6 Sept. 1591—Richter, *Canones et Decreta Conc. Trid.*, p. 71; *Sagonen.*, 21 June 1623—*Fontes*, n. 2442; *Capritana*, 16 Dec. 1730—*Fontes*, n. 3368.

The decree issued by Pope Clement VIII through the Sacred Congregations of Bishops and Regulars in 1600 had for its purpose the correction of abuses caused by delay in the execution of the ordinances of the Council of Trent. It repeated the injunctions regarding appeals as set forth in the Tridentine legislation and defined certain points more clearly relative to the competence of original and appellate judges, the formalities required in the placing and prosecution of an appeal, the proper effects of the appeal itself in certain cases and the contumacious conduct of the judge of first instance or the appellant.[29] The provisions contained in this decree appear later in the constitution *"Ad Militantis"* of Benedict XIV and in many of the rescripts of the Sacred Congregation of the Council.

The same Congregation issued decrees in 1835 and 1851 for the purpose of expediting the procedure relative to the interposition and prosecution of appeals in criminal causes, particularly those which were sent to the Congregation proper. While these decrees repeat in substance the provisions of the constitution *"Ad Militantis,"* the general tone of the prescriptions is not quite so rigorous as the former.[30] An important instruction was issued by Pope Leo XIII through this Congregation in 1880 permitting ordinaries to dispense with the formalities of a solemn canonical trial in disciplinary and criminal causes against clerics and allowing them to judge such causes by a summary process. It comprised all the essential rules of canonical procedure which the Roman Congregations of the preceding three centuries had held to be applicable and had in fact employed, when circumstances necessitated some departure from the ordinary method of procedure. The instruction regulated the proceedings in the lower court and also before the appellate tribunal. The provisions of the constitution *"Ad Militantis"* and the decree of the same Congregation published in 1835 again form the norm of appellate procedure.[31] A few years later, at the request of this Congregation, the instruction of 1880 became the norm governing canonical procedure in criminal and disciplinary causes in the United States

[29] S. C. Ep. et Reg., *decr.*, 16 Oct. 1600—*Fontes*, n. 1586.

[30] S. C. Ep. et Reg., *decr.*, 18 Dec. 1835—*Fontes*, n. 1908; encycl., 1 Aug. 1851—*Fontes*, n. 1961.

[31] S. C. Ep. et Reg., instr., 11 June 1880—*Fontes*, n. 2005.

and was reissued as the Instruction "*Cum Magnopere*" containing a few changes calculated to meet the requirements of certain circumstances peculiar to this country.[32] The Third Plenary Council of Baltimore incorporated the Instruction "*Cum Magnopere*" into its canons [33] and at the same time included the instruction on matrimonial procedure [34] issued by the Sacred Congregation of the Propagation of the Faith in 1883 for the United States.[35] This Instruction repeats substantially the provisions of the constitution "*Dei Miseratione*" relative to appeals.

## ARTICLE IV. THE ROMAN TRIBUNALS

The reorganization of the Roman curia was effected through the constitution "*Sapienti consilio*," issued by Pope Pius X in 1908.[36] At the same time, there appeared the "*Ordo Servandus in S. Congregationibus, Tribunalibus, Officiis Romanae Curiae*" [37] and the "*Lex Propria Sacrae Romanae Rotae et Signaturae Apostolicae*" [38] which introduced a general division of jurisdiction into the judicial power of the Tribunals and the administrative competence of the Congregations. This was further outlined in the "*Regulae Servandae in Iudiciis apud S. R. Rotae Tribunal*" [39] and the corresponding "*Regulae Servandae in Iudiciis apud Supremum Signaturae Apostolicae Tribunal.*" [40] Pope Benedict XV in 1915 [41] extended the competence of the Signatura in certain phases of matrimonial procedure

[32] S. C. de Prop. Fid., instr., 1883—*Collectanea S. C. de Prop. Fid.*, n. 1586.

[33] *Concilii Plenarii Baltimorensis III, Acta et Decreta*, nn. 298, 311.

[34] *Concilii Plenarii Baltimorensis III, Acta et Decreta*, n. 304.

[35] S. C. de Prop. Fid., instr., 1883—*Collect. S. C. de Prop. Fid.*, n. 1587. A comparison of this instruction with the "*Instructio pro Iudiciis Ecclesiasticiis Imperii Austriaci quoad Causas Matrimoniales*," commonly referred to as "The Austrian Instruction," drawn up by Cardinal Rauscher for use in Austria in 1855 and suggested as the norm for matrimonial causes in the United States by the Council of Baltimore in 1884 (cf. *Conc. Plen. Balt. III, Acta et Decr.*, n. 304), will show that the two have many points in common. Cf. *Collectio Lacensis*, V, 1286 ff.

[36] Pius X, const. "*Sapienti consilio*," 29 June 1908—*Fontes*, n. 682.

[37] *AAS*, I (1909), 36.

[38] *AAS*, I (1909), 20.

[39] August 4, 1910—*AAS*, II (1910), 783.

[40] March 6, 1912—*AAS*, IV (1912), 187.

[41] Benedict XV, chirog. "*Attentis expositis*," 28 June 1915—*Fontes*, n. 705.

particularly with regard to the *Restitutio in integrum* and the *Querela nullitatis* interposed against Rotal sentences.

The Rota is more frequently a tribunal of appeal.[42] While the Rota judges as a tribunal of first instance, causes which are reserved for its cognizance by the Code [43] or which the Roman Pontiff has reserved for Himself and committed to the Rota for judgment,[44] it acts as the court of second instance to receive appeals interposed against sentences rendered by inferior tribunals of first instance [45] or as the court of third or final instance for causes that have been judged in the second instance by inferior tribunals and appealed, not having become *res iudicatae*.[46] Moreover, the Rota receives the first, second or further appeal in causes that have been judged by another Rotal *turnus* and have not become *res iudicatae*.[47] If the Rotal sentence conforms to that pronounced by the previous tribunal whether the latter be a *turnus* of the Rota or an inferior court, no appeal is admissible, for the cause has become a *res iudicata*. Recourse may be had, however, to the Signatura by means of a *querela nullitatis* or a petition for a *restitutio in integrum*. The only exception to this rule respects causes that affect the state of a person for these never become *res iudicatae*.[48] If, however, a sentence of the Rota does not confirm the judgment of the preceding *turnus* or inferior tribunal, it may be appealed to another *turnus* consisting of three auditors distinct and different from the former in-

[42] It is obviously not within the confines of this dissertation to engage in any discussion relative to the origin, constitution and practise of the Rota from the point of view of history nor to present a commentary on the Rotal procedure of the present period. For further information regarding these points, reference may be had to Cerchiari, *Capellani Papae et Apostolicae Sedis Auditores Causarum Sacri Palatii Apostolici seu Sacra Romana Rota,* I, p. 1 ff.; Ojetti, *De Romana Curia,* p. 175 ff.; Martin, *The Roman Curia,* p. 137; Leitner, *De Curia Romana,* p. 25; Hinschius, *System des Katholischen Kirchenrechts,* I, 392 ff.; Monin, *De Curia Romana,* pp. 96, 336; Roberti, *De Processibus,* I, n. 128 ff.; Korr, *Die Appellation an die Sacra Rota Romana nach geltendem Kanonischem Recht,* p. 11; Cappello, *De Curia Romana,* I, p. 369 ff.; Schneider, *Die Römische Rota nach geltendem Recht auf geschichtlicher Grundlage.*

[43] *Lex Prop.*, can. 14, §1; C. I. C., can. 1557, §2.

[44] *Lex Prop.*, can. 14, §1; C. I. C., can. 1599, §2.

[45] *Lex Prop.*, can. 14, §2; C. I. C., can. 1599, §1, n. 1.

[46] *Lex Prop.*, can. 14, §3; C. I. C., can. 1599, §1, n. 2.

[47] *Lex Prop.*, can. 14, §1; C. I. C., can. 1599, §1, n. 2.

[48] *Lex Prop.*, can. 33, §1; *Reg. Serv. in iudic. apud S. R. Rotae Trib.*, §211.

stance.[49] The proceedings before the appellate instance as well as the method of interposing and prosecuting an appeal in the Rota differ but little from the present mode of procedure as contained in the Code. These differences will be pointed out in the course of the commentary on the appellate legislation in the Code.

## Conclusion

In conclusion, the general, historical outline of the evolution of appeal, brings to light certain developments worthy of note. In Roman Law, a real development took place with regard to this legal remedy. From the simple *provocatio ad populum* of the period of the Monarchy, this mode of defense against injustice progressed and unfolded gradually, with the result that by the middle of the sixth century, the Empire of Rome was in possession of a code of law in which the institution of appeal and the formalities of appellate procedure reached the highest degree of perfection and the greatest development it was ever to attain under the Roman standard.

In the history of this judicial remedy in ecclesiastical legislation, the same situation does not hold true. Many and varied evidences of the use of appeal are found both in the period preceding the Council of Sardica and subsequent to it. However, the legal niceties of judicial and formal procedure do not make their appearance until a much later date. Beyond the insistence on the right of appeal as belonging to all in ordinary cases and its complement, the prohibition of an appeal of any character from the sentence of the Pope, the determination of the several instances of appellate procedure and certain vague declarations relative to the suspensive effect of an appeal, no particular development in this institution was witnessed until the twelfth century which marked the appearance of the Decree of Gratian, and the convoking of the III Lateran Council. The IV Lateran Council and the promulgation of the Decretals of Gregory IX in the following century marked a further progressive and somewhat final step in this evolution. Thereafter, the Church had a sys-

[49] *Lex Prop.*, can. 33, §2; *Reg. Serv. in iudic. apud S. R. Rotae Trib.*, §211, n 1. The method of rotation of the *turni* is described in canon 12 of the *Lex Propria.*

tem of law, containing the formalities of appellate procedure that reached the position occupied by Roman Law some centuries previously. It cannot be said that this came about as the result of a slow, evolutionary process, particularly with regard to the judicial remedy under consideration. The development, if such it may be called, took place in a very short space of time, the formalities of appellate procedure, absorbed more or less unconsciously from Roman Law by the canonists of the time, making their appearance somewhat suddenly. Thereafter, the development is concerned with a more exact determination of the several instances in which appeals may be interposed and prosecuted, with a more efficient administration of justice as represented by this mode of redress, the effect of which was the discarding of useless, futile and inane appeals as well as appeals from interlocutory sentences and with the extension of this legal remedy to certain specified causes which are outlined in the Tridentine decrees, the various papal constitutions and the rescripts and instructions of papal congregations.

Only those phases of development which would serve to delineate the progress of this institution, have been touched upon. The present interpretation of this legislation as embodied in the Code of Canon Law, forms the subject of the remainder of this dissertation.

# PART II

## A JURIDICAL SURVEY OF THE APPELLATE LEGISLATION IN THE CODE

# CHAPTER VI

## THE RIGHT OF APPEAL

**Canon 1879. Pars quae aliqua sententia se gravatam putat, itemque promotor justitiae et defensor vinculi in causis in quibus interfuerunt, ius habent a sententia appellandi, id est provocandi ab inferiore iudice qui sententiam tulit, ad superiorem, salvo praescripto can. 1880.**

APPEAL is a legitimate means of defense and a legal protection of innocence and natural equity demands that this mode of redress be extended, subject to the prescriptions of the law, to all who are not otherwise rendered incapable of using it.[1] An appeal, generally speaking, is permitted by law to any and all parties interested in a suit if the sentence pronounced by the judge on the cause in question, is not considered to be in accordance with the requirements of justice.[2] Accordingly, the plaintiff or the defendant, the *actor* or the *reus*, and those associated with either party in the trial, the litigant who presses his suit with partial success but who thinks his rights have not been sufficiently vindicated as well as the party against whose interests the sentence has been pronounced, may file an appeal against the judicial pronouncement of the judge.[3] The same rights are enjoyed by the heirs or successors of either party to the suit.[4]

[1] Cf. Schmalzgrueber, lib. II, tit. XXVIII, nn. 6, 16; Reiffenstuel, lib. II, tit. XXVIII, nn. 32, 281.

[2] Wernz-Vidal, *De Processibus*, n. 602; Noval, *De Processibus*, n. 643; Roberti, *De Processibus*, II, n. 468; Vermeersch-Creusen, *Epitome*, III, n. 237; Blat, *De Processibus*, n. 409; Cocchi, *De Processibus*, n. 223; Schmalzgrueber, lib. II, tit. XXVIII, n. 7; Reiffenstuel, lib. II, tit. XXVIII, n. 32; Bouix, *De Iudiciis*, II, 248; Lega, *De Iudiciis*, I, n. 629.

[3] Wernz-Vidal, *De Processibus*, n. 602; Vermeersch-Creusen, *Epitome*, III, n. 237; Noval, *De Processibus*, n. 643.

[4] Can. 1733, §1, §2.

The exercise of this right occcurs when one of the litigants dies, changes his state of life or gives up the office by virtue of which he is involved in litigation. The counsel, attorney or procurator for either party has a similar right,[5] which is extended in like fashion to the tutors, guardians, etc., of the interested parties.[6] The right of appeal is so extended because the juridical status of the litigants is considered rather than the individual personality itself, and consequently, all who are in any way concerned with or interested in the point at issue may appeal from the sentence of the judge.[7] A third party who suffers some particular loss or undue abridgment of his rights through a sentence which he considers unjust, may avail himself of an extraordinary means of redress, called *oppositio tertii,* provision for which has been made in the Code.[8]

The defender of the marriage bond, *defensor vinculi,* and the promoter of justice, *promotor iustitiae,* may also have a just complaint to make against a judicial sentence and accordingly, each is permitted to interpose an appeal when acting in his official capacity and when convinced that the public welfare has not been sufficiently protected.[9] The question of appeals is of significant interest to the defender of the marriage bond.[10] It has not been considered necessary or relevant to the question under discussion to engage in any protracted examination of the obligations, rights and privileges of the *defensor vinculi* with regard to his office of protecting and defending the integrity of the marriage bond.[11] It will be sufficient to point out the obligation that is incumbent upon him of appealing from a sentence declaring for the nullity of a marriage in the first instance.

*The Defensor Vinculi and the Solemn Judicial Process.* Canon

[5] Can. 1664, §2.

[6] Wernz-Vidal, *De Processibus,* n. 602.

[7] Roberti, *De Processibus,* II, n. 468.

[8] Can. 1898-1901; cf. Lega, *De Iudiciis,* I, n. 630; Noval, *De Processibus,* n. 643.

[9] Roberti, *De Processibus,* II, n. 468; Blat, *De Processibus,* n. 409; cf. can. 1986, 1987, 1991, 1998, §2.

[10] Can. 1967. The institution of this office by Benedict XIV in the constitution "*Dei Miseratione,*" has been described in a previous article.

[11] Can. 1968, 1969, 1984, etc.

1986 [12] ordains that the *defensor vinculi* must, within the time granted by law, appeal to a superior tribunal, if the sentence of the first court defines the nullity of the marriage in question.[13] This is a solemn and strict obligation and it is binding whether the party against whom the sentence has been pronounced, appeals or not, and despite the absence of any juridical cause or reason for an appeal, v. g., an unjust sentence.[14] Vlaming [15] declares that the *defensor vinculi* must appeal only when the defendant whose marriage has been declared null, refuses to appeal. The Code does not mention this obvious qualification; it merely insists that the *defensor* appeal from a sentence in first instance decreeing the nullity of marriage to the extent that if he should neglect his duty in this respect, the judge is empowered to compel him to fulfill this obligation of his office, even by threatening to impose ecclesiastical penalties on him for his malfeasance or to have him removed from the office itself.[16] This canon seems to confer some punitive power on the judge for this particular case.[17] If, however, the sentence rendered on the merits of the cause, favors the validity of the marriage, the defender of the bond cannot interpose an appeal for he is present merely as a representative of the Church to protect the matrimonial tie. He is not permitted to attack it or to impugn its valid character in any manner whatsoever.[18] The party who is attacking the validity of his marriage, may appeal if the sentence pronounced by the judge favors the validity of the marriage in question.[19] The *promotor iustitiae* also enjoys this right because he is empowered by the Code to take

[12] Can. 1986. "A prima sententia, quae matrimonii nullitatem declaraverit, vinculi defensor, intra legitimum tempus, ad superius tribunal provocare debet; et si negligat officium suum implere, compellatur auctoritate iudicis."

[13] Cappello, *De Sacramentis,* III, n. 887; Noval, *De Processibus,* n. 868; Chelodi, *Ius Matrimoniale,* n. 179; Payen, *De Matrimonio,* III, n. 2715; Gasparri, *De Matrimonio,* II, n. 1506.

[14] Cappello, *De Sacramentis,* III, n. 887.

[15] *Praelectiones Iuris Matrimonii,* II, n. 802.

[16] Wernz-Vidal, *Ius Matrimoniale,* n. 703; Augustine, *A Commentary,* V, 432; Vlaming, *Praelectiones,* II, n. 802; cf. can. 1626.

[17] Noval, *De Processibus,* nn. 868, 219.

[18] Can. 1968. Cf. Wernz-Vidal, *Ius Matrimoniale,* n. 703; Payen, *De Matrimonio,* III, n. 2715; Cappello, *De Sacramentis,* III, n. 887; Chelodi, *Ius Matrimoniale,* n. 179.

[19] Vlaming, *Praelectiones,* II, n. 802; Wernz-Vidal, *Ius Matrimoniale,* n. 703; Gougnard, *Tractatus de Matrim.,* p. 543.

action against a marriage invalid by reason of an impediment that is *natura sua* public.[20] If the sentence favors the validity of the marriage, the *promotor* can appeal if he has any reason to believe that the valid character of the marriage has not been sufficiently demonstrated. There is no obligation on his part to appeal. It is merely his duty to see that, in the interests of the common good, a marriage be annulled if it has been invalidly contracted; or, if otherwise, confirmed.

Appeals in matrimonial causes, with the exception of some few concessions granted by law to the *defensor vinculi* in view of the character of his office, follow the prescriptions of the Code relative to appeals in general, as hereinafter explained.

*The Defensor Vinculi and the Documentary Process.* This particular process has been the subject of an extensive controversy since the appearance of the Code. Is the documentary process of canons 1990-1992 judicial or administrative in character? [21] The controversy is purely an academic question if the Ordinary himself reviews and decides on the merits, authenticity, etc., of the documents submitted in proof of the presence of one of the impediments *taxative* mentioned in canon 1990 or of the absence of any dispensation from the impediment in question, because the Ordinary possesses both judicial and administrative power.[22] However, the Code [23] declares that it is not always expedient for the Ordinary to preside over all cases that are brought to the curia for decision. Accordingly, the controversy has some practical value for the Ordinary can exercise his power *per se vel per alios.* Shall he refer the causes that are excepted from the solemn judicial process, to the vicar general, his representative in matters of an administrative nature, or to the *officialis,* the judge who acts for him in the diocesan curia? While it is true that the majority of canonists re-

[20] Can. 1971, §1, n. 2.

[21] Some authors mistakenly term this mode of procedure, the summary process. Cf. Roberti, *De Processibus,* I, p. 26, note 1. The summary process comprises rather the cases contained in the third part of the fourth book of the Code, can. 2142 ff.; cf. Noval, *De Processibus,* n. 35; Vermeersch-Creusen, *Epitome,* III, n. 4.

[22] Can. 335, §1.

[23] Can. 1578.

gard the process as administrative in nature,[24] the contrary opinion is held by commentators of equal weight and authority, who substantiate their stand on the question by sound reasoning and able arguments, a fact that is noticeably lacking in the contention of the former group. Noval [25] is particularly convincing in the reasons he advances for his attitude on the question. The controversy is thoroughly examined by Kay [26] who adopts the view that the process is strictly judicial in nature. This opinion is likewise shared by Triebs who advances solid arguments for his conclusion.[27]

There is no particular advantage to be gained, relative to the subject of this dissertation, by engaging in a thorough investigation of the different points of the controversy. It was judged sufficient merely to call attention to the dispute and to note the adoption by the writer of the opinion of Noval and others, to the effect that the documentary process as advocated by canons 1990-1992 is judicial in character.

Canon 1991 declares that the *defensor vinculi,* who has examined and investigated the nature and authenticity of the documents presented in support of the original contention, is obliged to appeal to the ordinary court of second instance if he is not satisfied with the sentence of the judge of the lower court decreeing the nullity of the marriage. The obligation of appealing from the sentence of nullity binds the *defensor* only if it appears to his prudent judgment that the alleged impediment did not exist or that a dispensa-

[24] Cappello, *De Sacramentis,* III, n. 891; Chelodi, *Ius Matrimoniale,* n. 180; Cerato, *De Matrimonio,* n. 169; Wernz-Vidal, *Ius Matrimoniale,* n. 704; De Smet, *De Sponsal. et Matrim.,* n. 702; Farrugia, *De Matrim. et Causis Matrim.,* nn. 164, 379; Payen, *De Matrimonio,* III, n. 2720; Vlaming, *Praelectiones,* II, n. 803 and Lanier, *Guide Pratique de la Procedure Matrimoniale,* pp. 2, 5. The last three authors mentioned are somewhat confused in regard to the distinct and precise meaning of the terms, "appeal," "recourse," "sentence," "declaration," "judge," "superior," etc.

[25] *De Processibus,* n. 873. Cf. also Blat, *De Processibus,* n. 551; Ferreres, *Institutiones Canonicae,* II, n. 864; Vermeersch-Creusen, *Epitome,* III, n. 297; Sipos, *Enchiridion Jur. Can.,* p. 884.

[26] *Competence in Matrimonial Procedure,* pp. 109-154. Cf. particularly p. 128, note 63 wherein Roberti is quoted as having expressed through the medium of a personal communication to the author, his opinion that the process is judicial in character.

[27] "De Interpretatione Canonum, 1990-1992"—*Periodica de Re Morali, Canonica, Liturgica,* XX (1931), pp. 93*-107*.

tion was granted from it. It is not required that he be absolutely certain or convinced of the non-existence of the impediment or the concession of a dispensation in the matter, to be obliged to appeal. A prudent doubt regarding the authentic nature of the documents and consequently of the existence of the impediment itself or the granting of a dispensation therefrom, would be sufficient to impel the defender to interpose an appeal against the sentence of nullity.[28] The defender cannot be forced to appeal as canon 1986 ordains. The entire matter is left to his prudent judgment and his conscience. It would be impossible to draw up exact rules to demonstrate when the defender of the bond should appeal and when he is not so obliged, for the question is referred to his discretion and judgment. He will naturally decide his stand on the problem when he inspects the documents, having in mind at the same time, the provisions of the Code relative to the proof established by various kinds of documents.[29] The *defensor vinculi* in appealing, should observe the general prescriptions of the Code with regard to appeals. All the acts of the cause are to be transmitted to the court of second instance with a notation to the effect that the sentence appealed was delivered in a documentary case wherein the ordinary formalities of a solemn judicial process were not observed.[30]

The promoter of justice may likewise appeal from the sentence of the Ordinary or the *officialis*. He is permitted by law to attack a marriage because of an impediment that is public by its nature.[31] and the impediments mentioned in this canon are regarded as such.[32] Similarly, either party in the case in question may appeal from the sentence in accordance with the ordinary provisions of the law.[33]

In general, all persons who are allowed to appear in court, not

[28] Noval, *De Processibus*, n. 874; Vermeersch-Creusen, *Epitome*, III, n. 296; Blat, *De Processibus*, n. 552.

[29] Can. 1812-1824.

[30] Can. 1991; Wernz-Vidal, *Ius Matrimoniale*, n. 704; Chelodi, *Ius Matrimoniale*, n. 180; Vlaming, *Praelectiones*, II, n. 803; Cappello, *De Sacramentis*, III, n. 891.

[31] Can. 1971, §1, n. 2.

[32] Can. 1037; Noval, *De Processibus*, n. 850; Augustine, *A Commentary*, V, 419; Chelodi, *Ius Matrimoniale*, n. 176; Vermeersch-Creusen, *Eptiome*, III, n. 286.

[33] Can. 1879.

only those who are permitted by law to become plaintiffs in an action [34] but also those who can stand in judgment, *in iudicio stare,* either personally or through the medium of a procurator, have the right to appeal from a sentence that appears unjust. Non-Catholics, heretics or infidels are included herein if they have received the permission of the Holy Office to institute a suit or file an action [35] or if they have been cited to appear as defendants in a suit. Excommunicated persons are likewise accorded the right to appeal if they have been allowed to take part in the litigation.[36] The enactments governing the lawfulness of excommunicated persons acting as plaintiffs are contained in the Code under a separate chapter—"*De actore et de reo convento.*" [37]

Appeal is a legitimate mode of defense and a legal protection of innocence, as has been declared previously, and as such, it can be denied to no one, except in so far as the law itself restricts the use of this means of redress.

Moreover, the sentence or judgment against which the appeal is interposed, must be definitive in character, that is, a judicial pronouncement on the principal cause that was proposed directly by the plaintiff and contained in the introductory *libellus.* It must be decisive and determined, settling the cause or controversy definitely for the plaintiff or for the defendant.[38] However, an interlocutory sentence that has been pronounced on an incidental question, raised during the course of the trial by one of the parties, or by the *defensor vinculi* or the *promotor iustitiae,* may partake of the nature of a definitive sentence or have definitive force. This occurs ordinarily in the following cases: when the interlocutory sentence defines one article of the principal cause; when it relieves a judge of further participation in the cause; when it admits or rejects a

[34] Can. 1646 ff.; cf. Vermeersch-Creusen, *Epitome,* III, nn. 76-79.

[35] S. C. S. Off., *resp.,* 18-27 Jan., 1928—*AAS.,* XX (1928), 75; cf. *Appollinaris,* I (1928), 214 ff.; Roberti, *De Processibus,* II, n. 468, note 1.

[36] Wernz-Vidal, *De Processibus,* n. 602; Vermeersch-Creusen, *Epitome,* III, n. 237; cf. c. 5, X, *de exceptionibus,* II, 25; Reiffenstuel, lib. II, tit. XXVIII. n. 35; Schmalzgrueber, lib. II, tit. XXVIII, n. 11.

[37] Title IV of Book IV—can. 1654. Cf. also can. 1628, §3; Noval, *De Processibus,* n. 262; Roberti, *De Processibus,* I, nn. 175, 205.

[38] Can. 1868, §1.

peremptory exception; when it imposes an obligation on one of the parties that cannot be remedied or corrected by the definitive sentence; and finally, when it is of such a nature that it so defines a point or question raised in the trial that the entire proceedings are thereby terminated, thus rendering a definitive sentence on the principal cause unnecessary.[39]

The sentence, finally, must be valid, that is, rendered in accordance with the requirements of canonical jurisprudence as contained in the Code.[40] No appeal is allowed from an invalid sentence.[41] It is admissible only if the sentence, valid in all respects, is considered unjust by the party in question who considers his rights as having been unlawfully restricted or injured by the sentence pronounced against him. The injustice may be the result of formal error,[42] ignorance or prejudice on the part of the judge, or negligence and carelessness on the part of the aggrieved person in the presentation of his case.[43] The aggrieved party may claim that the judgment or sentence, though formally valid in law, is yet materially unjust or unfair, that the law itself has been wrongly applied in the cause in question, that the law is no longer in force, that the present cause did not fall under the provisions of a certain law that were applied in the case; that the sentence is not sufficiently supported by the evidence produced, that the sentence is too severe and undeserved, etc. There can be no appeal against the law itself for this would amount to an impeachment of the law that was rightly applied in the case, as in itself unjust. Provision has been made in the Code[44] for the correction of material errors which appear in the sentence, by the judge who pronounced it.

The grievance against the sentence must be real, not imaginary, and must be supported by sound reasons. While canonists generally exclude all appeals that are filed with the intention of unnecessarily delaying the execution of a just sentence, appeals that are frivolous,

[39] Reiffenstuel, lib. II, tit. XXVII, n. 18 ff.; Wernz-Vidal, *De Processibus,* n. 606, note 61.

[40] Can. 1868-1877.

[41] Can. 1880, n. 3.

[42] Blat, *De Processibus,* n. 409.

[43] Bouix, *De Iudiciis,* II, 246.

[44] Can. 1878.

frustratory or based on inane or futile grounds, nevertheless, ecclesiastical legislation affords great latitude in this matter to those who consider the sentence pronounced on their case as unjust. In practise, it is frequently difficult to distinguish between the just or unjust, legitimate or frivolous reasons upon which an appeal is based and consequently, it would be a dangerous course for a judge to pursue, if he were to reject indiscriminately as unjust, appeals that were otherwise made legitimately and in accordance with the due forms of law.[45] If the appeal is based on a reasonably just cause and filed according to the prescriptions of the law, it should be accepted. It will often be left to the discretion of the judge of first instance whether or not, an appeal is to be allowed in a particular case and ordinarily, if the circumstances of the cause permit it at all, the benefit of the doubt concerning the probably legitimate character of an appeal, should be given to the appellant.[46] Similarly, an appeal that is made even in an important cause should be admitted without any question, if the prescriptions of the law in other respects are fulfilled.

[45] Wernz-Vidal, *De Processibus*, n. 600, note 11.

[46] Wernz-Vidal, *De Processibus*, n. 600, notes 10 and 11.

## CHAPTER VII

## LEGAL RESTRICTIONS ON THE RIGHT OF APPEAL

THE right to appeal, under the former discipline, was limited with respect to persons as well as with regard to the nature of certain causes.[1] The Code does not limit the use of this judicial remedy in this manner. The restriction is concerned not with the person of the litigant nor with the nature of the cause as such, but rather with the sentence that is rendered in certain particular cases. While some of the causes of the pre-Code legislation in which an appeal was inadmissible, are preserved in the present law, the latter is not quite as severe or rigorous in circumscribing this right as the former discipline. Appeal is considered as an ordinary remedy of law and a legal means of defense and is thereby conceded to all unless the law specifically provides otherwise and expressly excludes the use of this mode of redress. When the exercise of this right is prohibited by law, an appeal that is made contrary to the provisions of the Code, as contained in canon 1880, is not only unlawful but invalid. The direct exclusion of the right to appeal results in the cause becoming immediately a *res iudicata* and the sentence is forthwith to be executed.[2]

**Can. 1880. Non est locus appellationi:**

1. *A sententia ipsius Summi Pontificis vel Signaturae Apostolicae.* There is no appeal allowed from a sentence that is prononunced personally and directly by the Supreme Pontiff, for the reason that an appeal is an application made to a superior judge for redress against the sentence of an inferior tribunal and the Supreme Pontiff has no superior on earth. His tribunal is supreme and it sub-

[1] Cf. Lega, *De Iudiciis,* I, nn. 632, 633; Bouix, *De Iudiciis,* II, pp. 247-266; Schmalzgrueber, lib. II, tit. XXVIII, nn. 10-13, 20-31; Reiffenstuel, lib. II, tit. XXVIII, nn. 43-53.

[2] Can. 1902, n. 3; Noval, *De Processibus,* n. 644; Roberti, *De Processibus,* II, n. 469.

stantially excludes any superior court.[3] The Holy See may be judged by no one[4] and any appeal from its decisions is forbidden by divine law.[5] This follows from the primacy of jurisdiction enjoyed by the Pope. One cannot be judged by another unless he is subject to the latter *coactive* at least in the matter in dispute; the Vicar of Christ is *coactive* subordinate to no man, judge or tribunal.[6] For the same reasons, no appeal may be made from the sentence of the Roman Pontiff to a General Council.[7] There are numerous papal constitutions and epistles as well as decrees of councils that are indicative of the mind of the Church on this matter.[8] The mere interposition of an appeal constitutes a crime that is punishable by excommunication *latae sententiae,* reserved to the Holy See in a special manner.[9] When the Supreme Pontiff, however, judges a cause in the first instance, if the sentence is adverse to the interests of either contending party, the grace or benefit of a new hearing may be requested, during which the case will be subjected to a new examination.[10]

An appeal from a sentence pronounced by the Apostolic Signatura is likewise forbidden because this tribunal, by law, is supreme and represents the Roman Pontiff.[11] This prohibition is of ecclesiastical law only from which the Pope may dispense; such procedure, however, is somewhat unusual.[12] While an appeal is denied from the decisions of the Signatura, ample provision is made for the use of other remedies in order to correct or revise by means of a rehearing of the cause, the sentence that is alleged to be unjust.[13]

2. *A sententia iudicis qui a Sancta Sede delegatus est ad videndam causam cum clausula "appellatione remota."* An appeal is not

[3] Wernz-Vidal, *De Processibus,* n. 606.
[4] Can. 1556.
[5] Roberti, *De Processibus,* II, n. 469.
[6] Noval, *De Processibus,* n. 63.
[7] Can. 228, §2.
[8] Cf. Historical Conspectus, chap. III, art. II; chap. IV, art. III.
[9] Can. 2332; cf. Ayrinhac, *Penal Legislation,* pp. 232, 233.
[10] Roberti, *De Processibus,* II, n. 469; Wernz-Vidal, *De Processibus,* n. 606.
[11] Can. 1602; Noval, *De Processibus,* n. 644.
[12] Roberti, *De Processibus,* II, n. 469.
[13] Cf. can. 1569; Roberti, *De Processibus,* II, n. 469; Wernz-Vidal, *De Processibus,* n. 609, note 59.

admissible from the sentence of a judge delegated by the Holy See to take cognizance of a particular cause, if the special mandate of the delegated judge contains the clause "*appellatione remota.*" The use of this prohibitive clause is noticed frequently during the early middle ages under the law of the Decretals.[14] There was some dispute among canonists regarding the real significance of the prohibition, whether it was intended to exclude only useless and frivolous appeals [15] or whether the purpose of the clause was to remove entirely the possibility of appealing from any sentence whatsoever.[16] The general opinion seemed to be that frustratory or futile appeals were not the object of the restriction for appeals of this type were not to be admitted even under ordinary circumstances; [17] nor was it aimed at those causes which expressly and explicitly allowed the interposition of an appeal.[18] The main purpose of the prohibition was to prevent appeals being interposed against sentences that the law did not expressly declare to be appealable.[19] Bouix,[20] however, states that the clause was intended to exclude only the suspensive effect of a sentence, that the sentence as such could be appealed but only *in devolutivo;* moreover, this restriction affected only definitive sentences, not interlocutory judgments. The Council of Trent likewise made use of this clause in its disciplinary enactments [21] and it is also found in the constitution "*Ad Militantis*" of Benedict XIV.[22]

Under the present discipline, however, ordinaries do not, as a rule, delegate judges for particular causes with this restriction. The Holy See rarely delegates judges for particular cases and very sel-

[14] C. 8, X, *de rescriptis,* I, 3; c. 15, X, *de officio et potestate iudicis delegati,* I, 29; c. 8, X, *de officio iudicis ordinarii.* I, 31; cc. 4, 9, 41, X, *de appellationibus, recusationibus et relationibus,* II, 28.

[15] Schmalzgrueber, lib. II, tit. XXVIII, n. 29.

[16] Reiffenstuel, lib. II, tit. XXVIII, n. 287.

[17] Schmalzgrueber, lib. II, tit. XXVIII, nn. 29, 117.

[18] Schmalzgrueber, lib. II, tit. XXVIII, n. 29; Reiffenstuel, lib. II, tit. XXVIII, nn. 287, 288; Santi-Leitner, lib. II, tit. XXVIII, n. 13; Bouix, *De Iudiciis,* II, p. 263.

[19] Schmalzgrueber, lib. II, tit. XXVIII, n. 30; Reiffenstuel, lib. II, tit. XXVIII, n. 289.

[20] *De Iudiciis,* II, 265.

[21] Concil. Trident., sess. XIII, *de ref.,* c. 1; sess. XXIV, *de ref.,* c. 10.

[22] *Fontes,* n. 326.

dom with the clause *"appellatione remota."* [23] By the "Holy See" is understood in this regard, not only the Roman Pontiff but the ordinary Roman tribunals and congregations which exercise judicial power in the external forum.[24] When this clause is inserted in the rescript or mandate of delegation, it is to be interpreted strictly and the exceptions admitted in the Decretals are thereby excluded.[25] It deprives the litigants of the cause in question of the right of appeal under any circumstances; it does not, however, take away the privilege of using other legal remedies for the purpose of having an unjust sentence rectified, e. g., the *restitutio in integrum.*[26]

3. *A sententia vitio nullitatis infecta.* There can be no appeal from a sentence that is null and void. An appeal always presupposes a valid sentence; an invalid sentence is no sentence whatever, juridically considered.[27] A sentence may be null and invalid to such a degree that it cannot be rectified. Of this type are the following: a sentence which has been pronounced by a judge who was absolutely incompetent to render a decision on the cause; [28] a sentence rendered by a collegiate tribunal that lacks the proper number of judges prescribed by law; [29] a sentence that has been pronounced on a cause in which one of the interested parties was not entitled to bring suit in an ecclesiastical court; [30] a sentence that was rendered in a cause prosecuted by one party in the name of another without having been commissioned to do so by the latter. No procurator, counsel or administrator may prosecute a cause validly without a special and legitimate mandate.[31] Other sentences may be null and void for special reasons but in this case, the nullity of the judgment may be rectified. In this regard may be mentioned the following sentences which have curable defects: a sentence that is rendered on a cause wherein the legitimate summons or citation was omit-

[23] Noval, *De Processibus,* n. 644; Roberti, *De Processibus,* II, n. 469.
[24] Cf. Blat, *De Processibus,* n. 410; Noval, *De Processibus,* n. 644; can. 7.
[25] Wernz-Vidal, *De Processibus,* n. 606, note 60.
[26] Can. 1905; Augustine, *A Commentary,* VII, 320.
[27] Noval, *De Processibus,* n. 644; Vermeersch-Creusen, *Epitome,* III, n. 238.
[28] Can. 1611-1613.
[29] Can. 1576, §1; 1892, n. 1.
[30] Can. 1646, 1654, 1892, n. 2.
[31] Can. 1655-1666, 1892, n. 3; Roberti, *De Processibus,* II, n. 490.

ted; [32] a sentence in which the reasons and motives that prompted the judge in making his decision, are insufficiently stated or lacking altogether; [33] a sentence that does not contain all the signatures prescribed by law, i. e., the signature of the notary and of each judge of a collegiate tribunal; [34] a sentence that lacks all indication of the year, month and day on which, as well as the place where, the sentence was pronounced.[35] If only one of these items is omitted, the sentence is to be considered null.[36] Muniz [37] and Vidal [38] consider the enumeration of invalid sentences as contained in canons 1892 and 1894 to be exclusive. Roberti,[39] on the other hand, declares that there are other defects which either by positive or natural law, will annul a sentence and cites various decisions of the Rota in support of his contention. Although the claim of Roberti in this regard seems to be justified and strongly substantiated, it will be sufficient for the purposes of this work, to note that the type of defective sentence mentioned in canon 1892, i. e., *insanabilis,* calls for a *restitutio in integrum* in accordance with the provisions of canon 1905; whereas the kind of invalid sentence stated in canon 1894, i. e., *sanabilis,* may be remedied in a twofold manner, viz., by interposing a *querela nullitatis* against the judgment in question [40] or by joining the *complaint of nullity* with the motives which prompt an appeal and filing the latter within the proper time.[41] In this regard, however, care must be taken that the complaint of nullity be combined with the allegation of injustice as an accessory motive and not as the principal reason for the appeal; otherwise, the appeal will not be admitted.[42]

[32] Can. 1711, §2, 1894, n. 1.

[33] Can. 1873, §1, n. 3; 1894, n. 2.

[34] Can. 1874, §5; 1894, n. 3.

[35] Can. 201, §2; 1637; 1874, §5; 1894, n. 4.

[36] Roberti, *De Processibus,* II, n. 489.

[37] *Procedimientos Eclesiasticos,* III, n. 505.

[38] Wernz-Vidal, *De Processibus,* n. 623.

[39] *De Processibus,* II, n. 492, 493, 494.

[40] Can. 1895-1897.

[41] Can. 1895; cf. Roberti, *De Processibus,* II, n. 496; Wernz-Vidal, *De Processibus,* n. 606.

[42] Can. 1880, n. 3; Roberti, *De Processibus,* II, n. 500

4. *A sententia quae in rem iudicatam transiit.* A sentence that has become an adjudged matter, *res iudicata,* is not appealable. The very foundation and aim of a court trial is to settle an issue in pleading decisively for the plaintiff or for the defendant and it is contrary to the fundamental purpose of judicial procedure to protract or prolong these proceedings. It is for the interest of the public good that a judicial cause be ended speedily after it has been sufficiently investigated and examined and that the sentence, pronounced on the cause in question, all things considered, be firm and irrevocable. On the other hand, circumstances, varying with regard to different issues, may permit some delay or allow the judicial repetition or review of a cause in the interests of justice. An issue in pleading becomes adjudged under the following conditions: when two uniform sentences have been pronounced on the cause, either in the first and second or third instance or in the second and third instance; [43] when a sentence has not been appealed within the time specified by law, or, if appealed, it has not been prosecuted before the appellate judge within the appointed term; in either of these cases, the appeal is considered to have been abandoned, the cause becomes a *res iudicata* and the sentence is forthwith to be executed; [44] finally, when no appeal is admissible against even the first sentence pronounced on a cause, due to some legal restriction or prohibition of the right of appeal, as in canon 1880 which is now under discussion.[45] Appeal, as an ordinary mode of redress against an unjust sentence, cannot be used in the preceding cases; however, a petition for a *restitutio in integrum,* an extraordinary judicial remedy, may be filed with the judge who has rendered the decision.[46]

5. *A sententia quae iureiurando litis decisorio innexa est.* An appeal is not admitted from a definitive sentence that has been pronounced by virtue of a decisive oath which determines victory or defeat in a cause and which puts an end to the issue in question.

[43] Can. 1902, n. 1; Roberti, *De Processibus,* II, n. 510; Wernz-Vidal, *De Processibus,* n. 606; Vermeersch-Creusen, *Epitome,* III, n. 238.

[44] Can. 1902, n. 2. An appeal that is null and void due to some defect in the placing or prosecution of it, would have the same effect. Cf. Roberti, *De Processibus,* II, nn. 478, 489, 510.

[45] Can. 1902, n. 3.

[46] Can. 1905, 1906.

An appeal is denied here because of the sacredness of the oath itself and the reverence that is due the Holy Name.[47] An oath of this kind is a quasi-contract for it is similiar in nature to a compromise.[48] While it terminates the issue in pleading and while it may concern the principal cause or have reference merely to an incidental question, it must rest upon a mutual agreement between the parties interested in the case. If the litigants agree to settle the controversy by means of this oath, before the trial begins, it will be a compromise, according to canon 1925 and subject to the provisions therein contained. One party may demand that the oath be taken by his opponent at any time during the trial [49] and if the request is not complied with, it may be revoked by the party who made the demand; the party who was asked to swear, may agree to do so, or he may reject, or reverse it upon the original petitioner.[50] On account of the danger of perjury, an oath of this kind may be taken only in matters that of their nature admit a compromise and that are not of too great value or importance to the litigants.[51] It may be made by or demanded of those persons alone who can cede their rights or make a private settlement concerning them,[52] or who have not sufficient proof to establish the validity of their claims.[53] The oath is to be concerned with merely the knowledge of facts or actions personally known to the party who is asked to swear.[54] If it is refused by one party and not retorted by him on the other litigant, it is left to the discretion of the judge to ascertain the justice of the demand itself, to consider how much weight is to be attributed to the refusal and whether or not, this refusal is to be regarded as tantamount to a confession of guilt.[55] If the oath is

[47] Blat, *De Processibus*, n. 410, §5.

[48] Can. 1925 ff.; cf. Noval, *De Processibus*, n. 644; Vermeersch-Creusen, *Epitome*, III, n. 238, §5; c. 54, X, *de appellationibus, recusationibus et relationibus*, II, 28; c. 20, X, *de officio et potestate iudicis delegati*, I, 29; Santi-Leitner, lib. II, tit. XXVIII, n. 12, §2.

[49] Can. 1834.

[50] Can. 1836, §1.

[51] Can. 1835, n. 1; 1927, §1, §2.

[52] Can. 1835, n. 2.

[53] Can. 1835, n. 3.

[54] Can. 1835, n. 4; Noval, *De Processibus*, n. 573; Roberti, *De Processibus*, II, n. 390.

[55] Can. 1836, §3.

reversed or retorted upon the original petitioner and the latter refuse to swear, the refusal results in his defeat and the termination of the cause.[56] The sentence which is pronounced by virtue of the decisive oath, must be definitive in character, concerned with the principal issue of the controversy. It must, moreover, be based directly on the oath itself; if the sentence rests on other proofs instead of on the oath, or if only one or two points of the sentence rest on the oath, an appeal from the sentence may be admitted.[57] If it is found that perjury has been committed, a *restitutio in integrum* may be requested by the injured party.[58]

6. *A iudicis decreto vel a sententia interlocutoria, quae non habeat vim definitivae, nisi cumuletur cum appellatione a sententia definitiva.* An appeal is not permitted from a judicial decree or from an interlocutory sentence that has not definitive force unless it is joined with an appeal from a definitive or final sentence.

An appeal from a decree is inadmissible ordinarily because judicial decrees are concerned for the most part with matters of little importance.[59] This kind of decision may be revoked or corrected by the judge who rendered it, either of his own initiative or at the instance of either party with the consent, however, of the other litigant and the *promotor iustitiae* or the *defensor vinculi* if either is interested in the cause.[60] A decree, in this respect, is a judicial pronouncement or an informal ruling of a judge with regard to an incidental question that has arisen in the course of a trial. It has not for its purpose the final settlement of the principal cause. It is left to the discretion of the judge whether he shall decide an incidental question by a decree or by an interlocutory sentence.[61] He may decree that the incidental question is not to be allowed or, if it is admitted, he may issue a decree that will define and settle the point in question. In either case, no appeal is allowed from the

[56] Can. 1836, §4; Roberti, *De Processibus,* II, nn. 391, 392.

[57] Roberti, *De Processibus,* II, n. 469, §4.

[58] Can. 1905, §2, n. 3.

[59] Noval, *De Processibus,* n. 644.

[60] Can. 1841; cf. Roberti, *De Processibus,* II, n. 397.

[61] Can. 1840, §1; cf. also can. 1868, §2; Augustine, *A Commentary,* VII, 309, where a list of certain settlements that come under the name *"decretum"* is given; Roberti, *De Processibus,* I, n. 188, §2.

judge's decision unless the decree *per accidens* terminates the cause. The judge should refrain from defining any side issue or incidental question of merit by means of a simple decree; he should use rather an interlocutory sentence which has a more formal character than the decree. If it should happen that a simple decree or ruling of the judge on some particular point, contains the substance of the definitive sentence itself, an appeal from this decree should be admitted if there are sufficient grounds for an appeal.[62]

The question of allowing appeals from interlocutory sentences was long disputed by the jurists and canonists of the middle ages. In the first periods of Roman Law, appeals were admitted from sentences of this kind. Later, however, they were limited somewhat [63] and under Justinian, they were altogether abolished as being a hindrance to the true course of justice.[64] In ecclesiastical legislation, such appeals had been allowed under Decretal Law [65] but the Council of Trent prohibited the interposition of appeals from interlocutory sentences for the reason that they frustrated the ends of justice. The Council added that sentences of this kind could always be corrected or revoked by the same judge who rendered them.[66] The Code substantially repeats the Tridentine legislation with regard to interlocutory sentences and admits an appeal from a judgment of this kind only by way of exception.[67] An interlocutory sentence is a decision rendered by a judge on the merits of an incidental question of some importance that is proposed by one of the parties during the course of a trial. The Code orders that the general norms laid down for definitive sentences be observed likewise for interlocutory judgments.[68] It permits an appeal from an interlocutory sentence if the latter has definitive force. This condition is present when the nature

[62] Roberti, *De Processibus,* II, n. 469, §5 b; cf. also Roberti, *De Processibus,* II, n. 446. The Signatura Apostolica accepts this principle; cf. Signatura Apostolica in c. *Novarien,* 30 June 1911—*AAS.,* III (1911), 356.

[63] *Cod. Theod.,* 11, 36, 18.

[64] *Cod.,* 7, 62, 36; 7, 45, 16.

[65] Cc. 2, 5, 12, 59, X, *de appellationibus, recusationibus et relationibus,* II, 28.

[66] Concil. Trident., sess. XIII, *de ref.,* c. 1; sess. XXIV, *de ref.,* c. 20.

[67] Blat, *De Processibus,* n. 410, §6; Roberti, *De Processibus,* II, n. 469, 5.

[68] Can. 1875; cf. can. 1840, §2; Roberti, *De Processibus,* II, nn. 379, b; 445, 446, b; Wernz-Vidal, *De Processibus,* n. 587, note 8, §3.

of the interlocutory judgment is such that it puts an end to the cause itself; by terminating the proceedings, it renders a definitive sentence unnecessary. Similarly, when the sentence defines one article of the principal cause, when it relieves a judge of further participation in the trial, when it admits or rejects a peremptory exception and finally, when it imposes on one of the litigants an obligation that cannot be remedied by a definitive sentence, it has the force of a definitive judgment and as such, admits an appeal.[69] Moreover, in the event that an interlocutory sentence has not the force of a definitive judgment, an appeal from it will be allowed if it is joined with the appeal from the definitive sentence proper and interposed at the same time as the appeal from the definitive sentence.[70] This procedure will only be followed if the judge who pronounced the interlocutory sentence, refuses to correct or revoke it. Since under the circumstances, a sentence of this type has no definitive force and is not a final judgment, it does not terminate the jurisdiction of the judge in the cause in question. Consequently, he is empowered by the Code to revise or reverse his decision, subject, however, to the prescriptions of canon 1841.

7. *A sententia in causa pro qua ius cavet expeditissime rem esse definiendam.* There is no appeal from a sentence pronounced on a cause for which the law demands a speedy settlement. This restriction has been placed on the right to appeal in certain particular cases for the purpose of expediting the court proceedings and preventing needless and futile delays in matters of judicial importance. There are several canons in the Code where this procedure is expressly mentioned. It has always been the aim of ecclesiastical, judicial legislation to effect a speedy and equitable administration of justice. However, at no time, were the ends of justice sacrificed to the interests of a hasty and possibly inaccurate judicial sentence. Accordingly, the exception of suspicion taken against a judge for any of the reasons *taxative* determined in canon 1613, §1, must be investigated and decided as soon as possible.[71] The reason for this procedure is

[69] Cf. Reiffenstuel, lib. II, tit. XXVII, n. 18; Wernz-Vidal, *De Processibus,* n. 606, note 61; Roberti, *De Processibus,* II, n. 446.

[70] Noval, *De Processibus,* n. 644; Blat, *De Processibus,* n. 410, §6.

[71] Can. 1616.

that an exception of this kind is an incidental question and has an important bearing on the entire cause. It follows the special rules enacted for the speedy termination of such side issues.[72] Another case for which provision is made in the Code for an immediate settlement is that concerning attentates, *attentata*, or attempts made by one of the parties or by the judge, to prejudice the rights of another party while the cause is pending in court. No change as to the object of the controversy nor as to the terms or periods of time determined by law or by the judge for the performance of certain judicial acts, may be made without the consent of all parties concerned, once the suit has begun and the trial is pending.[73] An attempt of this kind is called an innovation if it alters the object of the trial. When such *attentata* occur,[74] the action against such an attempt or innovation must be brought by the party whom it affects and before the judge who is competent to hear it. The latter is ordered to settle the question as expeditiously as possible and there is no appeal allowed from his decision.[75]

8. *A sententia contra contumacem, qui a contumacia se non purgaverit.* A party who is contumacious or held to be in contempt of court, is not permitted to appeal from the sentence that is adverse to his interests as long as he does not abandon his contemptuous attitude. Authors regard as the reason for this prohibition the fact that a plaintiff or a defendant who despises or holds in contempt the lower court or tribunal of first instance has no right to be heard by the appellate court or tribunal of second instance.[76] Contempt of court is an incidental question that is occasionally raised in the course of a judicial process.[77] It is defined as grave disobedience toward an ecclesiastical judge who has legitimately summoned or cited a party to appear in court, which party for no just reason refuses to

[72] Roberti, *De Processibus,* I, n. 158; can. 1837-1841; Noval, *De Processibus,* n. 201.

[73] Can. 1725, n. 5.

[74] Cf. can. 1854-1857.

[75] Can. 1856, §2; 1840, §3; Roberti, *De Processibus,* II, nn. 433, 469, n. 6; Noval, *De Processibus,* n. 644; Blat, *De Processibus,* n. 410, n. 7.

[76] Noval, *De Processibus,* n. 644; Cocchi, *De Processibus,* n. 225; Vermeersch-Creusen, *Epitome,* III, n. 238, §8.

[77] Can. 1842-1851.

heed the legal summons either personally and directly or by proxy.[78] Contempt may be shown by the plaintiff as well as by the defendant.[79] Since this incidental question occurs more frequently than others, it would be useful to examine it more thoroughly particularly with regard to the special procedure leading up to the pronouncement of the sentence that is not appealable in accordance with the prohibition of the canon under consideration. It may be said at this point that the procedure in the question of contempt as lodged against a defendant is similar to that concerning the plaintiff.[80]

The declaration of contempt is made by the judge at the instance of one of the parties or of the *promotor iustitiae* or of the *defensor vinculi* if either is interested in the cause.[81] The party who is declared by a decree of the judge to be contumacious is to be notified of this action so that he may propose an exception to it or purge himself of his contempt within the time determined by the judge.[82] If the party remains *in contempt,* the judge is to proceed with the trial *servatis servandis* even to the pronouncement of a definitive sentence and its execution. The procedure to be followed here by the judge is that common to all normal proceedings,[83] with the sole omission of the role that the party *in contempt* would play if he were present at the trial. This is omitted because he is considered to have renounced his rights in the matter and to have abandoned himself to the justice of the tribunal.[84] If the defendant was contumacious from the very beginning before the *litis contestatio* has taken place, the sentence rendered by the judge can only be directed to the points contained in the original bill of complaint, that is, the judge may grant only what was requested in the introductory *libellus.* However, if the defendant has been declared to be in contempt after the *litis contestatio* or issue in pleading has begun, the sentence should take into account the complaint of the plaintiff and the denial

[78] Wernz-Vidal, *De Processibus,* n. 550.

[79] Can. 1842, 1849.

[80] Can. 1849; Roberti, *De Processibus,* II, n. 411.

[81] Can. 1844, §1. The party may be declared to be in contempt also by the judge *ex officio;* cf. *Reg. Servandae in iud. apud S. R. Rotae Trib.,* §26, n. 7.

[82] Can. 1729, §1; cf. also *Lex Propria,* can. 24, §1; *Reg. Serv. in iud. apud S. R. Rotae Trib.,* §26, n. 2.

[83] Can. 1844, §1.

[84] *Reg. Serv. in iud. apud S. R. Rotae Trib.,* §26, n. 6; §29, n. 1.

to the latter made by the defendant.[85] The party in contempt should be notified of the sentence, which is in itself not appealable.[86]

On the other hand, if the *defendant* appears in court before the final sentence has been pronounced, his claims and proofs must be recognized and admitted, but the proceedings that have progressed thus far, stand as they are and the defendant is bound by what already has been decided. He cannot therefore offer dilatory exceptions [87] or reject witnesses; [88] in short, the privileges granted to defendants [89] are denied him lest the court seem to look with favor upon his contumacy. He is not allowed to delay or protract the proceedings unnecessarily.[90] The judge can, of course, correct or revoke any interlocutory sentence by his final judgment on the cause and the defendant who was held to be in contempt, may appeal from this decision according to the ordinary norms of appellate procedure.[91] If the *defendant,* however, abandons or clears himself of his attitude of contempt, which he may do by proving that he had never received the summons or citation or that he was legitimately impeded from obeying it, all the effects attendant upon the decree of contempt of court issued by the judge, thereby cease and the defendant may obtain a *restitutio in integrum,*[92] after which the proceedings follow their normal course. The same norm is observed if the defendant has withdrawn from his contumacy due to penalties or punishment threatened by the judge.[93]

If the final sentence has been passed before the defendant decides to abandon his contumacy, he is allowed within the space of three months from the time at which he was notified of the sentence, to seek from the judge who rendered the sentence, a *restitutio in integrum* for the purpose of interposing an appeal against the sentence.[94] If this petition is granted, the investigation and hear-

[85] Can. 1844, §2.
[86] Roberti, *De Processibus,* II, n. 405; can. 1880, n. 8.
[87] Can. 1628, §1.
[88] Can. 1764, §4
[89] Can. 1786, 1861, §1.
[90] Can. 1846.
[91] Can. 1879-1891.
[92] Can. 1687 ff.
[93] Can. 1845.
[94] Can. 1847; 1906.

ing of the entire cause devolves on the appellate court or tribunal of second instance, which will pass on the justice or injustice of the sentence. The time allowed for the submitting of the petition for a *restitutio in integrum,* three months, is reckoned as in the calendar,[95] the first day on which the notification of the sentence was received, is not counted and the time expires at the end of the last complete day.[96] Vidal [97] declares that the three months should start with the publication of the sentence itself [98] and not with the intimation of it to the party in contempt because in the latter case, the court seems to regard with favor the contumacy of the party by allowing him privileges that are permitted only to one who observes all the requirements of judicial procedure—which seems to be the more just and more reasonable interpretation. The law, however, provides otherwise for the situation. There is no necessity of seeking a *restitutio in integrum* for causes that never become *res iudicatae;* [99] a reexamination of the cause may be sought, even if the defendant has not purged himself of his contempt, although in the latter case, new proofs and documents would have to be produced in order to reopen the case.[100]

It may be stated here that the procedure in the question of contempt lodged against a *plaintiff* is similar, *mutatis mutandis,* to that followed in the preceding case against the defendant.[101] Although the *plaintiff,* if declared to be in contempt, forfeits his right to prosecute the case, the prosecution may be continued by the promoter of justice or by the defender of the marriage bond, if either was interested in the cause. In this event, the proceedings are continued as if there were no declaration of contempt made by the judge.[102] The defendant, however, may demand that he be absolved, or that all the proceedings thus far be considered null and void or that he be freed definitely from the claims of the plaintiff as contained in the latter's

[95] Can. 34, §3, n. 1.
[96] Can. 34, §3, n. 3.
[97] Wernz-Vidal, *De Processibus,* n. 556, note 23.
[98] Can. 1724; 1720.
[99] Can. 1847.
[100] Can. 1903.
[101] Roberti, *De Processibus,* II, n. 411; can. 1849.
[102] Cf. Wernz-Vidal, *De Processibus,* n. 558.

petition or that the trial be brought to a close at once.[103] Any of these requests may be complied with by the judge in the form of a definitive sentence from which there is no appeal admissible.[104] If, however, the plaintiff abandons his contumacy and appears in court, the procedure outlined in a preceding paragraph should be observed.[105]

9. *A sententia lata contra eum qui in scriptis expresse professus est se appellationi renuntiare.* There is no appeal from a sentence pronounced against a party who has declared explicitly and in writing that he has renounced his right to appeal. The benefit of an appeal is granted by law to the plaintiff and to the defendant whose rights have been unjustly or unreasonably abridged or violated by reason of the sentence pronounced on his cause; each one is perfectly free to exercise or to renounce that right. The renunciation, however, from the nature of the act itself and all that it implies, must be clear and specific, devoid of all doubt as to the intention of the person and the extent of the renunciation.[106] This action is more or less governed by the same enactments that refer to the renunciation of further proceedings *in toto* or of certain procedural acts.[107] It may be made by the plaintiff or by the defendant in particular questions or causes that affect the private welfare of either. Since renunciation involves a certain species of alienation of one's rights, a special mandate is required by a proctor or attorney and explicit permission and consent is needed by a tutor, guardian or agent acting for a moral person,[108] to file such an action. No special faculty seems to be required for the acceptance of the renunciation. It must be communicated to, accepted or at least not opposed by the other party and admitted by the judge. The judge should accept all such abjurations if they affect only the private welfare of the parties concerned; if on the other hand, the cause concerns the public good, the renunciation of an appeal, besides being admitted by

[103] Can. 1850, §3.
[104] Can. 1880, n. 8; cf. Blat, *De Processibus,* n. 373.
[105] Can. 1849; cf. Roberti, *De Processibus,* II, nn. 410, 411.
[106] Blat, *De Processibus,* n. 410, §9.
[107] Can. 1740, §1, §2.
[108] Can. 1740, §2; cf. Roberti, *De Processibus,* II, n. 316.

the judge, must receive his direct approval.[109] The renunciation of the appeal may be made before or after the sentence is pronounced. In the event of the former, however, it is usually contingent upon the condition that the sentence be consonant with right reason and justice. Although the commentators on the Code do not mention this qualification, it is stated in the Decretals in connection with the oath taken by a person who renounces such a right. The case appears analogous here and it is within the demands of equity and justice, that the party who has renounced his right to appeal may at least expect a just sentence to be rendered in his case and, if this is not done, if the sentence is notoriously unjust, there is no reason why he should not be able to revoke his decision.[110] The renunciation of the appeal may also be made before the end of the ten day period allotted by law for the exercise of this right or prior to the termination of the thirty day interval allowed for the prosecution of the appeal people before the court of second instance.[111]

Although Decretal Law permitted renunciation of this type to be made tacitly,[112] the Code demands that for purposes of solemnity, it be made in writing and signed by the interested party or by his attorney or proctor, although no special form is required for either the renunciation or the appeal or for the acceptance of the same.[113] The written renunciation is given to the judge by the notary of the tribunal. The judge informs the other party of the action of his opponent and when he receives evidence of the acceptance of the renunciation by the other party, he admits it by means of a decree. If any question arise as to the value or the merits of the renunciation, it is discussed and defined according to the norms regulating the settling of incidental questions.[114] The simple and unqualified renunciation of an appeal is not to be understood as depending upon the condition that the other party likewise give up his right to appeal; nor may the renunciation be revoked on this pretext, in the

[109] Roberti, *De Processibus,* II, n. 469, §8; it is evident that the *defensor vinculi* cannot renounce his right to appeal, because it is more than a mere right; it is a duty and an obligation which he is held to fulfill; can. 1986.

[110] Schmalzgrueber, lib. II, tit. XXVIII, n. 13.

[111] Noval, *De Processibus,* n. 644.

[112] C. 20, X, *de officio et potestate iudicis delegati,* I, 29.

[113] Can. 1740, §2.

[114] Can. 1840; cf. Roberti, *De Processibus,* II, n. 316.

event that the other party had filed an appeal. An action of this kind is separate and independent and no relation exists between the two parties concerning it when it is made, accepted and admitted unconditionally. Roberti [115] declares that the renunciation of the right of appeal includes the abandonment of all other legal remedies for redress against an unjust or defective sentence. He offers no reasons to substantiate this opinion and the Code is silent on the matter. From the nature of appeal and pursuant to the demands of strict justice, a regulation of this type would appear to be somewhat stringent and severe; certainly, the party who renounces his right to appeal, could not be held to observe it unless he had incorporated in his written renunciation, the abjuration also of the other legal remedies.

The foregoing nine cases which are *taxative* [116] enumerated in canon 1880, comprise the peculiar and particular sentences that are exceptions to the general rule to the effect that appeals are to be admitted in every cause, whether important or insignificant. The Code admits no other exceptions, all limitations and prohibitions of the former discipline to the contrary notwithstanding. The effect of the restriction of this right as outlined in this canon, is that the cause immediately becomes a *res iudicata,*[117] thereby creating a true and just *presumptio iuris et de iure* which cannot be directly attacked and which may serve as an exception to be proposed by either party to any future action brought against them in the same matter.[118] It can readily be seen that the Code, in lessening the number of restrictions placed on the right of appeal by the former legislation, allows greater opportunities for the legal use of this mode of judicial redress to the end that the demands of justice and equity be more faithfully observed and the rights of the plaintiff and the defendant be more zealously safeguarded. On the principle that an appeal is a legitimate means of legal defense, there is little occasion under the present law for any gross miscarriage of justice.

[115] *De Processibus,* II, n. 469, §8.

[116] Vermeersch-Creusen, *Epitome,* III, n. 238.

[117] Can. 1902, n. 3; 1903.

[118] Can. 1904, §1, §2; cf. also can. 1825-1828; 1972; 1015, §2; 1086, §1; 1814.

## CHAPTER VIII

## THE INTERPOSITION OF AN APPEAL

WHEN the cause under discussion has been closed by a decree of the judge and the final pleading has been completed by the attorney for the defense, the judge is to pronounce his sentence on the merits of the entire cause, settling decisively the controversy proposed by the litigants and tried in accordance with the formalities of solemn judicial procedure. The sentence, conforming it may be presumed to all the conditions necessary for its validity, should be published and communicated to the interested parties as soon as possible.[1]

This may be carried out in any one of three ways:—by summoning the parties to the tribunal to hear the sentence solemnly read by the judge sitting in court; by notifying the parties that the sentence has been filed with the chancery office and granting permission to them to read the sentence and to have copies made of it; by sending a copy of the sentence to the parties concerned, by registered mail to be delivered personally to the addressee, care being taken to secure a "return receipt" which will show by the signature of the addressee affixed thereto, that the letter has been received.[2] If any of these methods is employed, the norms and regulations demanded by the Code for the serving of a citation should be observed, *mutatis mutandis*.[3]

When notice of the sentence has been communicated to the parties by any of the foregoing methods, and upon examination and investigation, it is regarded as unjust for any reason whatsoever, the aggrieved party has the right to interpose an appeal against the sentence, except in those sentences where this right has been circumscribed by law.[4] The *defensor vinculi* is not required to base his

[1] Can. 1876.
[2] Can. 1877.
[3] Can. 1724; cf. S. R. Rota in c. *Societatis*, 18 March 1922—*Decisiones S. R. Rotae*, XIV, dec. VII, nn. 3, 4; *Jus Pontificium*, I (1922), p. 136.
[4] Can. 1879; 1880.

appeal on any grounds of injustice, etc., for he is obliged by law to appeal *ex officio* from the first sentence declaring for the nullity of a marriage.[5]

**Canon 1881. Appellatio interponi debet coram iudice a quo sententia prolata est intra decem dies a notitia publicationis sententiae.**

### Article I. The Proper Tribunal

An appeal consists of a twofold action: the interposition or filing of the appeal with the judge *a quo,* the *officialis* who has rendered the sentence from which the appeal is made, whether it be the first, the second or further instance; and the prosecution of the appeal before the judge *ad quem,* upon whose court, of second or third, etc., instance as the case may be, devolves the rehearing of the cause appealed. Canon 1881 considers the first part of an appeal and defines that it must be filed with the judge *a quo,* or the *officialis* who pronounced the sentence on the merits of the cause in litigation. The appealing of a sentence does not cast any reflection on the character or the judicial integrity of a judge for it is regarded as a legitimate means of defense and a protection of innocence. However, although the impugning of a sentence is never intended to cause any embarrassment to the judge whose sentence has been called in question, yet it may be regarded as a legal protest against that sentence or any single feature of it that appears unjust to the aggrieved party. Moreover, an appeal ordinarily suspends the jurisdiction and competence relative to the sentence proper, of the judge who rendered it and it is the intention of the appellant to effect this suspension in order to obtain a satisfactory and just verdict.[6] Consequently, the appeal must be interposed before that judge who pronounced the sentence to which exception has been taken. The law states expressly that an appeal prohibits the judge in question from proceeding further in the case and ordains that all the acts performed by a judge after his sentence has been appealed, are

[5] Can. 1986.
[6] Lega, *De Iudiciis,* I, n. 639.

null and void; therefore, he must know when his sentence has been appealed so that he may desist from acting further in the cause.[7] Accordingly, an appeal is invalid if filed with any one but the judge who pronounced the sentence that is impugned, nor does such an appeal produce any effect either devolutive or suspensive.[8]

### §1. *The Judge* a quo *and the Appellant*

When the sentence has been pronounced and published as noted and the plaintiff or the defendant regards it as unjust in view of the testimony or evidence presented during the process or for any other reason, he is to incorporate this consideration in a judicial petition which he sends to the judge *a quo* who in turn is held by law to receive the appeal. If the appeal is made with due regard to all legal requirements, the judge should permit it to be filed.[9] If he is doubtful concerning the justice or the legitimate character of the appeal, he should likewise receive it and leave the approval or rejection of it to the decision of the appellate court.[10] Under the former discipline, the appellant was obliged to obtain from the judge, dimissorial letters or *apostoli,* in which it was stated that the judge *a quo* received the appeal and was sending the entire cause to the superior tribunal. This proceeding, however, gradually fell into disuse [11] and even before the Code, the judge *ex officio* carried out the provisions of the law in regard to appeals, with the sole exception of the *libellus appellatorius.*[12] The Code maintains this same arrangement. When the appeal interposed by the aggrieved party has been received by the judge *a quo,* the term allotted by law for the prosecution of the appeal, begins to be in effect.[13] At the same time, the judge *a quo* should notify the other party in the case, the appellee, of the interposition of the appeal. This notification should likewise be made to the procurator or attorney of the appellee. For,

[7] Schmalzgrueber, lib. II, tit. XXVIII, n. 42.

[8] Bouix, *De Iudiciis,* II, 268; Wernz-Vidal, *De Processibus,* n. 610, note 67.

[9] Roberti, *De Processibus,* II, n. 478.

[10] Wernz-Vidal, *De Processibus,* n. 612.

[11] Devoti, *Instit. Can.,* lib. III, tit. XV, n. 11.

[12] Roberti, *De Processibus,* II, n. 478; Schmalzgrueber, lib. II, tit. XXVIII, n. 74.

[13] Cf. can. 1883.

although a definitive sentence has been pronounced on the cause in question, yet the *mandatum ad lites* by which the attorney was employed at the beginning of the litigation to conduct the cause to its completion,[14] includes in addition the faculty of interposing an appeal unless the client has reserved this right to himself.[15] When an appeal has been filed, the attorney for the appellee still has the right and opportunity of interposing an incidental appeal. He continues to act for his client and accordingly should be informed of the interposition of the appeal by the other party. The notification should be sent to the address given by the litigant or his lawyer for the purpose of receiving communications from the court.[16] Any of the approved methods may be employed by the judge in transmitting a notice of this kind.[17] If the party who is to be notified of the filing of an appeal, should die, change his state in life or go out of the office by virtue of which he became a litigant in the cause in question, the notification should be made to his heir or successor in the suit.[18] This communication is intended for the adversary of the appellant and accordingly, it has no direct connection with canon 1885 in regard to the suspension or interruption of the period of time allowed by law for the interposition of the prosecution of the appeal proper. The law indicates merely that the judge *a quo* upon receiving an appeal, must inform all the parties to the suit of the placing of an appeal against his sentence.[19]

When an appeal is submitted by the aggrieved party to the judge *a quo,* in writing and by mail, special messenger or in person, the judge is to inform the appellant of the receipt of his petition, declare his intention of transmitting the *acta causae* to the tribunal of second instance, remind the appellant of the time limit within which he is held to prosecute his appeal and acquaint the appellant of his right to request an extension of this term if he can show any reasonable cause for such prorogation.

[14] Can. 1664, §1.

[15] Can. 1664, §2.

[16] Can. 1708, §3.

[17] Can. 1717, 1719, 1724.

[18] Can. 1733; cf. Roberti, *De Processibus,* II, n. 478.

[19] Roberti, *De Processibus,* II, n. 478.

### §2. *The Judge* a quo *and the Judge* ad quem

**Canon 1890. Interposita appellatione tribunal *a quo* debet ad iudicem *ad quem* actorum causae authenticum exemplar vel ipsamet originalia acta causae transmittere ad normam can. 1644.**

The purpose and aim of an appeal consists in a review and reexamination of the cause itself to the end that the entire sentence or any of its component parts, alleged by the appellant to be unjust, might be corrected, reversed or revoked. The evidence, testimony and proofs presented in the previous instance retain their value and legal influence in the appellate court.[20] Consequently, when an appeal has been successfully interposed by the aggrieved litigant, the judge *a quo* is required *ex officio* [21] to forward to the appellate court either an authentic copy of all the acts of the cause, or, if this cannot be effected without inconvenience, the original acts proper.[22]

While the canon under consideration uses the words *acta causae,* it is difficult to determine precisely the character of the acts that are to be transmitted to the appellate tribunal. Certainly, the *acta causae* as such are to be sent. These comprise all the relevant testimony, proofs and documents, public and private [23] that have been produced in court and that have some bearing on the merits of the cause; in addition, all decisions, decrees and sentences that similarly affect the merits of the cause, are to be transmitted.[24] While canon 1890 distinctly declares that the *acta causae* are to be sent to the superior court, some confusion exists with regard to this prescription in view of the directions contained in related canons. Canon 1644 to which reference is made in canon 1890 and which prescribes the method to be used in transferring the acts to the appel-

[20] Can. 1891, §1.

[21] Roberti, *De Processibus,* I, n. 190.

[22] Can. 1644: "In casu appellationis, actorum exemplaria . . . mittantur ad superius tribunal; si exemplaria sine gravi incommodo exscribi nequeant, mittantur cum opportunis cautelis acta ipsa originalia."

[23] Noval, *De Processibus,* n. 243; cf. can. 1812-1824.

[24] Roberti, *De Processibus,* I, n. 187; Cocchi, *De Processibus,* n. 58.

late court, merely mentions the word *"acta,"* omitting the qualification *"causae."* This is interpreted by some commentators to include also the *acta processus,* the judicial acts that pertain to the form or procedure proper, viz., the acts that admit judicial petitions and proofs, the citations, communications and decrees that bear on procedural questions, etc. Vidal [25] calls attention to the omission of the word *"causae"* in canon 1644 and states that the word *"acta"* as employed in canon 1644 indicates all the judicial acts of the controversy, the *acta causae* and the *acta processus* as outlined in canon 1642, §1.[26] He adds that the directions of canon 1890 are to be understood and interpreted in this light, that is, as including all the judicial acts. Roberti [27] noting particularly that the Code uses the expression *"acta causae"* in canon 1890, declares nevertheless that evidently all the judicial acts, the *acta causae* and the *acta processus,* are included thereby, just as they are in canon 1969, n. 1 where the Code employs the expression *"acta processus."* Blat [28] who declares that the canon in question should be interpreted in the light of the legislation of the Council of Trent,[29] proceeds thereupon to limit and restrict the *acta omnia* required by Trent to the *acta causae* alone. Although his conclusion somewhat contradicts his premise in the matter, he interprets canon 1890 in the light of canon 1642, §1, and quotes the first part of the canon, "actorum causae quae nempe sunt: 'acta iudicialia quae meritum quaestionis respiciunt, ex gr., sententiae et cuiusque generis probationes'," leaving no doubt as to his opinion. But, in commenting on canon 1644, he declares that the word *"acta"* includes all the judicial acts of the entire process, both *acta causae* and *acta processus.*[30] Either the author's ideas on the subject are confused or his use of terms is unfortunate. How-

[25] Wernz-Vidal, *De Processibus,* n. 612.

[26] Can. 1642, §1: "Acta iudicialia, tum quae meritum quaestionis respiciunt, seu *acta causae,* ex gr., sententiae et cuiusque generis probationes, tum quae ad formam procedendi pertinent, seu *acta processus,* ex gr., citationes, intimationes, etc., scripto redacta esse debent."

[27] *De Processibus,* II, n. 478, note 1.

[28] *De Processibus,* n. 420.

[29] Con. Trident., sess. XXIV, *de ref.,* c. 20: "Si quis in casibus a iure permissis appellaverit aut de aliquo gravamine conquestus fuerit . . . teneatur *acta omnia* coram episcopo gesta, ad iudicem appellationis expensis suis transferre."

[30] Blat, *De Processibus,* n. 118.

ever, apart from this, he evidently restricts the expression "*acta causae*" of canon 1890 to the acts of the cause which respect the merits of the question proper.

Cocchi[31] merely states that the *acta causae* signify the judicial acts of the cause, that is, the *actua causae* and the *acta processus*. Creusen [32] indicates that the acts of the process are to be transmitted to the appelate court—"Acta processus a tribunali a quo ad tribunal superius mittenda sunt." Muniz [33] states directly that the *acta causae,* not the *acta processus,* are to be transmitted to the superior tribunal. With the exception of Muniz and probably Blat, the authorities do not limit the expression "*acta causae*" of canon 1890 to the particular, technical meaning it possesses in the first part of canon 1642, §1. They interpret it to signify all the judicial acts of the cause, the *acta causae* and the *acta processus*. Creusen in making use of the expression "*acta processus*" evidently refers likewise to all the judicial acts. Otherwise he would be guilty of a glaring error for by no possible means could the expression "*acta causae*" of canon 1890 be understood to indicate merely the *acta processus* of canon 1642, §1. The legislator evidently intends to convey the meaning that the *acta causae* of 1890 signify all the judicial acts of the cause, for there is no qualifying or explanatory word to indicate that the meaning is to be restricted; particularly since canon 1969, n. 1 uses the expresses "*acta processus*" in the same wide sense, that is, referring to all the judicial acts of the cause.[34]

The conclusion, therefore, would seem to be that in view of the foregoing interpretation, the judge *a quo* is obliged to transmit to the superior judge either an authentic copy of all the judicial acts of the cause, that is, of the *acta causae* and the *acta processus,* or the original acts themselves, in the manner hereinafter to be indicated. However, it cannot be said that the neglect to include the *acta processus* would result in the nullity of the appeal, for there is

[31] *De Processibus,* n. 229.

[32] Vermeersch-Creusen, *Epitome,* III, n. 239.

[33] *Procedimientos Ecclesiasticos,* III, n. 474.

[34] Vermeersch-Creusen, *Epitome,* III, n. 283; Blat, *De Processibus,* n. 523; cf. also *Apollinaris,* I (1928), 188; cf. S. C. de Sac., instr. 7 Maii 1923—*AAS,* XV (1923), 412, where both *acta* are requested to be sent to the appellate court.

a *dubium iuris* here; on the other hand, it does not seem to be necessary for the complete examination or investigation of the cause in the appellate instance, to forward the *acta processus* to the higher tribunal. A report in the form of a letter may be drawn up by the notary for the purpose of acquainting the appellate tribunal of the observance by the lower court of all the norms of judicial procedure prescribed by the law. This method is actually in use in some of the diocesan curias of this country.

Relative to the requirements of canon 1890, canonists also discuss the problem concerning the private, secret deliberations of the lower collegiate tribunal prior to the pronouncement of a sentence with reference to the court of appeal.[35] Are these secret deliberations to be forwarded *ex officio* by the judge *a quo* along with the other acts of the case to the appellate tribunal? If not, may they be transmitted to the court of appeal upon a decree of the judge of this tribunal? Or is the *secretum servandum* of canon 1623, §2 and 1871, §2 of such a nature that it prohibits positively and absolutely the exhibition of these deliberations to any and all judges of whatever grade of judgment or instance?

In criminal causes, the judges and the court officers are always bound to secrecy, whatever be the nature of the trial or the crime; in civil or contentious causes, the same obligation to secrecy must be observed if the revelation of the proceedings would engender prejudice toward either party in the case.[36] The judges of a collegiate tribunal are likewise enjoined to secrecy concerning the secret opinions and deliberations, the nature and number of votes cast prior to the actual pronouncement of the sentence. All court officials are similarly included here if they happened to participate in this judicial discussion.[37] The judge can also bind by oath to secrecy, the witnesses, experts, litigants, procurators and advocates, if the nature of the cause or the evidence is such that the reputation of others would be endangered, or scandal, discord or other embarrass-

[35] Can. 1871, §2—"Assignata conventui die, singuli iudices scriptas afferent conclusiones suas in merito causae, et rationes tam in facto quam in iure, quibus ad conclusionem suam venerint: quae conclusiones actis causae adiungantur, secreto servandae."

[36] Can. 1623, §1.

[37] Can. 1623, §2.

ing situation would arise upon the publication or disclosure of the proceedings.[38] Canon 1625, §2 and §3 enacts penalties of a serious nature for violations of the law in this respect. This legislation demonstrates the care and caution which the Church uses to guard the integrity of ecclesiastical judicial proceedings and to protect at the same time the reputation of disinterested persons as well as of the litigants proper. The motive that prompted the enactment of this canon appears to be the desire and wish of the legislator to withhold from those who had no possible right to know, the nature and character of the trial, the evidence, documents and testimony. Special stress is laid on the injunction to secrecy concerning the private deliberations of the judges of the collegiate tribunal prior to the sentence proper, the latter are held *ad inviolabile secretum servandum*. This strict admonition is carried further in canon 1871, §2, where it is decreed that the private conclusions reached by the collegiate judges are to be joined to the *acta causae* and are to be kept secret. The reason for this is probably to permit the judges to engage in a free and unlimited discussion of the merits of the cause without the fear of criticism or embarrassment that might result if the deliberations were made public, all of which might possibly influence the judges in their respective decisions. It can readily be seen that in this case, the obligation to secrecy is an aid to the just and equitable solution of a cause in litigation. It moreover fosters the spirit of reverence and obedience that is due to the sacred majesty of an ecclesiastical tribunal.[39]

This *secretum officii* binds the collegiate judges perpetually and inviolably.[40] But is this obligation and injunction in its nature and aim, absolute? Canon 1623, §2 adds no qualifying or conditional statement to indicate otherwise; and canon 1871, §2 excludes all court officers, not excepting the notary, from these deliberations. One of the members of the tribunal is ordered to act as the *ponens* or referee who will reduce to writing the opinions, deliberations, votes, etc., of the tribunal. The final clause of this paragraph de-

[38] Can. 1623, §3.

[39] Cf. Roberti in *Apollinaris*, I (1928), 189.

[40] Wernz-Vidal, *De Processibus*, n. 155; Blat, *De Processibus*, n. 92; Roberti, *De Processibus*, I, n. 160.

crees that the conclusions, etc., are to be joined to the *acta causae* and kept secret. The Rota maintains the same regulations with regard to these deliberations.[41]

In spite of the apparent absolute character of the *secretum officii,* some canonists are inclined, and rightly so, to regard the restriction placed on the revelation of these secret deliberations as relative only. Noval[42] explains the word *"secreto"* of canon 1871, §2 by stating that the secret deliberations of the collegiate tribunal must *never* be divulged to the parties in the cause or to their advocates; "secreto: ita ut numquam communicentur partibus aut earum advocatis." Blat[43] gives a similar explanation of the expression *"secreto servandae"* of this canon. These opinions would permit the communication of the secret deliberations to the appellate court, the *secretum officii* being observed at the same time. Roberti[44] declares moreover that the practise of ecclesiastical courts is such that these deliberations and conclusions as a rule are not concealed or kept secret from the officers of the tribunal. This opinion is likewise in harmony with canonical legislation on the subject. Canon 1871, §2 declares that the conclusions of the judges of a collegiate tribunal must be joined to the *acta causae.* Canon 1890 states that the *acta causae* must be transmitted by the judge of first instance to the appellate tribunal. There is no reason to make an exception of the secret deliberations of the collegiate judges. The conclusion, therefore, would *seem* to be that the judge *a quo* should remit the entire body of judicial acts, including the secret deliberations, opinions and discussions of the collegiate judges, to the tribunal of second instance.

Muniz[45] stresses the secret character of the deliberations and declares that they must be preserved in the secret archives apart from the rest of the acts of the case, a notation being made in the

[41] *Reg. Serv. in iud. apud S. R. Rotae Trib.,* §178, n. 5: "Vota scripta dabuntur Ponenti aut Auditori cui sententiam exarare demandatum est. Publicata sententia, ista vota tradentur Domino Decano a quo asservanda sunt in Archivo secreto decanali." Cf. also *Lex Propria,* can. 31, §2.

[42] *De Processibus,* n. 626.

[43] *De Processibus,* n. 398.

[44] *Apollinaris,* I (1928), 189.

[45] *Procedimientos Eclesiasticos,* III, n. 444.

minutes of the trial indicating where they may be found. They should be enclosed in a separate and distinct envelope under the curial seal. The only reason for preserving them at all, he adds, is that they may be required by the superior tribunal in the event that the sentence is appealed. In which case, they should be forwarded to the appellate court upon the issuance of a decree to this effect by the latter tribunal. Noval [46] likewise would permit the transmission of these secret deliberations to the appellate court at the latter's request. Now, if the *secretum officii* and the injunction to secrecy mentioned in canon 1871, §2 is absolute in its scope, perpetual and inviolable, not even the decree of a judge could force its violation. If the nature of these deliberations is not to be kept secret from all persons, certainly a decree of the superior judge could effect the transference of the conclusions to the higher tribunal. They are either to be kept absolutely secret or they are not so to be preserved. The foregoing interpretation points to the fact that the prescriptions of the law indicate merely a relativc secrecy, that is, with regard to certain persons, as the parties of the cause and their advocates; in view of this, the conclusion *is* that the provisions of the law should be observed; the judge *a quo* may upon a request or decree from the superior court, remit the secret deliberations of the collegiate tribunal to the latter tribunal along with the other acts of the cause. However, these secret deliberations should be enclosed in a separate folio and preserved apart from the other judicial acts. This is the more acceptable opinion for the reason that the secret deliberations and conclusions are not acts, *acta,* properly so-called of the trial. Even though they are to be joined to the *acta causae* it cannot be said that they are *acta* in the same sense as the rest of the judicial proofs, testimony, decrees, etc. A perusal of the appellate causes prosecuted before the Rota discloses the fact that at no time is any mention made of an examination or investigation into the secret deliberations of the judges of the lower tribunal.

Objection may be made to this method of procedure, first, because of the possibility that the appellate tribunal might be unduly swayed or influenced in their judgment by examining the secret deliberations of the lower collegiate court to the end that the appeal,

[46] *De Processibus,* n. 626.

instead of being a consideration of the evidence, testimony, proofs and documents bearing directly on the merits of the cause, would result principally in an investigation of the various opinions and conclusions of the judges of the inferior tribunal. But the primary aim of an appeal is to obtain above all a just sentence through the reversal of the previous verdict if it is found to be unjust as alleged. This might be more easily effected if the court of appeal deemed it necessary, through the investigation by the court of second instance of the evidence presented, together with an examination of the conclusions and deliberations of the judges of the court of first instance. The statement that the examination made by the higher court would be confined to the deliberations at the expense of an investigation into the evidence presented is merely a presumption without any foundation in fact. Moreover, if there is a dissenting opinion or conclusion in the judgment of the lower tribunal, an examination of the deliberations of the dissenting judge will certainly help to throw new light on the solution of the cause particularly if he be a canonist of merit and ability.

Another objection is concerned with the freedom of discussion that should be enjoyed by the collegiate judges of the court of first instance. Would the knowledge that their secret deliberations and conclusions might be communicated to the higher court, prevent the judges of the lower instance from freely discussing and examining the relative merits of the cause from every angle? There is no reason to assume that such would be the case. Every judge is obliged by law [47] to render his decision according to the *acta* and *probata* of the cause in question, and their relation to the law and to the original complaint. Proofs are not to be sought outside the acts and allegations of the trial because it is not as a private citizen but as a public ecclesiastical official that the judge must pronounce sentence. Personal prejudice or antipathy toward any member of the trial must not influence the decision of the judge.[48] Actually, the fact that the secret conclusions of the lower tribunal may be made known to the appellate court, will compel the judges of the former to adhere

[47] Can. 1868-1870.

[48] Cf. Roberti, *De Processibus*, II, nn. 443, 448, 451-456; Noval, *De Processibus*, nn. 621, 622.

to the prescriptions of the law relative to the drawing up of a sentence or verdict on the cause proper. If they comply with the provisions of the law in this respect, they will have nothing to fear in the way of subsequent criticism or embarrassment that might perchance follow upon the possible communication of their secret deliberations and conclusions to the appellate tribunal.

The manner of remitting the judicial acts of the trial is regulated by canon 1644. This canon ordains that an authentic copy of the *acta,* faithfully transcribed and bound in such a manner that all the documents and pages of testimony will be preserved intact and in their proper place, must be transmitted to the appellate tribunal. Each individual *act* should bear the signature of the notary and of the judge; if the tribunal is collegiate in nature, the signature of the *officialis* or the president of the college of judges will suffice, except in regard to the final definitive sentence.[49] This regulation holds for each act, even if there are two or more inscribed on one page.[50] Each page must bear the seal of the tribunal, which should be distinct and different from that used for other curial matters.[51] Each page of the entire process should be numbered and an index made of all the judicial acts and the particular documents. When a document contains two or more pages, this fact should be noted in the index. Old documents that may be in a poor state of preservation, should be held together by transparent manuscript tissue. When such documents are of great importance or value, it might be advisable to have photostatic copies made of them for the use of the appellate tribunal. The written guarantee of the notary or the chancellor must likewise be included, testifying to the faithful transcription and integrity of the *acta.*[52] The fascicle is then wrapped, sealed and despatched to the appellate tribunal by registered mail, a request being made at the same time for a "return receipt" indicative of the safe delivery of the *acta.*[53] While this is

[49] Can. 1874, §5.

[50] Can. 1643, §2.

[51] Can. 1643, §1. When a diocesan court acts as an appellate tribunal, it should have a special seal for that function; the seal used when it sits as a court of first instance, should not be employed when it hears a case on appeal.

[52] Can. 1644, §2.

[53] Can. 1719; cf. also can. 1724.

a safe and secure method of transmitting the acts of the cause, the court may permit the interested party to deliver them, with every precaution being taken to insure their safe transit and to prevent any tampering with the documents or evidence.[54] If a copy of the transcript of testimony cannot be made without great inconvenience, the original acts may be sent, with due provision being made for their safe delivery, so that they will not be lost, abused, damaged or seen by others than those for whom they are intended.

The Code moreover ordains that if the *acta* are to be sent to a tribunal, e. g., the Rota, where the vernacular tongue is not known or not recognized officially, they should be faithfully and correctly translated into the Latin language.[55] In this regard, it is well to remark that explanatory notes should accompany this translation to elucidate the meaning of "catch phrases," slang, peculiar idioms and colloquialisms that occur in the presentation of evidence and testimony by witnesses, and that are difficult to translate, or if translated, would be devoid of the proper meaning.

The minute observance of these prescriptions and regulations is an important matter because judicial acts that are not drawn up in the proper form and style, may be rejected by the appellate tribunal; in which case, those through whose negligence this has occurred, are held to have them transcribed or translated again and forwarded to the proper tribunal at their own expense.[56]

## Article II. The Proper Time

When the definitive sentence, pronounced by the court on the cause in question, has been communicated to the interested parties by any of the approved methods[57] that have been explained in a previous article, the litigant who wishes to appeal from the sentence, is granted by law a period of time within which he may exercise this right.

[54] Roberti, *De Processibus,* I, n. 190.

[55] Can. 1644, §2.

[56] Can. 1644, §3.

[57] Can. 1877.

## §1. *The Legal Term for an Appeal*

In the early imperial period of Roman Law, the appellant if acting for himself was allowed two days in which to file an appeal, three if he acted as a proxy or proctor.[58] This period of time was computed from the time the sentence was communicated to him.[59] In the later Empire, under Justinian, the term was extended to ten days,[60] the period likewise being computed from the time that notification of the sentence was received. Similar enactments may be traced through the later periods of ecclesiastical law.[61]

The Code has incorporated this feature into the prescriptions governing the interposition of an appeal. This period of ten days is a legal term, permitted by law[62] to enable an aggrieved litigant to seek the proper redress against an unjust sentence.[63] During this delay, the judge who pronounced the sentence, cannot act on it, that is, execute it, because the delay is allowed for the interposition of an appeal against the sentence itself. The law permits a judge to proceed to the execution of a sentence only when it becomes an adjudged matter, *res iudicata*,[64] which occurs if the ten day period has elapsed without an appeal having been placed against the sentence.[65]

The legal term, so-called because it has been determined by law,[66] is absolutely peremptory,[67] that is, it has been conceded by the law for a definite, particular purpose,[68] viz., for the exercise of the right to appeal[69] and the non-fulfillment of that end within the legal period of time, i. e., ten days, results in the absolute abatement

[58] *Dig.*, 49, 7.

[59] *Dig.*, 49, 5, 2, 5, 4.

[60] *Nov.* 23, pr; 119, 5; 123, 21.

[61] C. 28, C. II, q. 6; c. 15, X, *de sententia et re iudicata*, II, 27; cc. 3, 7, *de appellationibus*, II, 15 in VI°; Conc. Trident., sess. XXII, *de ref.* c. 7.

[62] Can. 1634; 1881.

[63] Noval, *De Processibus*, n. 228.

[64] Can. 1917.

[65] Roberti, *De Processibus*, II, n. 547; Wernz-Vidal, *De Processibus*, n. 659.

[66] Roberti, *De Processibus*, I, n. 180.

[67] Wernz-Vidal, *De Processibus*, nn. 185, 610.

[68] Noval, *De Processibus*, n. 228.

[69] Wernz-Vidal, *De Processibus*, nn. 184, 187, §7; Noval, *De Processibus*, n. 229.

and annulment of that right.[70] It comes under the *fatalia legis*[71] so that if no effort is made to interpose an appeal within the time allowed, the right to do so is thereby extinguished and it is not within the power of the judge to restore this right.[72] The term is, moreover, *improrogabilis*[73] in that it cannot be prolonged or extended arbitrarily by the judge beyond the period of time legally allotted for the exercise of the right to appeal; similarly, the judge cannot limit or restrict it at his pleasure. The only exceptions to these regulations are those permitted by the Code. These particular ordinances are not of recent origin. Their development begins with the Decretals[74] and probably before that time.[75] They were evolved slowly through controversial discussion[76] to their present clear and concise state. They represent the mind of the Church with regard to the speedy yet right administration of justice to the end that all parties may avail themselves of this particular form of defense and that, at the same time, suits and trials will not be unduly protracted and prolonged by the negligence of judges or litigants at the sacrifice of either the public or the private welfare.

The period of ten days mentioned in this canon, is considered by the Code as *tempus utile,* that is, the time is granted for the exercise of one's right, e. g., of appeal, in such a way that it does not *run* if one is prevented from using it through ignorance or some other legal cause.[77] This is a special concession of law, since time of its very nature, *runs* continuously. The idea prompting this legal

[70] Roberti, *De Processibus,* I, n. 180; Wernz-Vidal, *De Processibus,* nn. 185, 610.

[71] Can. 1634, §1.

[72] Noval, *De Processibus,* n. 229; Wernz-Vidal, *De Processibus,* n. 185.

[73] Can. 1634, §1; cf. Wernz-Vidal, *De Processibus,* nn, 185, 610; Roberti, *De Processibus,* I, n. 185.

[74] C. 15, X, *de sententia et re iudicata,* II, 27; c. 8, *de appellationibus,* II, 15 in VI°; c. 3, *de appellationibus,* II, 12 in Clem.

[75] C. 28, C. II, q. 6.

[76] Schmalzgrueber, lib. II, tit. XXVIII, nn. 70, 89; Pirhing, lib. II, tit. XXXVIII, n. 153; Bouix, *De Iudiciis,* II, 281 ff.; Lega, *De Iudiciis,* I, n. 638.

[77] Can. 35; cf. Matthaeus a Coronata, *Institutiones Jur. Can.,* I, n. 56; Ayrinhac, *General Legislation,* n. 129; Chelodi, *De Personis,* n. 89; Maroto, *Institutiones Jur. Can.,* I, n. 260; Michiels, *Normae Generales,* II, 158; Cicognani, *Jus Canonicum,* II, 199; Ojetti, *Commentarium,* I, 205; Vermeersch-Creusen, *Epitome,* I, n. 121.

favor is to allow anyone to make full use of the time granted to him for the exercise of his rights in a particular case. From this point of view, it is not to be interpreted strictly; the concession is rather to be amplified if it may be effected legitimately.[78] Roberti[79] claims that the time allowed by this canon, runs continuously, that, once begun, it is *tempus continuum* (as opposed to *tempus utile*), and that it can only be interrupted by the cases mentioned in canon 1733, which interruption is permitted by canon 1885, §1. Vidal[80] similarly states that the time runs continuously in as much as the *dies feriati* that occur during the period are counted as part of the ten days, the tenth day alone excepted. This opinion is probably based on the gratuitous distinction that is made by some canonists in this matter, *scil.*, that the time conceded by canon 1881 is useful, *tempus utile*, by reason of its beginning, that is, it does not run as long as a party is ignorant of the fact that he can exercise or prosecute his rights in a particular case, but continuous, *tempus continuum*, in its course or running, thereby permitting no interruption except that allowed by law, as in canon 1733. This distinction is made in a general way by Matthaeus a Coronata,[81] Chelodi[82] and Cicognani.[83] The last named canonist cites canon 432, §1 and §2 as an example of time that is *tempus utile ratione initii*, in that the obligation of a chapter to elect a vicar capitular does not begin to run until notice has been served on it concerning the death of the bishop; once the news of the bishop's death has been communicated to the chapter, however, this same time is continuous, *tempus continuum*, so that it admits no interruption whatever. If the chapter for any cause whatever shall fail to elect a vicar capitular within the eight days following the receipt of the notice, the case devolves on the metropolitan. It is difficult to see any parallel between this case and canon 1881.[84] The latter canon has no qualifying clause nor does it express any condition that would merit such an interpreta-

[78] Maroto, *Institutiones*, I, n. 260, §6; Michiels, *Normae Generales*, II, 161.
[79] *De Processibus*, II, n. 478.
[80] Wernz-Vidal, *De Processibus*, n. 610.
[81] *Institutiones*, I, n. 56.
[82] *Jus de Personis*, n. 89, c. note 1.
[83] *Jus Canonicum*, II, 200.
[84] Michiels, *Normae Generales*, II, 160.

tion. It merely states that an appeal ought to be interposed within ten days from the time that notice of the sentence has been received and it declares it in such a manner that the term is understood according to the norms of law and regarded by practically all canonists as *tempus utile.* It should therefore, possess all the beneficial qualities which the Code and canonical jurisprudence ascribe to *tempus utile.* This is the sound opinion of Michiels [85] who rejects the above mentioned distinction and of Creusen,[86] Maroto,[87] Cocchi [88] and De Meester [89] who do not admit it. Therefore, after a sentence has been communicated to the interested parties, and one of the latter has the right to appeal from the sentence but does not know that he may exercise this right, the *tempus utile* does not run; the days during which this ignorance persists are not counted as being part of the ten day period. Ignorance, however, will not be admitted if it is due to culpable negligence. Similarly, when a party is cognizant of his rights but is prevented from taking advantage of them, using or prosecuting them, the days on which the impediment exists, are not reckoned to be part of the *tempus utile* of ten days, provided there is no evidence of fraud or deceit.[90]

Moreover, the aggrieved party must be able to exercise his right of appeal during the whole of every one of the ten days. If the use of this right be impeded during a notable part of any particular day, that day is not counted in the general computation of the period. For each day not counted, another day is added to the time allotted by the Code.[91] This does not oppose or contradict what was stated previously regarding the fact that this time cannot be prorogued or prolonged. The statement was made to the effect that this term could not be arbitrarily extended by the judge; the latter can only permit a protraction of the time if the law permits or orders him to do so.

[85] *Normae Generales,* II, 160.

[86] Vermeersch-Creusen, *Epitome,* I, n. 121; III, n. 239.

[87] *Institutiones,* I, n. 260.

[88] *De Processibus,* n. 236.

[89] *Compendium,* I, n. 288.

[90] Cicognani, *Jus Canonicum,* II, 199; Michiels, *Normae Generales,* II, 158.

[91] Maroto, *Institutiones,* I, n. 260, §6; Michiels, *Normae Generales,* II, 161; Matthaeus a Coronata, *Institutiones,* I, n. 56, §3.

The period of ten days is computed in accordance with the regulations stated by the Code in canon 34, §3, n. 3, which explicitly mentions this term. When the *terminus a quo,* i. e., the exact time at which notification of the sentence is received, does not coincide with the beginning of a day, i. e., midnight, then the day on which the sentence was received is not counted in the ten day period and the allotment of time is completed at the expiration of the tenth full day on which the litigant could exercise his right of appeal.[92] Although the first day of this period is not counted, nevertheless an appeal may be interposed lawfully on that day.[93]

On the other hand, even days on which the court is not in session or the tribunal does not *sit,* are counted in the general computation of the ten day period.[94] It is this feature that prompts some authorities to regard the term under consideration as *tempus continum.*[95] Holidays of this order are determined by the Code,[96] or by the Ordinary of the diocese.[97] The Code prohibits the performance of certain acts on Sundays and feast days of precept but this list of proscribed acts is not *taxative* enumerated in the Code. *De facto,* all judicial acts are forbidden on *dies feriati* because the court remains closed on these days.

## §2. *Legal Exceptions to the Prescribed Term*

In addition to the circumstances of ignorance and the inability to exercise one's rights, as considered in the preceding section, there are certain other causes that may legitimately impede the course of the *tempus utile.*

Certain definite exceptions may be noted in regard to the fore-

92 Matthaeus a Coronata, *Institutiones,* I, n. 55; Cicognani, *Jus Canonicum,* II, 195; Michiels, *Norma Generales,* II, 155-160; Roberti, *De Processibus,* II, n. 478.

93 Maroto, *Institutiones,* I, n. 260, §5; Matthaeus a Coronata, *Institutiones,* I, n. 56, §3.

94 Roberti, *De Processibus,* II, n. 478; Wernz-Vidal, *De Processibus,* n. 610; cf. also Schmalzgrueber, lib. II, tit. XXVIII, n. 72; Reiffenstuel, lib. II, tit. VII, n. 80; Leurenius, lib. II, tit. XXVIII, q. 1119, n. 2.

95 Wernz-Vidal, *De Processibus,* n. 610; Ferreres, *Institutiones Canonicae,* II, n. 803.

96 Can. 1247, §1; 1639, §1.

97 Can. 1638, §1; cf. Roberti, *De Processibus,* I, n. 185.

going regulations. It may be remarked, first, that if the sentence which was communicated to the parties who were involved in the suit, was null and void, due to the presence of a material error which may have occurred in the transcription of the dispositive part of the verdict or which may have crept into the record in any other manner, the communication of this sentence to the interested parties is not regarded as the canonical *notitia publicationis* demanded by canon 1881. Accordingly, the *tempus utile* does not begin to run or to be in effect. The sentence should be returned for correction to the judge who will himself rectify the mistake in accordance with the provisions of canon 1878. Whereupon, it will be communicated to the parties again and the *tempus utile* for the appeal will be in effect when notice of the sentence has been received.

Similarly, if the method used in publishing the sentence is not in accord with the prescriptions of canon 1877 and is thereby nullified, the *tempus utile* for the appeal will not be in effect until notification has been made according to the provisions of the Code.[98] However, the fact that a sentence that has been communicated or published in an invalid manner will not nullify an appeal that is interposed against it.[99]

**Canon 1885, §1. Si casus de quo in canone 1733 contigerit intra terminum ad appellandum utilem sed antequam appellatio interposita sit, sententia debet iis quorum interest denuntiari eisque concessi intelliguntur termini a iure statuti a die denuntiationis computandi.**

The first section of canon 1885 concerns an interruption in the *tempus utile* of this term that happens occasionally. It refers to canon 1733 which treats of this case of interruption in connection with the proceedings proper. The *tempus utile* of canon 1881 may be interrupted by the death of one of the parties, by the change of state of any of the persons concerned in the trial or by the fact of resigning or otherwise withdrawing from an office by virtue of which

[98] Cf. S. R. Rota in c. *Societatis,* 18 March 1922—*Decisiones S. R. Rotae,* XIV (1922), dec. VII, n. 4.

[99] Roberti, *De Processibus,* II, n. 212, note 2.

one became a party to the suit in question. The change of state must be such that it will affect the juridical capacity of the one concerned. Marriage, ordinarily is not regarded as a change of state in this regard. The change mentioned here signifies, e. g., the transition from the lay to the clerical state, or from the lay or the clerical to the religious state, for the reason that the religious form a state of their own and are regarded in some respects as minors in ecclesiastical law. This rule, however, would not apply to novices because they still retain to a certain extent their juridical capacity, at least by proxy.[100] A change of state could likewise occur in the case of a minor, represented at court by a parent, a guardian or an attorney,[101] who would become of age during the course of a trial and so be able to act for himself.[102] The surrender or giving up of an office by reason of which the incumbent became a party to the suit, e. g., as a representative of a moral person, may occur in several ways, by death, resignation, dismissal, renunciation, or any other legitimate reason. This does not hold with regard to the *defensor vinculi* or the *promotor iustitiae,* for in these cases, the office, not the individual person is considered by the law.[103]

When any one of these circumstances occurs, the *tempus utile* is not only interrupted but entirely abated. The judge should be notified concerning the death, the change of state or the abandonment of the office in question, whereupon he will reissue or republish the sentence and communicate it to the heirs or successors of the litigants.[104] A new delay or term of ten days, *tempus utile,* is likewise granted by law, and it is in effect when knowledge of the sentence has been received by the heirs or successors. Similarly, it would be regulated by the ordinances of the preceding section of this work.[105] On the other hand, if any of the foregoing circumstances should occur in the case of the *defensor vinculi* or the *promotor*

[100] Can. 1652; cf. Augustine, *A Commentary,* VII, 181.

[101] Can. 1648-1651.

[102] Wernz-Vidal, *De Processibus,* n. 411.

[103] Roberti, *De Processibus,* II, n. 310; Wernz-Vidal, *De Processibus,* n. 411; Blat, *De Processibus,* n. 231.

[104] *Reg.* XLVI, R. J. in VI°—"Is qui in ius succedit alterius, eo iure quo ille, uti debebit."

[105] Roberti, *De Processibus,* II, n. 478; Wernz-Vidal, *De Processibus,* n. 610.

*iustitiae,* the term would not be interrupted, but merely suspended until a new official was named for the office.[106]

Another exception that is recognized by the law is stated in canon 1635. If the last day of this ten day period is one of the *dies feriati,* on which the court is closed for the transaction of any and all judicial matters, the term is prorogued or extended by law to the first subsequent day on which the tribunal is in session and it expires with the completion of that day.[107]

### §3. *The Lapse of the Term*

**Canon 1886. Inutiliter elapsis fatalibus appellatoriis sive coram iudice *a quo,* sive coram iudice *ad quem,* deserta censetur appellatio.**

The *fatalia legis*[108] are those peremptory terms or delays conceded by law to a party for the purpose of enabling the latter to perform some particular action in law, with this result, that if this right is not exercised within the interval of time granted, the right to perform the action is abated and extinguished forever as far as that particular act in a particular cause is concerned. Although the expression "*fatalia*" with reference to appeal is not found in the Decretals, the norm that is indicated thereby was first ordained by the Roman jurists of the Classical Period. It is to be found in the *Digest, Code* and *Novels* of Justinian and in all subsequent legislation concerning the right to appeal.[109] The expression itself is used by all the foremost commentators on the Decretals particularly with regard to appeals.[110] The terms permitted by law for the exercise of a right are called *fatalia* because they prove *fatal* to a cause if not

[106] Roberti, *De Processibus,* II, n. 310; Wernz-Vidal, *De Processibus,* n. 411.

[107] Roberti, *De Processibus,* I, n. 184. Before the Code this exception was not recognized and the term expired on the tenth day, regardless of whether or not this was a *dies feriatus;* no extension was made for this purpose. Schmalzgrueber, lib. II, tit. XXVIII, n. 72; Leurenius, lib. II, tit. XXVIII, q. 1119, n. 2.

[108] Can. 1634, §1.

[109] Cf. Article II, §1 of this chapter.

[110] Cf. Schmalzgrueber, lib. II, tit. XXVIII, n. 70; Reiffenstuel, lib. II, tit. XXVIII, n. 152; Devoti, *Jus Canonicum Universum,* lib. II, tit. XXVIII, n. 18; Santi-Leitner, lib. II, tit. XXVIII, n. 25.

observed.[111] In accordance with this legislation, canon 1886 ordains that if a litigant allows the term of ten days to lapse without taking advantage of the time granted him to interpose an appeal, he is considered by the law to have forfeited or abandoned his right to appeal in the case in question.[112] Whereupon, the sentence passed on his cause becomes a *res iudicata* [113] and is to be executed.[114] The *lapsus terminorum* is regarded as a matter of public right in that it cannot be renounced or formally abandoned by the parties themselves for the purpose of effecting the immediate execution of a sentence. The matter must first become a *res iudicata* following which, the judge will by decree, order its execution.[115]

With regard to the *defensor vinculi* and the *fatalia* of an appeal, it may be said that the *fatalia* of appeal affect those who have the right, *ius*, of appealing; they do not hold in the case of the *defensor vinculi* for he not only has the right to appeal but it is his duty to do so when the first sentence declares for the nullity of a marriage. This distinction between the *ius* and the *officium* is to be noticed in the constitution *"Dei Miseratione"* [116] and particularly in the instruction of the Sacred Congregation of the Holy Office to the Oriental bishops.[117] Consequently, although the defender of the marriage bond is obliged to appeal from the first sentence of nullity in a matrimonial cause within the legitimate time, i. e., ten days, according to canon 1986, yet if he neglects to do this, it cannot be said that the sentence of nullity becomes a *res iudicata*. Sentences of this type that affect the state of a person never become *res iudicatae* and the appeal of the *defensor vinculi,* even if made after the lapse of the ten day term, is to be received by the judge who pronouncd the appealed sentence.[118] The question does not seem to be

[111] Augustine, *A Commentary,* VII, 324.
[112] *Reg.* XXV, R. J. in VI°—"Mora sua cuilibet est nociva."
[113] Can. 1902, n. 2.
[114] Can. 1917, §1.
[115] Can. 1902, 1918. Canon 1903 contains the exception to this rule.
[116] Bened. XIV. const. *"Dei Miseratione,"* 3 Nov. 1741, n. 8—*Fontes,* n. 318.
[117] S. C. S. Off., *instr.,* a. 1883, n. 25—*Fontes,* n. 1076. "Quamvis appellationi interponendae nulli fatales dies vinculi defensori statuti sint, curandum tamen, ut quantocius id fiat."
[118] Cf. Roberti, in *Apollinaris,* II (1929), 516; Haring, "Gelten die Notfristen auch für den Defensor Vinculi in Eheprozess?", *Theol. praktische Quartalschrift,* LXXXIII (1930), 597, 598.

practical for the reason that the judge by the force of canon 1986 is empowered to compel the defender to fulfill his obligation even by threat of punishment or removal from office.[119]

### Article III. The Proper Form

The interposing of an appeal is an important judicial act, provision for which has been made by the Code. It is intimately connected with the solemn judicial process and as such, it should be endowed with the formalities required by law.

#### §1. *The Oral Appeal*

**Canon 1882. §1. Appellatio fieri potest oretenus coram iudice pro tribunali sedente, si publice sententia legatur, statimque ab actuario scriptis redigenda est.**

Canon 1877 provides for the public reading of the sentence by the judge. This is to be performed by the latter in a solemn manner, the interested parties having been cited to appear to hear the verdict of the court. When the sentence has been read by the judge, the party who is dissatisfied and desires to appeal, is permitted by law to stand and declare his intention of doing so orally or vocally. He may interpose his appeal by exclaiming "I appeal" or by using any similar expression which will inform the judge clearly of the opposition of the litigant to the sentence and of his intention to appeal therefrom.[120] This method of appealing was sanctioned by Roman Law[121] and was likewise incorporated into Decretal Law,[122] possibly through the Decree of Gratian[123] for there is no evidence of it in the early ecclesiastical sources.

[119] Can. 1986; cf. also can. 1935, §1 and 1625, §3; Roberti in *Apollinaris,* II (1929), 517, 518.

[120] Bouix, *De Iudiciis,* II, 274; Lega, *De Iudiciis,* I, n. 640; Noval, *De Processibus,* n. 646; Roberti, *De Processibus,* II, n. 478; Vermeersch-Creusen, *Epitome,* III, n. 239; Wernz-Vidal, *De Processibus,* n. 611.

[121] *Dig.,* 49, 1, 3, 4, 7; *Nov.,* 23, pr.; 119, 5; 123, 21.

[122] Cc. 34, 59, X, *de appellationibus, recusationibus et relationibus,* II, 28; cf. Schmalzgrueber, lib. II, tit. XXVIII, n. 65; Santi-Leitner, lib. II, tit. XXVIII, n. 18.

[123] C. 41, C. II, q. 6.

This vocal appeal must be made immediately after the verdict has been pronounced and before the judge leaves the tribunal proper. Canon 1877 declares that the judge is to read the sentence solemnly while sitting on the *bench* and the aggrieved party has the right to interpose the appeal immediately.[124] If, however, the judge has left the bench even though he may still be in the court room, it would appear that the appeal would not be heard or recognized and a written, formal notice of appeal would then be necessary. This seems to be indicated by the fact that the position occupied by the judge in the court, that is, on the *bench* or tribunal proper, is closely and intimately associated with the exercise of the office itself; that he acts as a judge in a given cause only when he occupies the formal position, location or place set aside for the exercise of that office. A formal judicial trial is a solemn matter and all the formalities of solemn judicial procedure should be observed strictly. The same feature is intimated by canonists who assert that the oral appeal must be made immediately without the lapse of any interval, after the reading of the sentence, that is, while the judge is still *on the bench,* and acting in his proper judicial capacity relative to the cause in litigation.[125] When the appeal is made in this manner from a definitive sentence, it is not necessary for the appellant to give the judge the reasons for his action, although he is at liberty to do so if he wishes. The judge whose sentence is appealed is to determine solely if the appeal has been made in a legitimate manner. If an interlocutory sentence is appealed, on the other hand, it is within the province of the judge who rendered the decision to know the reasons upon which such an appeal is based so that he himself may remedy the alleged injustice by correcting or changing the sentence.[126]

If the appeal has been interposed vocally or orally, the judge will order the notary to reduce to writing this oral notice of appeal,

[124] Cf. c. 5, *de sententia et re iudicata,* II, 14 in VI°; Wernz, *Jus Decretalium,* V, n. 669. The judge is obliged to sit while reading the sentence; however, whether he assumes a sitting or standing posture, it will not interfere with the solemn pronouncement of the sentence.

[125] Roberti, *De Processibus,* II, n. 478; Noval, *De Processibus,* n. 646; Vermeersch-Creusen, *Epitome,* III, n. 239; cf. also Reiffenstuel, lib. II, tit. XXVIII, n. 119.

[126] Noval, *De Processibus,* n. 646; cf. c. 59, X, *de appellationibus, recusationibus et relationibus,* II, 28.

and it thereby becomes a part of the permanent record of the cause. The notice of appeal should contain all the necessary elements of a written appeal, which will be noted in the following section. The notary is then to read the written notice to the appellant and if it has been correctly transcribed, the latter approves it, which approval is likewise noted by the actuary.[127] The statement that the notice as written must be approved, indicates that the appellant is to sign it. The law does not expressly direct that this be done but in as much as an appeal is similar in nature to a judicial petition,[128] it is to be executed, *mutatis mutandis,* according to the legal provisions and formalities governing that proceeding.[129] The signatures of the judge or of the *praeses* of a collegiate tribunal and the notary are likewise affixed to this notice.[130]

## §2. *The Written Appeal*

**Canon 1882. §2. Aliter facienda est in scriptis, salvo casu de quo in canone 1707.**

When the notice of the sentence has been received by the parties after the court has adjourned, and either litigant desires to interpose an appeal from the sentence in question, he must do so ordinarily in writing. It must be filed with the judge who pronounced the verdict and within the period of time specified by the law. According to Vidal,[131] no special formalities have been prescribed relative to the drawing up of this petition; on the other hand, Roberti [132] declares that the enactments governing the introductory *libellus* or original bill of complaint,[133] are to be applied likewise to petitions which invoke any legal favor of the law against an unjust sentence, with due regard, however, to the observance of appropriate changes necessitated by the peculiar circumstances of a particular cause. He

[127] Can. 1707, §3; Vermeersch-Creusen, *Epitome,* III, n. 144.
[128] Can. 1724; cf. Roberti, *De Processibus,* I, n. 278.
[129] Can. 1708, §3.
[130] Can. 1643, §2; cf. Roberti, *De Processibus,* I, n. 105.
[131] Wernz-Vidal, *De Processibus,* n. 611.
[132] *De Processibus,* II, n. 478; cf. I, n. 278.
[133] Can. 1706-1710.

quotes canon 1724 in support of this contention and his opinion seems to be substantiated thereby. Since a judicial petition is an act by which one seeks the aid of a judge in the execution of a particular law in a concrete case, it may be said with Roberti, that the interposition of an appeal assumes the character of a judicial petition. Accordingly, the petition in this case should manifest the litigant's intention of appealing from the verdict pronounced on the cause in which he participated. It should contain the names of the appellant and his opponent, the appellee; the entire sentence or its particular clause or section, whichever is appealed, is to be determined clearly; the name of the judge who rendered the verdict and to whom the petition is directed, as well as the name of the appellate court or tribunal before which the appeal is to be prosecuted, are to be likewise included. The motives which prompt the appeal or indicate the unjust character of the sentence, *in facto vel in iure*, may also be expressed in the petition but this proceeding is optional with the appellant since the judge *a quo* only looks to the legitimate form of the appeal and ascertains if it were interposed within the proper period of time prescribed by law. The petition should also contain the date on which the sentence was received by the appellant in addition to the date, day, month and year, on which the appeal is made; and finally, the signature of the appellant, whether the latter be the litigant himself or his procurator, should be affixed to the petition. What has been declared in a previous article regarding the procurator and the relation of the latter to his client in the matter of appeal, may be recalled here.

In order to appeal from a sentence, the attorney or proctor is not required to have a special mandate to that effect, unless the client has reserved that right to himself.[134] The original *mandatum ad lites* [135] under ordinary circumstances, includes the power of interposing an appeal.[136]

The petition may be deposited with the judge or the president of a collegiate tribunal or with the chancellor of the diocese by the appellant personally, or it may be transmitted by other means. In

[134] Can. 1664, §2.
[135] Can. 1659, §1.
[136] Roberti, *De Processibus*, I, n. 210.

either case, the appellant is responsible for its secure delivery and consequently, he should use the safest possible method of transmitting the petition to the proper person.[137] He should make use of the same means as described in a previous article with regard to the transmission of the *acta causae* to the appellate court; he may register the letter bearing his application and request at the same time a "return receipt" which will certify that he despatched his petition within the time required for it to reach its proper destination and indicate to him in addition, the reception of the letter by the party concerned. The receipt of the petition, together with the different elements and formalities contained therein, are to be transcribed by the notary in the *acta causae*.[138] While the foregoing recommended formalities, with the exception of the simple notice of appeal given orally or in writing to the judge *a quo* within the required term, do not seem to be necessary for the valid interposition of an appeal, however since the entire process is conducted along solemn lines, the legal formalities of solemn judicial procedure should be employed. This observance will assure the interested parties of a secure and regular as well as a rapid and direct recognition of their rights and privileges.

If the appellant is illiterate or unable to write for any reason, and if he has not appointed an attorney to act for him, he may appear before the notary of the court or tribunal wherein his case was heard, within the required period of time and interpose his appeal in accordance with the formalities mentioned in a preceding section relative to oral appeals. In this event, the notary shall, after having read the dictated notice to the appellant, reduce to writing the latter's approval of the transcribed petition, noting at the same time in the record the inability of the appellant to write.[139] He shall affix his signature to the notice and submit it to the judge to sign likewise.[140]

[137] Roberti, *De Processibus,* II, n. 478.
[138] Roberti, *De Processibus,* II, n. 478.
[139] Can. 1659, §2.
[140] Can. 1707, §1 and §3.

# CHAPTER IX

## THE EFFECTS OF AN APPEAL

THE primary purpose of interposing an appeal against a sentence that is alleged to be unjust, is to remedy the injustice by seeking to have the sentence reversed, revoked or revised. Appeal, as such, is a judicial mode of legal redress and a legitimate means of defense and its principal, however general aim is the reparation of the unjust verdict. However, this judicial remedy, where legitimately interposed, produces other and more immediate results. These particular effects are concerned directly with the contesting parties to the cause and with the cause itself.

### ARTICLE I. THE EFFECTS OF AN APPEAL RELATIVE TO THE LITIGANTS

The Code does not introduce any new features with regard to this element of an appeal. Under Decretal Law, the right to appeal was accorded to anyone who had a particular grievance against the verdict pronounced on his case,[1] for an appeal, then as now, was considered as a kind or species of natural defense against injustice. Both defendant and plaintiff enjoyed this right [2] so long as either could substantiate or support his allegation of injustice. On appeal, the cause *in toto* was judged by the superior tribunal and the investigation made by the latter, extended to all parts of the impugned sentence. However, an appeal could be directed against some particular section or phase of the sentence and at the same time, or later, the appellee could appeal from that part of the sentence excluded by the principal appeal.[3] The present legislation on the subject does not change this mode of procedure; rather it extends and

[1] C. 61, X, *de appellationibus, recusationibus et relationibus*, II, 28.

[2] C. 7, X, *de appellationibus, recusationibus et relationibus*, II, 28.

[3] C. 7, X, *de appellationibus, recusationibus et relationibus*, II, 28; cf. Santi-Leitner, lib. II, tit. XXVIII, n. 5; Heiner-Wynen, *De Processu Criminali Ecclesiastico*, p. 130; Grandclaude, *Jus Canonicum*, II, 153; Schmalzgrueber, lib. II, tit. XXVIII, n. 9.

amplifies it with resultant beneficial effects on the rights of the appellee in the case.

### §1. *The Appellee*

**Can. 1887. §1. Appellatio facta ab actore prodest etiam reo, et vicissim.**

**§2. Si interponatur ab una parte super aliquo sententiae capite, pars adversa, etsi fatalia appellationis fuerint transacta, potest super aliis capitibus incidenter appellare; idque facere potest etiam sub conditione recedendi, si prior pars ab instantia recesserit.**

**§3. Si sententia plura capita contineat, et appellans quaedam tantummodo capita impugnet, cetera capita exclusa habeantur; si nullum determinavit caput, appellatio presumitur facta contra omnia capita.**

The principal appeal is that which is interposed by the aggrieved party, apart from and independent of the appeal of the other litigant. The principal appellant may determine which part of the sentence is unjust and as such, appealed, or he may impugn the entire sentence. The writ of appeal, the *libellus appellatorius,* should state definitely which section or phase of the sentence is appealed; in which event, the new examination and rehearing of the cause conducted by the appellate tribunal, will extend only to that part of the sentence that has been appealed and to the questions implicitly contained therein.[4] The other portions of the sentence are excluded; and since the *litis contestatio* of the appellate instance extends to the reformation of that part of the sentence appealed, the judge of the superior tribunal may not include the remainder of the sentence in his judgment.[5] If the appeal is not directed against any particular portion of the sentence, it will be presumed by the appellate court that the entire sentence has been appealed, whereupon the judgment of the higher tribunal will extend to the whole sentence.[6]

[4] Roberti, *De Processibus,* II, n. 485.

[5] Can. 1891, §1; 1726; cf. Noval, *De Processibus,* nn. 650, 655; Wernz-Vidal, *De Processibus,* n. 613; Roberti, *De Processibus,* I, n. 301; II, n. 471.

[6] Can. 1887, §3; Cocchi, *De Processibus,* n. 230; Blat, *De Processibus,* n. 417; Wernz-Vidal, *De Processibus,* n. 608; cf. also S. R. Rota in c. *Policastren.,* 6 July 1915—*AAS.,* VII (1915), 500.

Moreover, since the cause in which the litigants are contending, binds both parties, an appeal placed by one of the latter may benefit the other. When an appeal has been made legitimately and prosecuted before the appellate court, the appellee enjoys the same rights as he would otherwise have if he had interposed the appeal himself.[7] Consequently, if the appellant is later found guilty of contempt of court, the appellee may plead that the instance be continued and a sentence more favorable to himself rendered.[8] Both parties may appeal as principals from different sections of the sentence, and in this event, both individual appeals will be governed by the regular appellate procedure of the Code.[9]

Furthermore, an added privilege is extended to the appellee by this canon, in the form of an incidental appeal. This is an appeal that is filed by the appellee against the appellant for the revision of that part of the sentence excluded by the principal appeal of the latter. It is termed "incidental," *incidenter,*[10] because it depends entirely on the principal appeal. In fact, it cannot be validly admitted, according to Noval,[11] unless the *incidental* appellant demonstrates and proves that his appeal is in some manner at least, connected with the principal appeal. He may do this by showing that if the principal appeal is successfully prosecuted, the subsequent sentence will result in some unjust injury to himself.[12] The incidental appeal depends on the principal appeal to this extent, that if the latter were not prosecuted before the court of appeal within the time required by law which would result in the appeal being regarded as abandoned or deserted, the incidental appeal would likewise be extinguished. However, once the incidental appeal is admitted, it is probably more or less independent of the main appeal, in this respect, that if the principal appeal is renounced by the ap-

[7] Can. 1887, §1; Noval, *De Processibus,* n. 651; Blat, *De Processibus,* n. 417.

[8] Noval, *De Processibus,* n. 651; cf. canon 1844, 1849; c. 44, X, *de appellationibus, recusationibus et relationibus,* II, 28.

[9] Can. 1879-1891.

[10] Can. 1887, §2.

[11] *De Processibus,* n. 651.

[12] Wernz-Vidal, *De Processibus,* n. 608, note 62; Vermeersch-Creusen, *Epitome,* III, n. 240.

pellant, the incidental would not necessarily be quashed, unless it had been interposed on the condition that it would be withdrawn if and when the principal appeal was formally renounced.[13] Noval[14] states in this regard that the party who appeals *incidenter* from a sentence, may withdraw his appeal when the principal appeal has been renounced or abated through renunciation, regardless of whether he appealed conditionally or not. He leaves the incidental appellant entirely free in the matter, regarding the latter as having been forced in the first place to appeal in order to defend himself or his interests and consequently, in equity, he should not be held to continue the prosecution of his appeal, if the principal appellant has receded from the case.

An incidental appeal may be proposed by any party who has the right to interpose a principal appeal. It may be filed even after the lapse of the terms allowed by law for the interposition[15] or the prosecution[16] of a principal appeal.[17] It is to be prosecuted before the ordinary tribunal of second instance which has taken cognizance of the principal appeal and prior to the *conclusio in causa.*[18] Roberti[19] claims that the incidental appeal should be made before the appellate *litis contestatio* has taken place for this act determines the scope of the appellate instance and the extent of the discussion or controversy. Noval,[20] on the other hand, permits the incidental appeal to be filed after the *litis contestatio* but before the sentence of the appellate court has been rendered and particularly before the *conclusio in causa.*[21] This would seem to be sufficient for the defense proper or *discussio in causa*[22] would afford ample opportunity to discern and determine the relative merits of the incidental appeal.

[13] Can. 1887, §2; Roberti, *De Processibus,* II, n. 472; Blat, *De Processibus,* n. 417; Wernz-Vidal, *De Processibus,* n. 608; Vermeersch-Creusen, *Epitome,* III, n. 240.

[14] *De Processibus,* n. 651.

[15] Can. 1881.

[16] Can. 1883.

[17] Can. 1887, §2.

[18] Can. 1860.

[19] *De Processibus,* II, n. 472.

[20] *De Processibus,* n. 651.

[21] Can. 1860-1861.

[22] Can. 1862-1867.

The incidental appeal differs from the principal appeal in the following manner: the *fatalia legis* [23] do not have to be observed in the interposition of the appeal; it is made by the appellee; it has the nature somewhat of a counter-plea. Vidal [24] and Roberti [25] admit this resemblance but the latter canonist declares that it is not to be confused with the *actio reconventionalis* [26] properly so-called. Noval [27] states directly that it is a *causa reconventionalis* since it is aimed to affect or curtail the claims made by the appellant in his *libellus appellatorius.* This is merely another method of stating the view of Roberti and Vidal for Noval does not declare that the incidental appeal is an *actio reconventionalis* but a *causa reconventionalis.* The incidental appeal is a necessary element to complete the judgment of a partial appeal for it enables the appellate tribunal to extend its investigation and examination to those parts of the sentence that were excluded by the principal appeal. Its usefulness will be seen when consideration is given to the fact that it will enable a party to place an appeal to offset a probable unjust appellate sentence, when otherwise he would be unable to do so on account of the lapse of the ten day term or for some other reasonable cause.

## §2. *The Co-appellants*

**Canon 1888. Si unus ex pluribus correis aut actoribus sententiam impugnet, impugnatio censetur ab omnibus facta,** ***quoties res petita sit individua aut obligatio solidalis;*** **expensas vero iudiciales ille tantum sustinere debet qui appellavit, si iudex appellationis primam sententiam confirmaverit.**

When several persons are jointly engaged in an action, *litis consortes, collitigantes,* either as co-plaintiffs or as co-defendants for the vindication or defense respectively of some right,[28] one or more of

[23] Can. 1881, 1883.

[24] Wernz-Vidal, *De Processibus,* n. 608, note 62.

[25] *De Processibus,* II, n. 472.

[26] Can. 1690 ff.

[27] *De Processibus,* n. 651.

[28] Cf. Roberti, *De Processibus,* I, nn. 193, 194; Wernz, *Jus Decretalium,* V, n. 156.

these parties may interpose an appeal against an obnoxious sentence. The question arises regarding the juridical effect of this appeal. If the appeal interposed by one of the *collitigantes,* is upheld and the sentence reversed, does this revision benefit the rest of the parties jointly united with the appellant in a common cause (which may be called the *effectus realis*), or does it affect the party alone who made the appeal (the *effectus personalis*)?

Roberti[29] who treats this problem at some length, contends that the principle, *viz.*, that an appeal made by one of several co-defendants or co-plaintiffs as the case may be, extends to all who are jointly united with him so long as the *res petita* or the cause of the action is the same for all, is founded on the fact that part of a statement made on this point by Ulpian [30] had been misunderstood. The influence of Teutonic law further augmented the confusion and in this condition, the principle was incorporated into Decretal Law.[31] It had the force of law and became the practical norm for this particular case. Toward the end of the last century, however, certain scholars subjected the text of Ulpian to a new examination and declared that in view of the general principles of Roman Law which constantly tend to restrict and limit the effects of a sentence, an appeal produced only a personal effect and that it affected those alone who interposed it. Notwithstanding this consideration, the old principle of Decretal Law was adopted by the Rota unconditionally.[32] The Code, however, according to Roberti,[33] rejects this principle and states that as a general rule, when one party of several jointly united in a cause, appeals from a sentence, the appeal affects that party alone, *effectus personalis.* It does not extend to the other *consortes,* except in two cases, *scil., quoties res petita sit individua* and *(quoties) obligatio (sit) solidalis.* Noval [34] states that the Code corrects or determines

[29] *De Processibus,* II, nn. 473, 474.

[30] *Dig.,* 49, 1, 3.

[31] C. 72, X, *de appellationibus, recusationibus et relationibus,* II, 28—"Una sententia pluribus condemnatis, si unus solus ad appellationis beneficium convolaverit, illius victoria, iure communi, ceteris suffragatur, si communi iure iuventur, idemque negotium et eadem causa defensionis existat."

[32] *Reg. Serv. in iud. apud S. R. Rotae Trib.,* §220, n. 2.

[33] *De Processibus,* II, n. 473, p. 206.

[34] *De Processibus,* n. 652.

more strictly this principle of the previous law as contained in the Decretals of Gregory IX.[35]

Bouix[36] had adopted this principle of the pre-Code legislation, citing in support of it the Roman and Decretal Law.[37] He arrived at practically the same conclusion as Roberti some years later, namely, that an appeal made successfully by one of several litigants united together in a common cause, benefited all upon the fulfillment of certain conditions. An investigation of the latter will show the similarity between the exceptions noted as such by Roberti and the conclusions of Bouix. For the effects of a victorious appeal to extend to the other parties jointly united with the appellant *(effectus personalis)*, it is required that the parties be *correi* or co-litigants or condemned by the same sentence in the same cause; that the sentence pronounced by the court of appeal be favorable to the appellant; that the *collitigantes* make use of the common law, for if one of their number is aided by a particular or special ordinance, v. g., on account of being a minor, his appeal, if successful and based on this particular law, will not benefit the other parties; that the object of the trial or suit, be the same for each party, otherwise the sentence could not be given for all; that each party have the same means of defense for if there were many and varied lines of defense, all litigants would not come under one and the same sentence; finally, that the sentence of the first court be not approved tacitly or explicitly by any one of the co-litigants who has not exercised his right of appeal, for a sentence that is approved becomes a *res iudicata* for the party who assents to or approves of it. When these conditions are present and fulfilled, declared Bouix, an appeal made successfully by one of the co-litigants, benefits the other parties jointly united with him, even though none of them had appealed. The qualifications, herein discussed, certainly appear to contain the conditions expressed in canon 1888.

Apart from the principle of law involved and regardless of

[35] C. 72, X, *de appellationibus, recusationibus et relationibus*, II, 28.

[36] *De Iudiciis*, II, 248.

[37] *Dig.*, 49, 1, 10; *Cod.*, 7, 68, 1; 7, 68, 2; c. 72, X, *de appellationibus, recusationibus et relationibus*, II, 28; Schmalzgrueber, lib. II, tit. XXVIII, nn. 14, 15.

whether or not the Code introduced a new principle in this canon, the opinion of Roberti relative to the interpretation of the canon in question, will serve as a sufficient foundation on which to base the commentary of this particular ordinance.

The effects of a successful appeal are communicated to all the co-litigants of the appellant *quoties res petita sit individua.* The claim or complaint contained in the introductory *libellus,* or the denial or defense produced by the co-defendants, must be distinct, one and incapable of separation or division. It would not be sufficient for the purpose of gaining the advantage of this privilege, if the co-plaintiffs or the co-defendants entered the trial on a common basis or to vindicate a common right. That right or basis must be in itself and with respect to the litigants using it, indivisible, coherent and singular [38] with the result that the sentence rendered on the cause could not be divided or separated, or in any manner regarded by the parties as relating to and affecting one of them and not the others.[39]

The second condition respects the obligation which binds the co-litigants, *quoties . . . obligatio (sit) solidalis.* This quality is somewhat similar to the preceding. The obligation by which the parties are jointly united in a common cause, must extend to and bind all collectively and each party individually,[40] with the result that the sentence pronounced on the cause will affect each party to the same extent and in the same degree. This *obligatio solidalis* may come about by means of an agreement previously entered into by the co-litigants [41] or by the direct will of the law.[42] In neither of the above mentioned cases would the effects of an appeal interposed by one of the parties be communicated to the others, if the reason for

[38] Noval, *De Processibus,* n. 652; Roberti, *De Processibus,* II, n. 474.

[39] Blat, *De Processibus,* n. 418.

[40] Blat, *De Processibus,* n. 418.

[41] Roberti, *De Processibus,* II, n. 474.

[42] Noval, *De Processibus,* n. 652. Cf. can. 2211, 2230, 2231, 2346; Ayrinhac, *Penal Legislation,* n. 26; Vermeersch-Creusen, *Epitome,* III, n. 394; S. R. Rota in c. *Aegypti,* 20 June 1922—*Decisiones S. R. Rotae,* XIV (1922), dec. XIX, nn. 7-10, or *AAS.,* XIV (1922), 606, 607. In this decision of the Rota, the effect of an appeal interposed by the *defensor vinculi* was communicated to the party who had not appealed.

the appeal was proper or peculiar to the appellant, v. g., a defect of age, lack of consent, etc.[43]

An appeal of this character is subject to all the prescriptions of the common law relative to this judicial remedy; wherefore, the terms of ten and thirty days, etc., run, not concurrently, but separately for each party. Each litigant may take full advantage of the *tempus utile* [44] but at least one of the litigants must interpose and prosecute an appeal within the time allotted by the law.[45]

If the appealed sentence is confirmed by the appellate tribunal, the appellant alone is held liable for all the expenses incurred by the placing of the appeal proper [46] as well as his share of the expenses of the previous instance.[47] The co-litigants are not responsible for the appeal and accordingly they are not bound to provide for the cost of the second trial.[48] They are held to compensate the victorious party of the original instance.[49] By the same process, it would seem that if the appealed sentence is reversed or revoked, the appellant would not only be relieved of his share of the expenses of the first trial but reimbursed by the appellee for the cost of the second instance. Similarly, equity would demand that if the appeal was successful, the expenses of the first trial should be shared by the appellee and those co-litigants of the appellant who did not appeal from the first sentence. It is true that the juridical effects of a successful appeal extend to the latter but since they would not be forced to stand for the expenses of the appellate instance if the appeal was unsuccessful, inversely they should not be entirely relieved of the expenses of the previous instance in the event that the sentence of the first court was reversed.

## Article II. The Effects of an Appeal on the Cause Proper

A party aggrieved at the injustice of a sentence pronounced against his interests, appeals from that sentence in order to prevent

43 Roberti, *De Processibus*, II, n. 474.

44 Can. 34, §3, n. 3; 35.

45 Roberti, *De Processibus*, II, n. 474.

46 Roberti, *De Processibus*, II, n. 532.

47 Can. 1910, 1912, 1913, §2.

48 Vermeersch-Creusen, *Epitome*, III, n. 240; Cocchi, *De Processibus*, n. 230; Wernz-Vidal, *De Processibus*, n. 608.

49 Can. 1910, 1912.

its execution and the subsequent undue restriction of his rights. He aims, by interposing an appeal, to avert or delay the threatened injury until such time as the cause can be reviewed and the alleged unjust features of the sentence corrected or reformed. The Code recognizes this primary and immediate legal effect of a legitimately interposed appeal and declares in canon 1889 that an appeal has a twofold effect, suspensive and devolutive.

### §1. *The Suspensive Effect of an Appeal*

**Canon 1889. §1. Appellatio *in suspensivo* exsecutionem appellatae sententiae suspendit ac propterea in suo robore permanet principium: "lite pendente nihil innovetur"; appellatio autem *in devolutivo* tantum, non suspendit exsecutionem sententiae, licet lis adhuc pendeat circa meritum causae.**

**§2. Omnis appellatio est *in suspensivo,* nisi aliud in iure expresse caveatur, firmo praescripto canonis 1917, §2.**

The suspensive effect of an appeal consists primarily in this, that the jurisdiction of the judge who rendered the verdict is stayed relative to the cause in question and the sentence pronounced by the judge and appealed, cannot be executed. An appeal legitimately made, withholds the legal force of an otherwise valid sentence, prevents the execution thereof and hinders the judge from taking any further steps in the matter. This particular effect *in suspensivo* of an appeal was accorded full recognition in Roman Law.[50] It appears likewise in early ecclesiastical legislation [51] and later in the Decree of Gratian [52] and the Decretals of Gregory IX.[53] This particular feature of an appeal gave rise to many abuses which were subsequently abolished by the Council of Trent.[54] Benedict XIV in his

[50] *Dig.*, 49, 5, 6; 49, 5, 7; 49, 7, 1; *Cod.*, 7, 62, 3.

[51] Council of Sardica, can. 4—Mansi, III, 23 ff.; Hardouin, I, 637 ff.

[52] C. 3, C. III, q. 6; c. 12, C. II, q. 1; c. 2, C. II, Q. 6.

[53] C. 24, X, *de officio et potestate iudicis delegati,* I, 29; c. 19, X, *de iureiurando,* II, 24; cc. 16, 55, X, *de appellationibus, recusationibus et relationibus,* II, 28.

[54] Conc. Triden., sess. XXIV, *de ref.*, c. 10.

constitution *"Ad Militantis,"* [55] further regulated the suspensive effect of an appeal but in this constitution, it may be seen that reference is made to extra-judicial appeals or recourse against episcopal decrees rather than to appeal properly so-called from a judicial sentence. These enactments were incorporated also in the instruction issued in 1880 [56] and in the *"Cum Magnopere"* of 1883.[57] The Third Plenary Council of Baltimore included the *"Cum Magnopere"* among its canons as a norm for judicial procedure in the United States.[58] The Code establishes the general principle that every appeal is *in suspensivo* unless the law expressly provides otherwise.

The execution of the sentence is delayed or deferred until the entire cause is reviewed in the appellate instance and the sentence of the lower court either confirmed or reformed.[59] The suspensive effect of the appeal extends to this entire process with the result that the cause is left *in statu quo,* that all further proceedings of the lower court in the matter appealed, become so many *attentata* in law when instituted either within the ten days allowed for an appeal or after the notice of appeal has been given. Such acts are called *attentata* to indicate that they are merely *attempts* made to prejudice the legal rights of a party and as such devoid of any legal effect or force. They are unlawful attacks upon the safety or immunity of the appellant, granted by the law in the case of a suspensive appeal. This immunity demands that pending an appeal, no action of this type be made by the judge of first instance to execute the sentence or otherwise prejudice the rights of the appellant.[60] The *remedium attentorum* is not strictly so-called an effect of appeal

[55] 30 March 1742—*Fontes,* n. 326.

[56] S. C. Ep et Reg., *instr.,* 11 June 1880—*Collect. S. C. de Prop. Fid.,* n. 1534.

[57] S. C. de Prop. Fid., *instr.,* a. 1883—*Collect. S. C. de Prop. Fid.,* n. 1586.

[58] *Conc. Plen. Baltimorensis III, Acta et Decreta,* nn. 298, 311.

[59] Noval, *De Processibus,* n. 653.

[60] Roberti, *De Processibus,* II, n. 476; Vermeersch-Creusen, *Epitome,* III, n. 240; Blat, *De Processibus,* n. 419; Wernz-Vidal, *De Processibus,* n. 607. Cf. also Wernz, *Jus Decretalium,* V, n. 697; Lega, *De Iudiciis,* I, n. 625; Bouix, *De Iudiciis,* II, 288 ff.; Schmalzgrueber, lib. II, tit. XXVIII, n. 108; Reiffenstuel, lib. II, tit. XXVIII, n. 249; Leurenius, lib. II, tit. XXVIII, q. 1134.

proper, as Schmalzgrueber appeared to believe.[61] Bouix,[62] Wernz [63] and Vidal [64] follow the opinion of Schmalzgrueber in this respect. It is rather a direct result and consequence of the suspensive effect of an appeal, as declared by Reiffenstuel,[65] Lega [66] and Roberti.[67]

The canon under consideration declares that the principle "lite pendent, nihil innovetur" [68] exerts its full force with regard to an appeal that is pending before the superior tribunal. The jurisdiction of the inferior judge is stayed and he is regarded as incompetent relative to the cause appealed.[69] This opinion seems somewhat severe for the reason that the judge is permitted by law to take any precautionary measures necessary in his judgment to protect the rights of both parties concerned in a cause that has been appealed, as, for example, the sequestration [70] with a third person, of an object, the possession or ownership of which is controverted and the immediate use of which by one party might injure the rights of the other litigant by working harm to the object itself; or the temporary prohibition restricting the exercise of a particular right, decreed by the judge if he foresees that the use of this right by one party would be detrimental to the interests of the other litigant.[71] Similarly, in matrimonial causes, when a marriage is doubtfully valid, the parties should not be deprived in the external forum, of their proper rights, while an appeal is pending; in the internal forum, however, when the married parties are doubtful concerning the presence of a diriment impediment to their marriage, they should be

[61] Lib. II, tit. XXVIII, n. 108.
[62] *De Iudiciis,* II, 288.
[63] *Jus Decretalium,* V, n. 697.
[64] Wernz-Vidal, *De Processibus,* n. 607.
[65] Lib. II, tit. XXVIII, n. 206.
[66] *De Iudiciis,* I, n. 626.
[67] *De Processibus,* II, n. 476.
[68] Can. 1725, §5; cf. Noval, *De Processibus,* n. 408; Blat, *De Processibus,* n. 419; Roberti, *De Processibus,* I, n. 297.
[69] Lega, *De Iudiciis,* I, n. 625.
[70] Roberti, *De Processibus,* II, n. 476.
[71] Can. 1672 ff.—"De rei sequestratione et inhibitione exercitii iuris"; cf. Noval, *De Processibus,* n. 311; Wernz-Vidal, *De Processibus,* n. 269, ff.; Roberti, *De Processibus,* I, n. 232; c. 40, X, *de appellationibus, recusationibus et relationibus,* II, 28; cc. 4, 6, 7, *de appellationibus,* II, 15 in VI°.

directed in the question of the exercise of their proper rights, by their respective consciences; the party who is certain of the existence of a diriment impediment cannot request or render the *debitum*.[72]

An appeal is pending from the very moment that a sentence is rendered, even before any appeal is interposed against the sentence in question. For as soon as the notice of the verdict is communicated to the litigants, the term of ten days [73] allowed by the Code for the placing of an appeal, is in effect or begins to run and during this time, even before an appeal is made, the judge cannot move to execute the sentence, or perform any action detrimental to the rights or interests of the appellant, or even of the appellee.[74] The appeal continues to be pending when it is *de facto* interposed before the judge of first instance and until it is finally and decisively settled by the appellate tribunal.[75] The principle stated in this canon is similar to that of canon 1854 and the prescriptions contained therein relative to the *attentata* committed while the cause itself is pending, are to be applied, *mutatis mutandis*, to the matter of the *attentata* performed while the appeal is pending,[76] for canon 1854 refers directly to the terms allowed for the interposition of an appeal [77] and the prosecution thereof.[78]

Attempts, *attentata*, of this kind are *ipso iure* null and void,[79] not merely voidable as some authors maintained before the Code.[80] Such prejudicial acts are of themselves substantially defective and

[72] Wernz-Vidal, *De Processibus*, n. 572; Roberti, *De Processibus*, II, n. 431; Vermeersch-Creusen, *Epitome*, III, n. 221; Lega, *De Iudiciis*, I, n. 563; Reiffenstuel, lib. II, tit. XVI, n. 11; cc. 3, 5, 13, X, *de restitutione spoliatorum*, II, 13.

[73] Can. 1881.

[74] Roberti, *De Processibus*, II, n. 476; Bouix, *De Iudiciis*, II, 289; Lega, *De Iudiciis*, I, n. 625. This prohibition is subject to the provisions of the Code contained in canons 1902 and 1917.

[75] Bouix, *De Iudiciis*, II, 289; Lega, *De Iudiciis*, I, n. 625.

[76] Roberti, *De Processibus*, II, n. 476; cf. also Lega, *De Iudiciis*, I, n. 626.

[77] Can. 1881.

[78] Can. 1883; Can. 1854: ". . . sive respiciat terminos partibus a iure vel a iudice assignatos ad ponendos certos actus iudiciales"; cf. Noval, *De Processibus*, n. 602.

[79] Can. 1855, §1.

[80] Cf. Reiffenstuel, lib. II, tit. XVI, nn. 20, 21; Bouix, *De Iudiciis*, II, 288.

are null and void from the very beginning,[81] according to the principle "quae contra ius fiunt, debent utique pro infectis haberi."[82] The nullity of the *attentata* should be decreed[83] by the appellate court before the latter proceeds to act on the admission of the appeal proper.[84]

The Code declares that every appeal is *in suspensivo;* this is the general principle. However, it is not in itself absolute, for there are several exceptions noted by the law in this regard. The canon under consideration declares that it may be expedient for the sentence to be wholly or partially executed, due to certain particular, attendant circumstances. When this proceeding is found to be necessary, the appeal is not thereby extinguished or abated; it is still considered as *pending* before the superior or appellate instance.[85]

The first exception to be noted occurs when the judge orders the provisionary execution of a sentence.[86] This feature was not considered important under the pre-Code discipline, for judicial sentences for the most part could be appealed only *in devolutivo* or they were denied this right entirely and explicitly.[87] The Rota[88] made this feature a general principle and ordered the provisionary execution of a sentence where circumstances warranted such an action. This occurred usually in possessory judgments and others that were concerned with the sustenance or maintenance of litigants, where the non-execution of an appealed sentence would place the party in question in dire straits. The Code retained the principle

[81] Roberti, *De Processibus,* II, n. 432; Noval, *De Processibus,* n. 603; Vermeersch-Creusen, *Epitome,* III, n. 221.

[82] *Reg.* LXIV, R. J. in VI°.

[83] There is no appeal admissible from this decree; cf. can. 1856, §2; 1880, n. 7.

[84] Can. 1679-1682. This is not an *actio rescissoria.* Cf. can. 1684, 1685; Noval, *De Processibus,* n. 603.

[85] Roberti, *De Processibus,* II, n. 476.

[86] Can. 1917, §2—"Iudex tamen potest sententiae, quae nondum transiit in rem iudicatam, provisoriam exsecutionem iubere:

1. Si agatur de provisionibus seu praestationibus ad necessariam sustentationem ordinatis;

2. Si alia gravis urgeat necessitas, ita tamen ut, concessa provisoriaria exsecutione, per cautiones, fideiiussiones aut pignora satis consultum sit indemnitati alterius partis casu quo exsecutio revocanda sit."

[87] Noval, *De Processibus,* n. 702.

[88] *Reg. Serv. in iud. apud S. R. Rotae Trib.,* §84.

and declares that the judge may order the provisional execution of a sentence under certain conditions.

First, the sentence in question must not yet have become a *res iudicata,* that is, its execution is suspended for the reason that the term allowed by law for an appeal is pending, or *de facto,* an appeal has been interposed against the sentence in question.[89] Otherwise, if the sentence had already become an adjudged matter, it would have to be executed.[90] The sentence should in all probability be definitive in character; however, an interlocutory sentence does not appear to be excluded thereby, if circumstances demand the provisional execution of the sentence. The sentence should likewise be condemnatory, for otherwise, there would be no particular need for provisional execution. The second necessary condition is concerned with the urgency of the need depending on the execution of the sentence. This exigency would be present if the execution pertained to payments or warrants that were necessary for the support of a litigant who would otherwise be lacking the necessities of life, were the execution of the sentence to be delayed or temporarily suspended. This provision applies to all who would be placed in such an emergency.[91]

Certain authors, notably Muniz,[92] Eichmann,[93] Haring[94] and Perathoner,[95] interpret the word "ordinatis" as referring to *ordained* men and restrict this particular condition to clerics only. This word, according to Woywod,[96] is never used by itself in the Code to indicate clerics except with regard to and in connection with the laws that are concerned specifically with the clergy. Any other urgent

[89] Can. 1917, §2; cf. Roberti, *De Processibus,* II, n. 546; Blat, *De Processibus,* n. 455; Noval, *De Processibus,* n. 704; Wernz-Vidal, *De Processibus,* n. 659; Cocchi, *De Processibus,* n. 252.

[90] Can. 1902; 1917, §1. There is no reason to regard the clause "quae nondum transiit in rem iudicatam" of canon 1917, §2 as referring exclusively to the particular causes mentioned in canon 1903, that never become *res iudicatae.*

[91] Roberti, *De Processibus,* II, n. 546; Cocchi, *De Processibus,* n. 252; Blat, *De Processibus,* n. 455; Vermeersch-Creusen, *Epitome,* III, n. 250.

[92] *Procedimientos Eclesiásticos,* III, n. 527.

[93] *Prozessrecht,* p. 190.

[94] *Grundzüge des Katholischen Kirchenrechtes,* II, n. 230.

[95] *Kirchliches Gerichtswesen,* p. 60.

[96] *A Practical Commentary,* II, 318; cf. *Reg. Serv. in iudic. apud S. R. Rotae Trib.,* §84.

reason or grave necessity, apart from the question of sustenance, would likewise suffice to allow the judge to order the provisional execution of a sentence. It is left to the judgment and discretion of the court to determine the extent of the necessity and the gravity thereof. The judge is to consider and weigh well all the circumstances of the case; nor should he be unmindful of the rights of the other party in the matter. If the judge decrees the provisional execution of a sentence, he should see to it that a guarantee in the form of bail, bonds, securities, etc., is posted for the indemnification of the other party, should the sentence be reversed in the final instance and the execution thereof revoked.[97] The Code in no instance demands specifically the provisional execution of a sentence, the matter being left to the wisdom and discretion of the judge. This mode of execution, moreover, is to be requested by the interested party himself. Only in causes respecting the public good, may the judge act *ex officio* in the matter.[98] The provisional execution of a sentence is the first legal exception to the suspensive effect of an appeal; the second is concerned with appeals that are conceded only *in devolutivo* by the law.

### §2. *The Appeal in devolutivo*

The devolutive effect of an appeal consists in this, that the cause is brought before the court of the superior or appellate judge. The latter takes cognizance of it, passing on its admissibility or legality; if he admits it, he will eventually decide the issue itself, confirming, modifying, reversing or revoking the sentence of the lower court.[99] Every appeal when it is admitted into the appellate tribunal naturally has a devolutive effect. The sentence, however, is executed,

[97] Can. 1917, §2, n. 2; Roberti, *De Processibus,* II, n. 546; Blat, *De Processibus,* n. 455; Wernz-Vidal, *De Processibus,* n. 659.

[98] Cf. Suprem. Signat. Apost. Trib., in c. *Manilen.,* 28 April 1917—*AAS.,* X (1918), 41.

[99] Noval, *De Processibus,* n. 653; Wernz-Vidal, *De Processibus,* n. 607; Vermeersch-Creusen, *Epitome,* III, n. 240; Roberti, *De Processibus,* II, n. 477; Blat, *De Processibus,* n. 419; Cocchi, *De Processibus,* n. 231; cf. also Santi-Leitner, lib. II, tit. XXVIII, n. 34; Bouix, *De Iudiciis,* II, 254; Lega, *De Iudiciis,* I, n. 627.

regardless of the appeal. If the appeal is upheld and the sentence reversed, the effects of the latter are likewise revoked.[100]

Under the former discipline, as now, the entire cause was transferred from the inferior tribunal to the appellate court on the occasion of an appeal from a definitive sentence; moreover, the competence of the superior judge extended, in the event of an appeal from an interlocutory sentence, to the parts of the principal cause that were not yet defined by the judge of first instance; if the appellate court confirmed the interlocutory sentence, it was the custom to remit it to the judge of the lower court.[101] If, however, the sentence were reformed, the judge would at the same time define the principal cause [102] in order to safeguard the interests of the appellant for the opinion was that, due to the reformation of his sentence, the inferior judge might be antagonistic to the interests of the appellant.[103] If the first sentence was confirmed, the judge of first instance could renounce his right to hear the cause and remit the entire matter to the judgment of the superior tribunal, unless the latter had remanded the cause to the lower court to be adjudged and completed therein.[104]

Under the present discipline, however, due to the precise and explicit determination of the grades of jurisdiction and the several instances, and similarly, owing to the direct prohibition against the introduction of new causes into the appellate instance,[105] the judgment of a cause in the first instance can never be omitted. Consequently, interlocutory sentences that have definitive force, if appealed and reformed by a superior tribunal, must be returned to the first instance for final judgment; if, however, the sentence is confirmed, ordinarily, the process is extinguished and the cause abated. Otherwise, a sentence rendered on the principal cause by the appel-

[100] Roberti, *De Processibus,* II, n. 476.

[101] Santi-Leitner, lib. II, tit. XXVIII, n. 45; cf. c. 59, X, *de appellationibus, recusationibus et relationibus,* II, 28; *ASS.*, XVI (1883), 328; XVIII (1885), 56.

[102] Lega, *De Iudiciis,* I, n. 627; this mode of procedure was the practise of the S. C. C. and the Rota; cf. Santi-Leitner, lib. II, tit. XXVIII, n. 45; Pirhing, lib. II, tit. XXVIII, nn. 124, 237.

[103] Roberti, *De Processibus,* II, n. 477.

[104] Lega, *De Iudiciis,* I, n. 627; Reiffenstuel, lib. II, tit. XXVIII, n. 234 ff.; cf. c. 5, *de appellationibus,* II, 15 in VI°.

[105] Can. 1569 ff.; 1891.

late court, the previous grade of judgment having been omitted, would be null and void.[106] Therefore, under the present law, the scope of the appeal cannot be greater in extent in the appellate instance than it was in the inferior tribunal. It may be limited or restricted, as when only one part of a sentence is appealed, the remainder being thereby excluded.

Although there are few cases of appeal *in devolutivo* in the Code, attention may be directed to one of the more important examples of this type of complaint, *viz.*, canon 2243.[107] This canon is concerned with censures or medicinal penalties that are inflicted through the medium of a judicial sentence or precept.[108] Censures that are contracted *latae sententiae* are not included here; such censures permit no appeal for an appeal in this case would be a complaint against the law itself.[109] Moreover, there could be no foundation or reason on which to base an appeal in this instance, for no question could arise regarding the injustice of the punishment or any defect of procedural formality.[110] The censure is executed and binding in the external and internal forums as soon as the crime, forbidden under

[106] Cf. S. R. Rota in c. *Treviren.*, 7 Feb. 1913—*Decisiones S. R. Rotae,* V (1913), dec. X, n. 15; S. R. Rota in c. *Biturgen.*, 27 April 1917—*Decisiones S. R. Rotae,* IX (1917), dec. X, nn. 4, 5, 13; S. R. Rota in c. *Mauranen.*, 13 July 1918—*Decisiones S. R. Rotae,* X (1918), dec. XI, nn. 5, 6; *Apollinaris,* I (1928), 116-118.

[107] §1. Censurae inflictae per *sententiam* iudicialem, statim ac latae fuerint, exsecutionem secumferunt, nec ab eis datur appellatio, nisi in devolutivo; item a censuris ad modum praecepti inflictis datur recursus, sed in devolutivo tantum.

§2. Appellatio vero vel recursus a sententia iudiciali vel praecepto comminante censuras etiam latae sententiae nondum contractas, nec sententiam aut praeceptum nec censuras suspendunt, si agatur de re in qua ius non admittit appellationem vel recursum cum effectu suspensivo; secus censuras suspendunt, firma tamen obligatione servandi id quod sententia aut praecepto mandatur, nisi reus appellationem vel recursum interposuerit non a sola poena, sed ab ipsa quoque sententia vel praecepto.

[108] Canon 2287 states that an appeal *in suspensivo* is permitted from a judicial condemnatory sentence that imposes a vindicative penalty, unless the contrary is explicitly declared by the law. Cf. Noval, *De Processibus,* n. 807; Ayrinhac, *Penal Legislation,* n. 156; Vermeersch-Creusen, *Epitome,* III, n. 490; Sole, *De Delictis et Poenis,* p. 191; Blat, *De Delictis et Poenis,* n. 117; Ferreres, *Institutiones Canonicae,* II, n. 1052; Claeys Bouuaert et Simenon, *Manuale Iur.* Can., n. 1298.

[109] Ayrinhac, *Penal Legislation,* n. 80.

[110] Vermeersch-Creusen, *Epitome,* III, n. 439.

the threat of censure, is committed [111] and the delinquent is conscious of his guilt.[112] If, however, the delinquent cannot observe the censure without infamy or loss of reputation he is not bound to do so until a declaratory sentence has been passed on his case.[113] The effect of this declaratory sentence is to proclaim that the person in question has really committed the crime and consequently has incurred the penalty attached thereto. It does not of itself inflict the penalty but declares that the penalty has been incurred and that from the very moment at which the delict was perpetrated.[114]

There is no reason to deny the right of appealing from a declaratory sentence of this kind, but the appeal can be *in devolutivo* only, for the censure must be observed in the external forum.[115] Ayrinhac [116] asserts that there might be an appeal *in suspensivo* according to the common opinion of canonists; however, he gives no authorities for this statement, nor can the latter be understood in the light of canon 2243 and the fact that a censure, incurred *ipso facto* is immediately executed. The declarative sentence of itself does not impose the penalty. Noval [117] also states that an appeal *in suspensivo* could be admitted, on the general principle that every appeal is *in suspensivo* unless the law explicitly provides for the contrary.

Canon 2243 refers directly to censures that are inflicted by a condemnatory sentence, and accordingly, censures that are imposed *ferendae sententiae*.[118] A condemnatory sentence is a declaration by which a judge imposes a *ferendae sententiae* penalty on a delinquent for a crime that has been committed and of which he has been convicted.[119] It really inflicts or imposes a penalty, for, prior to the

[111] Can. 2217, §1, n. 2.

[112] Can. 2232, §1.

[113] Cf. can. 2217, 2222, 2223; Ayrinhac, *Penal Legislation*, n. 57; Cappello, *De Censuris*, n. 74; Chelodi, *Jus Poenale*, n. 28; Noval, *De Processibus*, n. 807.

[114] Can. 2232, §2; cf. Hyland, *Excommunication*, pp. 50, 51.

[115] Vermeersch-Creusen, *Epitome*, III, n. 439; De Meester, *Compendium*, III, pars 2, n. 1735; Bouuaert et Simenon, *Manuale Iur. Can.*, n. 1272; Lega, *De Iudiciis*, I, n. 635; Schmalzgrueber, lib. II, tit. XXVIII, n. 109; Santi-Leitner, lib. II, tit. XXVIII, n. 38; c. 53, X, *de appellationibus, recusationibus et relationibus*, II, 28.

[116] *Penal Legislation*, n. 80.

[117] *De Processibus*, p. 541.

[118] Blat, *De Delictis et Poenis*, n. 67; can. 2217, §1, n. 3.

[119] Cerato, *Censurae Vigentes*, n. 8.

sentence, the party in question was not under the censure. But the moment the sentence is pronounced, the penalty takes effect and must be observed immediately. No particular act of execution is needed.[120] The canon under consideration declares, therefore, that there is no appeal *in suspensivo* from such a sentence; an appeal *in devolutivo* only is permitted,[121] for a censure once inflicted obtains its effect immediately and can be removed only by absolution.[122] When a judicial sentence threatens the imposition of a censure whether *latae* or *ferendae sententiae,* an appeal may be interposed against a *sentence* of this character. The censure is not yet contracted for the incurring of it will depend on the fulfillment of a condition placed by the judge in his sentence. The appeal here will be *in devolutivo* if the cause in question or the sentence itself admits only an appeal of this kind.[123] If, however, the nature of the case is such that it would admit a suspensive appeal, an appeal interposed against the sentence, would suspend and delay the execution of the sentence as well as the threatened censure.[124]

An appeal against the *threatened censure* alone would suspend the execution of the censure if it were to be inflicted *ab homine,* regardless of whether the obligation or condition on which the threat was based, was fulfilled or not. For the appeal would suspend the jurisdiction of the judge in the case and consequently, he would not be able to inflict the censure. If, however, the censure that was threatened, was to be inflicted *a iure,* an appeal against the threatened censure would suspend the latter only if the obligation or condition imposed by the judge in his sentence was fulfilled. If it were not obeyed, the censure would be incurred in spite of the appeal;

[120] Sole, *De Delictis et Poenis,* n. 164; Vermeersch-Creusen, *Epitome,* III, n. 439; Ayrinhac, *Penal Legislation,* n. 80. This applies to censures only, not to vindicative penalties.

[121] Ferreres, *Institutiones Canonicae,* II, n. 996; Blat, *De Delictis et Poenis,* n. 67; Sole, *De Delictis et Poenis,* n. 164.

[122] Can. 2248, §1.

[123] Can. 1395, §2; 1498, §3.

[124] Noval, *De Processibus,* n. 807; Cappello, *De Censuris,* n. 82; Chelodi, *Jus Poenale,* n. 32; Cerato, *Censurae Vigentes,* n. 13; Vermeersch-Creusen, *Epitome,* III, n. 439; Ayrinhac, *Penal Legislation,* n. 81; Sole, *De Delictis et Poenis,* n. 165; Blat, *De Delictis et Poenis,* n. 67; Ferreres, *Institutiones Canonicae,* II, n. 996.

for though the appeal would suspend the jurisdiction of the judge over the matter, the services of the judge would not be required to execute or impose a censure that was to be incurred *a iure*. In this case, the appeal would be *in devolutivo* only.[125]

It may be remarked at this point that while the Code prescribes a special mode of procedure for the conduct of criminal trials and causes,[126] it states [127] that relative to the interposition and prosecution of appeals in criminal trials, the general norms of appellate procedure [128] are to be observed.

[125] Bouuaert et Simenon, *Manuale Iur. Can.*, n. 1272; Blat, *De Delictis et Poenis*, n. 67; Chelodi, *Jus Poenale*, n. 32; Cappello, *De Censuris*, n. 82; Vermeersch-Creusen, *Epitome*, III, n. 439; Noval, *De Processibus*, n. 807.

[126] Can. 1933-1959. Cf. Vermeersch-Creusen, *Epitome*, III, nn. 257-275; Wernz-Vidal, *De Processibus*, nn. 690-736; Cocchi, *De Processibus*, nn. 266-286; and particularly Noval, *De Processibus*, nn. 735-830.

[127] Can. 1959.

[128] Can. 1879-1891.

## CHAPTER X

## THE PROSECUTION OF AN APPEAL BEFORE THE ORDINARY COURT OF SECOND INSTANCE

It has been noted in the Historical Conspectus of the present work that during the ancient period of Roman Law when justice was administered directly by the king or by a popular and supreme tribunal, there was but one judicial instance or grade of judgment which issued decrees and decisions and pronounced sentences on controversial or criminal matters, with the result that its judgment was regarded as final and decisive. Appeal, as it was understood in the light of later development, was not known. In ecclesiastical circles, in the early days of Christianity, a situation of almost like character existed; for the only exception to this condition of things was the recourse or appeal to the Pope, a privilege that was accepted by all. Practical judicial organization, however, was effected by slow progressive stages, that were characterized by an ever increasing realization of the principal purpose and object of distributive as well as vindictive justice and the eager desire to see these aims satisfied and fulfilled. Organization with regard to the ecclesiastical administration of justice, consisted of a multiplex system of graded jurisdiction; however, the jurisdictional limits and the juridical competence of these respective grades were not well defined until the Council of Trent remedied somewhat the confused notions prevalent at the time relative to the competence of the respective grades of judgment. It enacted legislation determining the number of competent instances for the hearing and rehearing of a judicial cause, defining at the same time the scope and power of each grade or instance.

The Code of Canon Law, in turn, changed several aspects of the Tridentine legislation and perfected a more definite and more efficient system of judicial instances with the result that the administration of justice is more speedily and accurately accomplished. This reformation consists principally in permitting, subject to the restrictions of the law in particular cases, a cause to be taken through three separate grades of judgment or instances, or until two conformable sentences have been pronounced on the merits of the cause in question.[1] Causes which are concerned with the state in life of a person, whether clerical, religious or married, never become *res iudicatae* and consequently they may be tried in further instances provided new and weighty evidence is produced.[2]

## Article I. The Ordinary Tribunal of Appeal

**Canon 1883. Appellatio prosequenda est coram iudice *ad quem* dirigitur intra mensem ab eius interpositione, nisi iudex *a quo* longius tempus ad eam prosequendam parti praestituerit.**

The Code ordains that ordinarily a cause becomes a *res iudicata* after two conformable sentences.[3] Accordingly, a cause may go through three or more instances or grades of judgment wherein it is examined and its merits determined by a definitive sentence, until two conformable verdicts have been obtained. The first process ordinarily takes place before the lowest, *ratione gradus*, competent tribunal, with the exception of those causes which the Roman Pontiff has reserved for his own judgment.[4] The review of the cause upon appeal is regularly conducted by the ordinary tribunal that is immediately superior. Special enactments of the Code explicitly determine that tribunal or court of second instance and regulate the rehearing of the appealed cause therein. The petition through which the aggrieved party files his appeal with the judge *a quo* must determine the judge *ad quem*, the superior tribunal to which the appeal is directed. This feature is absolutely necessary for the reason that it is a matter touching on the competence of the judge of the appeal, *ratione gradus*. The interposed appeal will be invalid if the appellate judge is not *de facto* determined by the appel-

[1] Can. 1902.
[2] Can. 1903.
[3] Canon 1902, n. 1.
[4] Can. 1557.

lant. The Code contains several general enactments relative to the appellate instance and tribunal and attention will be directed to an investigation of these ordinances before proceeding to an interpretation of the canon under consideration.

## §1. *The Question of Competence*

Canon 1571 states that a judge who takes cognizance of a cause in one grade cannot render a decision on the same cause in another instance. The question here is one of competence. Competence implies jurisdiction for the competent judge has the power to apply the prescriptions of the law to individual persons in particular causes; accordingly, the competence of a judge in any one cause extends only to a particular grade of judgment. It cannot be prorogued or extended beyond its legitimate confines. This prohibition is absolute and renders any judgment or sentence pronounced by a tribunal that has already seen the cause in one grade, whether that tribunal consists of but one judge or is collegiate in nature, not only unlawful and illicit but null and void, because the judge who rendered the verdict was absolutely incompetent to do so.[5] Appeals are made from grade to grade. When the diocesan court has taken cognizance of a cause in one instance, it thereby becomes incompetent to judge the same cause in another grade.[6] The competence of the court in question is restricted to one instance. This particular feature of judicial procedure is prescribed for the public good and it holds even when the membership of a tribunal has been changed and replaced. The change of personnel of any court, the Rota excepted,[7] does not alter or convert the grade or instance.[8] This absolute limitation of competence is maintained for the tribunal that judges a cause in any instance or grade, whether that tribunal consists of one judge or of a college of judges; the complete change of personnel does not render the court in question competent to judge

[5] Noval, *De Processibus,* n. 105; Burke, *Competence in Ecclesiastical Tribunals,* pp. 6, 25.

[6] Can. 1571.

[7] Can. 1599, §1, n. 2.

[8] Noval, *De Processibus,* n. 105; cf. Lega, *De Iudiciis,* I, nn. 318, 325; can. 1615, §1.

the cause; the same prohibition holds also for an *Official* who, having judged the cause in the first instance, would be a member of the collegiate tribunal of second instance. In any case, therefore, the court or judge that adjudicates a matter in one instance is by law absolutely incompetent of judging the same matter in another grade, i. e., the grade of appeal or the appellate instance.[9]

Canonists discuss in this connection, the possibility of a bishop's legally taking cognizance of a cause in two different grades, the original and the appellate. If a bishop from whose sentence an appeal has been taken were in the meantime promoted to the metropolitan see, authors generally declare that he could judge the cause again in the appellate instance because "quasi alius homo videtur," he would be occupying another office; he would be the same person, but clothed with new dignity. However, at the same time, they recommend that in the interests of justice, he should delegate another to hear the cause. He might also simply leave the matter to his *Officialis,* for even though the latter forms one tribunal with his Ordinary, yet he is a *persona diversa.* Nothing would prevent the Ordinary from taking the cause to the Holy See in order to avert all suspicion in the matter.[10]

### §2. *The Ordinary Appellate Tribunal*

In accordance with the foregoing principle, the Code ordains that if a cause was tried in the first instance[11] before the court of a suffragan bishop, the appeal from the sentence pronounced by that court is to be taken to the tribunal of the metropolitan. If the cause was heard in the first instance by the metropolitan court, the appeal is to be made before the court of the local Ordinary whom the metropolitan, with the approval of the Holy See, has designated once and for all time, as the court of appeal. This need not be one of his suffragans or even the neighboring metropolitan. If the metropolitan lacks suffragans or if the Ordinary of the place is immedi-

[9] Roberti, *De Processibus,* I, n. 58; Wernz-Vidal, *De Processibus,* n. 68; Noval, *De Processibus,* n. 105.

[10] Wernz-Vidal, *De Processibus,* n. 605; Roberti, *De Processibus,* I, p. 151, note 2.

[11] Can. 1594; 1572.

ately subject to the Holy See, appeals from sentences pronounced by their respective tribunals are to be taken to the court of the nearest metropolitan in accordance with canon 285 which prescribes similar regulations for synods and councils.[12] This is the ordinary and regular procedure for appeals and the designating of appellate instances.

However, the selection of the ordinary court of second instance for the review of a cause on appeal, is not obligatory for an appeal may be taken to the Roman Rota from all sentences pronounced by local Ordinaries in the first instance.[13] The Rota may be the second instance for appeals of this kind that are interposed legitimately. This holds, however, only in the case of judicial sentences validly and lawfully pronounced, for canon 1601 declares inadmissible recourse made to the Rota from the decrees or extra-judicial decisions of an Ordinary. Recourse is usually had to a particular Congregation, according to the nature of the case. The Rota is likewise competent to take cognizance of appeals in the third and further instances where a cause of its nature cannot become a *res iudicata*.[14] The Apostolic Signatura does not receive appeals from ordinary diocesan courts or metropolitan tribunals. It is the court of appeal solely for causes concerned with the violation of the *secretum officii* on the part of an Auditor of the Rota or with the injury or damage caused by the Auditors of the Rota in rendering an unjust verdict, fraudulently or negligently conceived.[15]

In addition to the previous instances, canon 1569 enunciates a principle that has been recognized from time immemorial, the right to appeal to the Supreme Pontiff. The right to accept and decide appeals rests on the primacy of the Roman Pontiff and is co-extensive with his legislative and judiciary power.[16] The series of in-

[12] Roberti, *De Processibus*, pp. 146-148, gives a partial list of appellate courts approved by the Holy See shortly after the appearance of the Code; they may be found in the *AAS*., from XII (1920), 14 to XIII (1921), 356.

[13] Can. 1599, §1, n. 1.

[14] Can. 1599, §1, n. 2; cf. can. 1903.

[15] Can. 1603, §1, n. 1; 1604; cf. *Lex Propria*, can. 9, 37.

[16] Conc. Vatican., sess. IV, c. 3, *de vi et ratione primatus*. The exercise of this right has been traced through the various historical epochs in the Historical Conspectus of the present work.

stances ordained by the Code, is limited only by the Supreme Pontiff. His power is not confined or restricted by the hierarchy of tribunals, nor by procedural norms, nor by judicial sentences that may become *res iudicatae*. Consequently, any of the faithful, in any part of the world, not excluding nor excepting those under ban of excommunication, suspension or interdict, can appeal any cause, whether civil or criminal, from an ordinary judge or a delegated official, at any stage of the trial proper or in any grade or instance, to the Roman Pontiff.[17] The Pope may hear this appeal himself,[18] entrust it to the ordinary tribunals regularly established for the Holy See[19] or assign it to a delegated judge who will act in his name.[20] The appeal, governed as it is by the ordinary norms of appellate procedure, suspends the jurisdiction of the trial judge relative to the appealed cause. It is evident, however, that while the Supreme Pontiff, has the right to receive appeals that are made in this manner, he will not make use of this power except in very grave matters; otherwise, the order of judicial grades and instances, set up for the purpose of serving the ends of justice, speedily, thoroughly and regularly, would prove ineffective and futile.[21]

## §3. *The Mutual Relation of Tribunals*

Canon 1570, §2 adds a further provision relative to appellate procedure. It is concerned with the cooperation that should exist between tribunals in the interests of justice and decrees that any court of justice that is competent to act on or judge a particular cause, e. g., an appellate court, has a right to the cooperation and assistance of any other tribunal, e. g., the tribunal *a quo*, in the matter of supplying necessary information regarding the litigants, the examination of witnesses, citations, the investigation of documents, and other matters of a similar character. The tribunal whose

[17] Roberti, *De Processibus*, I, n. 88; Noval, *De Processibus*, n. 101; Wernz-Vidal, *De Processibus*, n. 68; Vermeersch-Creusen, *Epitome*, III, n. 27; Blat, *De Processibus*, n. 25.

[18] Can. 1597.

[19] Cf. cc. 1598-1605.

[20] Can. 199, §1, §2.

[21] Roberti, *De Processibus*, I, n. 88.

aid has been requested, must use the ordinary norms and prescriptions of law in fulfilling this obligation to prevent the interposition of dilatory exceptions in the appellate instance and the consequent undue extension of the appellate trial. In the question of appeals, letters of this kind which request the information, are called "*remissoriales*" if sent to a tribunal of equal authority or grade, "*supplicatoriae*" if to a superior court and "*hortatoriae*" or "*imperativae*" if despatched to an inferior tribunal.[22] This right and consequent obligation rest today on the precise determination of the law and should be studiously observed.

## §4. *Canonical Regulations for Appellate Courts*

For the conduct and prosecution of an appeal, canon 1595 decrees that the tribunal of appeal must be constituted along the same lines as the court of first instance. It must have its *Officialis*,[23] a notary,[24] a *promotor iustitiae* and a *defensor vinculi*,[25] messengers, etc.,[26] in short, all the court officials necessary for the right conduct of a trial before the appellate tribunal. Furthermore, the same laws and regulations relative to citations, witnesses, evidence, documents, and the process in general, must be observed in the appellate instance in as much as they apply to the cause appealed or can be accommodated to the circumstances of the trial; for example, the *libellus appellatorius* will take the place of the introductory *libellus* or bill of complaint of the first instance, and will be subject, more or less to the norms governing the latter; likewise the prosecution of the appeal proper will include the *contestatio litis* and the subsequent *instruction* of the process as carried out in the lower court and will be subject *mutatis mutandis* to the regulations prescribed for the latter in the inferior tribunal.

Finally, the Code ordains that a cause tried before a college of judges in the original instance, must likewise be heard before a col-

[22] Noval, *De Processibus*, n. 104; Wernz-Vidal, *De Processibus*, nn. 71-75; Roberti, *De Processibus*, I, n. 89, applies the name "*rogatoriae*" to all such letters.

[23] Can. 1573.

[24] Can. 1585.

[25] Can. 1586.

[26] Can. 1591 ff.

legiate appellate tribunal of three or five judges, depending on the number in the court of first instance.[27] However, the neglect of this observance will not affect the validity of the acts; nor does it follow from this prescription that a cause tried before one judge in the first instance, could not be heard by a collegiate tribunal in the appellate instance. The appellate judge, if he were the Ordinary, could use the power granted to him by canon 1576, §2, which permits him to entrust to a collegiate tribunal of three or five judges the cognizance of a cause that was difficult or important by reason of circumstances of time, place, persons involved, etc.[28]

### §5. *The Principle: "A Delegato Appellatur ad Delegantem"*

The problem herewith presents itself relative to the prosecution of an appeal that has been interposed against a verdict rendered by a delegated judge. Is this appeal to be taken to the *delegans* or is it to be introduced into the metropolitan or ordinary court of appeal? The Code contains a special chapter on delegated tribunals [29] but no mention is made of this particular question. Does the principle *"a delegato appellatur ad delegantem"* hold under the present legislation? Certainly it does not apply when the sentence is given by the ordinary diocesan tribunal, presided over by the Ordinary, the *Officialis* or the vicar *Officialis*. Such a tribunal acts with ordinary, not delegated power.[30] Even the prescriptions of the pre-Code legislation prohibited appeals from the vicar general or the *Officialis* to the bishop, on the ground that they both formed one tribunal.[31] But the problem here concerns the appeal

[27] Can. 1596.

[28] Noval, *De Processibus,* n. 159; Roberti, *De Processibus,* I, n. 108; Wernz-Vidal, *De Processibus,* nn. 89, 126.

[29] Tit. II, cap. IV, "De Tribunali Delegato," can. 1606, 1607. The first canon declares that the rules contained in canons 199-207, 209, are to be observed by all delegated judges. Cf. Roberti, *De Processibus,* I, n. 146 ff.; Noval, *De Processibus,* n. 180 ff.; Blat, *De Personis,* n. 148; *De Processibus,* n. 72 ff.; Wernz-Vidal, *De Personis,* n. 368; *De Processibus,* n. 139; Vermeersch-Creusen, *Epitome,* I, n. 222; III, n. 57.

[30] Can. 1572, §1; 1573, §1; cf. Roberti, *De Processibus,* I, n. 148; Noval, *De Processibus,* nn. 110, 113.

[31] C. 2, *de consuetudine,* I, 4 in VI°; c. 3, *de appellationibus,* II, 15 in VI°; Schmalzgrueber, lib. II, tit. XXVIII, n. 54.

from a sentence pronounced by a delegated judge; would the appeal be taken to the Ordinary or delegans, or to the regular court of appeal?

Many commentators [32] pass over the problem in silence, while others [33] allude to it without attempting to propose a solution. Roberti and Vidal put forth variant opinions on the subject which will be treated presently. Creusen [34] merely states what appears to him to be the regulating principle. Noval [35] asserts that the Code contains no explicit prescription concerning the principle and proceeds in accordance with the rules laid down in canon 20, to solve the problem by pre-Code principles. He declares that, since appeals are to be made to the judge who is immediately superior, not *per saltum, omisso medio,*[36] an appeal is to be taken from the sentence of the delegated judge to the *delegator, ad delegantem,* and likewise from a subdelegated judge to the *subdelegator, ad subdelegantem,* unless the latter had subdelegated his jurisdiction *in plena,* in which case, the appeal was to be taken to the original *delegator* or *delegans.*[37] He concludes with the statement that an appeal from the delegate of the bishop, is to be taken to the *Officialis* of the bishop, unless the bishop has ruled otherwise; for although the *Officialis* was deprived of jurisdiction over the cause in the first instance, it does not follow that he cannot exercise it over the same cause in the second instance. He quotes Schmalzgrueber [38] as the authority for this statement. Noval commits himself to the observance of the pre-Code principle, "*a delegato appellatur ad delegantem.*" He excludes any appeal to the superior of the *delegans,* "*a delegato appellandum ad delegantis superiorem,*" that is, to the ordinary court of appeal. He asserts that some propose this latter principle because

[32] Viz., Blat, Eichmann, Augustine, Haring, Ferreres, Simenon et Bouuaert, et al.

[33] Cocchi, *De Processibus,* n. 29; De Meester, *Compendium,* III, pars 2, n. 1530.

[34] Vermeersch-Creusen, *Epitome,* III, n. 57—"Iudex immediate superior ad quem a delegato appellatur, est qui delegavit."

[35] *De Processibus,* n. 157.

[36] C. 3, *de appellationibus,* II, 15 in VI°; Conc. Trident., sess. XXII, *de ref.,* c. 7; sess. XXIV, *de ref.,* c. 20.

[37] Cf. c. 10, *de officio et potestate iudicis delegati,* I, 14 in VI°.

[38] Lib. II, tit. XXVIII, n. 54.

they confuse jurisdiction that is delegated, delegata or *data* as understood in Roman Law, with jurisdiction that is *mandata,* such as is possessed by the vicar general.[39] Apart from his statement relative to the misunderstanding of delegated jurisdiction in the matter under consideration, Noval presents the usual objection to the abolition of the principle *"a delegato appellatur ad delegantem,"* *scil.*, that the Code does not explicitly abrogate it and consequently it will have to be retained as a norm of judicial procedure.

Vidal [40] repeats the view of Noval to the effect that the Code contains no special rule relative to an appeal from the sentence of a delegated judge, and decides likewise that it is to be settled according to the prescriptions of the former discipline, which were not, in this instance, revoked by the Code. He cites the Decretals,[41] the Tridentine legislation [42] and some of the older canonists who comment on the question,[43] to the effect that it was a principle of Decretal Law which has been since observed, that an appeal is to be made *gradatim,* to the next immediate superior, not *per saltum,* omitting the intermediate tribunal. The purpose of this principle was to prevent confusion in the matter of jurisdiction and competence as well as to spare the litigants any unnecessary expense. Although the faculty of appealing directly to the Holy See was at all times admitted, appeals from the ordinary tribunal of the archdeacon to the metropolitan, the intermediate tribunal of the bishop being omitted, were forbidden by law. In consequence thereof, appeals are to be taken from the verdict of a delegated judge to the next higher superior, the *delegans* but in the same grade of tribunals. Accordingly, if a bishop delegated a judge to hear a cause, an appeal from the sentence of the latter, is to be taken to the delegating bishop or to his *Officialis,* not to the metropolitan. And whatever the sentence of the bishop will be in the matter, whether it confirms or revokes that of the delegated judge, it will still be the

[39] Cf. Lega, *De Iudiciis,* I, n. 622, note 2.

[40] Wernz-Vidal, *De Processibus,* n. 128.

[41] C. 27, X, *de officio et potestate iudicis delegati,* I, 29; c. 66, X, *de appellationibus, recusationibus et relationibus,* II, 28.

[42] Conc. Trident., sess. XXII, *de ref.*, c. 7; sess. XXIV, *de ref.*, c. 20.

[43] Schmalzgrueber, lib. II, tit. XXVIII, nn. 53, 54; Leurenius, lib. II, tit. XXVIII, q. 1064; Bouix, *De Iudiciis,* II, 270-272.

sentence of the first grade not the second. Otherwise, continues Vidal, any bishop would have the opportunity of subjecting a cause to a two-fold instance in his court and of exercising jurisdiction of the first and second grades. Vidal declares that this procedure was recognized by Wernz [44] who declared that delegated judges, apart from the *Officialis* who with the bishop formed one tribunal,[45] were regarded as *judices instructores*,[46] not as ordinary judges of the first instance. This would be in harmony with the Code with this exception [47] that the Code prohibits the *iudex instructor* or *auditor* from passing sentence on the cause in question, whereas Wernz would allow the delegated judge to render a verdict on the case and permit this sentence to be appealed to the delegating bishop, declaring that this procedure would form a complete instance. This conclusion does not harmonize with the Decretal Law as closely as does that of Creusen and Noval. There is some confusion, moreover, in the attempt made to distinguish between the grades of judgment and the grades of tribunals. It seems in short to be rather an awkward and somewhat labored effort to combine the principles of the pre-Code discipline with the legislation of the Code on the subject as set forth in canons 1571 and 1594.[48]

Roberti [49] acknowledges that the foregoing principle, "*a delegato appellatur ad delegantem*," was in force under the former law but declares that the principle does not hold in view of the present enactments on the question. His remarks on the origin and subsequent use of this principle as a guiding norm, will be omitted as irrelevant to the present discussion. The reasons set forth by this eminent canonist in support of his contention follow: canon 1571 (commented upon previously), seems to exclude the accomplishment of two instances before one and the same tribunal, even if the personnel of the tribunal was changed completely. The word "*qui*"

[44] Wernz, *Jus Decretalium*, V, n. 695, note 53. This is reproduced in Wernz-Vidal, *De Processibus*, n. 605, note 51.

[45] Cf. can. 1573, §2.

[46] Cf. can. 1580-1582.

[47] Can. 1582.

[48] Cf. Wernz-Vidal, *De Processibus*, n. 128, n. 605, notes 47, 51 and 52; cf. Lega, *De Iudiciis*, I, n. 622, §6.

[49] *De Processibus*, I, n. 148.

used in this canon, is to be taken in its widest sense, so as to include not only *persons* but *tribunals*. The Code has carefully defined a series of instances and tribunals, the first instance before the local Ordinary, the second ordinarily before the metropolitan or regular court of appeal and the third before the Holy See,[50] with each grade complete and distinct in itself, permitting no change of the general order by the substitution of persons or judges. The Code regards the Ordinary as the judge of first instance whether he exercises his power personally and directly or through others; even if he delegates a judge to take cognizance of a cause, before the law he is considered to have tried and defined the cause himself. Accordingly, any appeal from the sentence of a judge so delegated, must be taken to the metropolitan court or to the regular tribunal of second instance, or to the Rota as the case may warrant. This principle was in force likewise in pre-Code legislation with regard to matrimonial causes although Roberti does not note this fact. The Council of Trent abolished all inferior tribunals in this matter, establishing the bishop alone as the ordinary judge of first instance in matrimonial causes.[51] The constitution *"Dei Miseratione"* of Benedict XIV decreed that two conformable sentences were to be obtained in causes of this kind, before distinct grades of judgment[52] which similarly points to the same conclusion. Canonists interpreted this legislation to indicate that if the bishop delegated a judge in matters of this character, the delegation was *in totum* and an appeal from the sentence of the delegated judge was taken, not to the delegans, the bishop, but to the regular court of appeal, the second instance.[53]

Furthermore, continues Roberti, the enactments of the Code concerning appeals, refer always to the grade, not to the person. The appeal is from grade to grade rather than from inferior to superior, for example, *"a tribunali episcopi,"*[54] *"coram metropolita,"*[55] *"coram*

50 Can. 1572, 1573, 1594, 1597-1599.

51 Conc. Trident., sess. XXIV, *de ref.*, c. 20.

52 Bened. XIV, const. *"Dei Miseratione,"* 3 Nov. 1741, n. 8—*Fontes*, n. 318; cf. *Jus Pontificium*, XI (1931), 254.

53 Peries, *Procédure Matrimoniales*, p. 49, note 13.

54 Can. 1594, §1.

55 Can. 1594, §2

*archiepiscopo, coram ordinario immediate Sedi Apostolicae subjecto,"*[56] *"coram superiore provinciali, coram abbate locali."* [57] The preceding titles comprise those persons who exercise ordinary jurisdiction in their respective tribunals. No mention is made here of any delegated judge. While it is true that an appeal is always made from grade to grade, Roberti fails to mention the fact that such terms as the following are used in the canons dealing directly with appeals as such; *"ab inferiore judice," "ad superiorem,"* [58] *"coram iudice,"* [59] *"iudicis superioris,"* etc.[60] This fact rather weakens his argument though his contention is not affected thereby. Moreover, if the grades of jurisdiction were allowed to be multiplied by the practise of delegating judges for particular causes, it could easily happen that the second and third instances could be committed to delegated judges with the result that all the instances would be completed without the cause proper proceeding beyond the limits of the first tribunal. This plurality of instances in the same tribunal would not be regarded as the proper exercise of ordinary jurisdiction. The causes would be tried almost entirely by delegated jurisdiction, a very exceptional proceeding to say the least. This practise would subvert the entire procedure advocated and prescribed by the Code and demanded by the public good. Finally, the observance of the pre-Code principle would utterly confuse the procedure relative to the other remedies of law conceded to litigants aggrieved or dissatisfied by unjust verdicts or invalid sentences. Where the person of the delegated judge rather than the grade of judgment in which he acts occupies the first consideration in delegation, the question is asked regarding the manner in which the other means of legal redress are to be proposed. The *querela nullitatis,*[61] the *oppositio tertii,*[62] the *restitutio in integrum,*[63] incidental questions relative to the execution of a sentence,[64] must all be presented to the judge who

[56] Can. 1594, §3.
[57] Can. 1594, §4.
[58] Can. 1879.
[59] Can. 1881, 1883.
[60] Can. 1884, §1.
[61] Can. 1893.
[62] Can. 1899, §1.
[63] Can. 1906.
[64] Can. 1919.

pronounced the questionable sentence. The difficulty of carrying out this procedure is manifest when it is realized that some of the remedies, e. g., the *querela nullitatis insanabilis*, can be proposed even after a long interval. The observance of the pre-Code principle of delegation with relation to the application of these remedies, would obviously result in great confusion, for the judge in question would have to retain his delegated status for an indefinite period.

Consequently, maintains Roberti, to each grade of tribunals should correspond one judicial instance. Only in this manner will the prescriptions of canon 1571 be observed—that, *ratione gradus*, the incompetence of a *tribunal* which has already taken cognizance of a cause in one grade is absolute in regard to subsequent instances.[65] The only exception admitted is the case of the Rota wherein the various *turni* are the tribunals of appeal. However, in this regard, the Rota, while conforming to the general norms of the Code, is also regulated by particular and special ordinances.[66]

The crux of the controversy lies in the question whether or not there can be two instances or grades of judgment before one and the same tribunal. Roberti denies this stating that it is not in harmony with the prescriptions of the Code. He adds that there should be one judicial instance to each of the series or grades of tribunals established by the Code, that is, one grade of judgment before the ordinary tribunal of first instance,[67] one grade of judgment before the ordinary tribunal of second instance,[68] and one, or more according to the nature of the cause itself, before the ordinary tribunal of the third instance.[69] Consequently, an appeal should be taken from the verdict of a delegated tribunal, the court of first instance or of the first grade of judgment, not to the *delegans*, the bishop, but to the tribunal that is superior, *ratione gradus*, that is, to the

[65] Cf. Roberti, *De Processibus*, I, nn. 54, 55, 58; Noval, *De Processibus*, n. 105; Wernz-Vidal, *De Processibus*, n. 68.

[66] Cf. Roberti, *De Processibus*, I, n. 136; Ojetti, *De Romana Curia*, p. 185; Cappello, *De Curia Romana*, I, 391; *Lex Propria*, can. 12; *Reg. Serv. in iud. apud S. R. Rotae Trib.*, §211 ff.

[67] Can. 1572, §1.

[68] Can. 1594.

[69] Can. 1569, 1597-1599. This would not prohibit the appellant from taking his cause directly to the Rota from the court of first instance, for the law provides for this proceeding.

ordinary court of appeal. Vidal[70] is not in sympathy with this opinion and clings religiously to the pre-Code principle. He claims against Roberti, whose view has little force in his opinion, that two sentences, one in an inferior grade, the other in a superior grade, can be given in the same tribunal. In view of this contention, the principle of the former legislation, *"a delegato appellatur ad delegantem,"* can be and should be applied, *scil.*, that an appeal from the sentence of a delegated judge should be taken to the *delegans*. He concedes to Roberti the fact that this principle is not found in the Code; but on the other hand, it is not excluded by the notion of appeal given in canon 1879 and accordingly the prescriptions of canon 6 with regard to the relation between the former legislation and the Code, should prevail and this particular norm should be observed. He concludes: "nihil tamen mirarer, si data occasione prodiret declaratio conformis doctrinae a cl. Roberti propositae; qua declaratione adveniente Ordinarii consultius iudicem delegatum constituerent (distinctum ab Officiali) ad modum iudicis instructionis, reservata sibi sententia vel saltem eius essentiali confirmatione."[71]

The view of Roberti is favored. The Code seems to have carefully defined the ordinary tribunals of appeal, at the same time determining the different instances or grades of judgment. An appeal is ordinarily made from grade to grade, from an inferior tribunal to a superior, *ratione gradus*. This holds for general procedure[72] as well as for matrimonial[73] and criminal causes.[74] Moreover, it expressly declares in canon 1571 that a *tribunal* that judges a cause in one instance is absolutely incompetent to take cognizance of the same cause in a superior grade, even though the personnel of the court is completely changed. Kay,[75] likewise asserts that the opinion of Roberti is more acceptable. Certainly it aims to prevent confusion and makes for a more orderly observance of the norms of appellate procedure.

[70] Wernz-Vidal, *De Processibus,* n. 128, note 8. Vidal substantially reproduces the opinion of Wernz on this question; here, in a footnote, he criticises Roberti's stand on the matter.

[71] Wernz-Vidal, *De Processibus,* n. 128, note 8.

[72] Can. 1594, 1599, §1, n. 1; 1879-1891.

[73] Can. 1986, 1987.

[74] Can. 1959.

[75] *Competence in Matrimonial Procedure,* p. 103.

## ARTICLE II. THE PRESCRIBED FORM

**Canon 1884. §1. Ad prosequendam appellationem requiritur et sufficit ut pars ministerium invocet iudicis superioris ad impugnatae sententiae emendationem, adiuncto exemplari huius sententiae et libelli appellatorii quem iudici inferiori exhibuerat.**

After an investigation of the foregoing facts and principles, the necessity of determining the court of appeal in the petition interposing the appeal itself, may readily be seen. It is a necessary feature because it is concerned with the question of competence *ratione gradus,* the incompetence of the inferior tribunal being absolute and because the neglect of this required provision would result in the nullity of the appeal proper. The form required for the introduction of the appeal into the court of second instance and the time prescribed for this introduction may now be considered.

To prosecute an appeal legitimately, the Code requires that the appellant implore the superior tribunal to change or remedy the obnoxious sentence. The judge of the appellate instance is requested formally to exercise his ministry to the end that the rights of the aggrieved party may be vindicated through the revision or reversal of the impugned sentence. This is done by means of a judicial petition. The petition must contain the name of the party against whom the appeal is directed; it should determine the particular part of the sentence appealed, otherwise it shall be presumed that the entire sentence is appealed;[7a] the reasons upon which the appeal is based should be included in the petition. These reasons do not necessarily have to be developed to any great length; it is sufficient if they be sound, clearly and concisely stated so that the appellate judge may recognize immediately the justice of the claim. They may not be omitted, however, for the appellate judge may reject the appeal as frivolous or frustratory in character if no reason is advanced in support of the appeal. In accordance with what has been stated in a previous section, since the law permits an appeal from all sentences, whether the cause in question is important or

[7a] Can. 1887, §3.

insignificant and unless such appeal has been expressly forbidden by the law, the basis of the appeal or the reason or reasons put forth in support of it are not required to be absolutely convincing. It is sufficient, practically speaking, if the judge of the appellate instance knows that the appeal has not been interposed merely for the sake of delaying the execution of a just sentence or that the appeal is not of a frivolous or futile nature.

If, during the term allowed for the interposition of an appeal or during the period of time allotted by law for the prosecution thereof, the judge *a quo* had attempted in any way contrary to law to execute the sentence he had rendered on the cause or to perform any act detrimental to the interests or the rights of the appellant, the latter should include in his petition a plea that these acts, *attentata*, null and void by law,[77] be declared so by the appellate judge. They are devoid of any legal force and are regarded as unlawful attacks on the immunity granted by law to an appellant, in accordance with the principle, "*lite pendente, nihil innovetur.*" [78] This petition may be made orally under the same circumstances that it was permitted in the first instance. The notary must similarly reduce the oral statement to writing, repeat it to the appellant and obtain the latter's approval as to the correctness of the petition.[79]

A question arises here with regard to the proctor or attorney and the prosecution of the appeal he has previously filed. Is it necessary for him to obtain from his client a new mandate or the confirmation of the commission under which he conducted the cause in the first instance? Canon 1664, §2 states that the attorney is entitled to interpose an appeal after a final sentence has been pronounced on the cause in question, if his client does not object or has not reserved that right to himself.[80] May he likewise prosecute the appeal

[77] Can. 1855, §1. This presupposes that the sentence required execution and that the appeal interposed, was *in suspensivo* (canon 1889), or that it was not against the prohibition of canon 1880. Due allowance must be made also, for the provisional execution of a sentence when such action is justified by circumstances—canon 1917, §2.

[78] Can. 1889, §1; 1854; cf. Wernz-Vidal, *De Processibus*, nn. 569, 607; Noval, *De Processibus*, n. 602; Roberti, *De Processibus*, II, nn. 430, 476.

[79] Cf. can. 1707; 1882, §1.

[80] C. 14, X, *de procuratoribus*, I, 38; cf. *Il Monitore Ecclesiastico*, XXXIII (1921), 70.

and conduct the cause through the appellate instance without obtaining a new mandate? Roberti [81] asserts that the proctor or attorney needs at least a confirmation of the mandate that he possesses. He admits that probably it is not strictly necessary, on account of the procedural bond that exists between the cause itself and the different instances through which it might be taken. But from a practical point of view, a confirmation of the attorney's mandate is preferable because of the fact that appeals oftener than not are tried in widely scattered places and attorneys require the approval of the judge of the appellate court. Noval [82] arguing from the fact that the Code [83] does not draw any distinction between the interposition and the prosecution of an appeal as did the former legislation, asserts that the original mandate confers upon the attorney the office of interposing the appeal and likewise of conducting it through the appellate process. The word "appeal," according to Noval, includes, as it appears in this canon, both ideas. However, to safeguard the interests of the client and to prevent any untoward interruption in the appellate instance, the mandate should explicitly grant permission to the proctor to prosecute the appeal that he has interposed, or at least the mandate in question should be formally confirmed after the appeal has been filed. This confirmation should be drawn up in the usual legal manner, bearing the day, month, year, place, the names of the client and the attorney and the signature of the former. It should be presented to the appellate judge for his approval and preserved in the acts of the cause.[84]

A copy of the petition that had previously been submitted to the judge of the lower court, should accompany the application invoking the aid of the superior judge for the revision of the alleged unjust sentence. This copy should be similar in all points to the original, containing all the necessary data and information. If the appeal had been interposed vocally before the judge *a quo*, a copy of the

[81] *De Processibus*, I, n. 210; II, n. 479.

[82] *De Processibus*, n. 287.

[83] Can. 1664, §2.

[84] Can. 1559, 1560; cf. Wernz-Vidal, *De Processibus*, n. 613; Noval, *De Processibus*, n. 648; Roberti, *De Processibus*, II, n. 479; Cocchi, *De Processibus*, n. 227; Blat, *De Processibus*, n. 414.

written transcript executed at the time by the notary of the lower court, should be included with the abovementioned petition.

Finally, an authentic copy of the impugned sentence, rendered by the judge of the first instance, should be transmitted together with the petition and the *libellus appellatorius*. This procedure is likewise to be followed if the sentence appealed is interlocutory in character and joined with a definitive sentence for the purpose of an appeal. The transmission of these three prescribed documents is required by this canon for the valid prosecution of the appeal. This procedure shows the good faith of the appellant since continued action on the part of the aggrieved litigant confirms the interposition of the appeal.

When the judicial petition has been submitted to the appellate tribunal, the judge of the latter should first act on the illegal attempts, if there were such, made by the judge of the previous instance to execute his sentence contrary to the prescriptions and provisions of the Code. Such attempts or *attentata* [85] as they are called, may also consist of other acts detrimental to the cause of the appellant. When the latter petitions that the *attentata* be declared null by the appellate judge, he may do so in either of two ways, either as an *exceptio praejudicialis*, proposed in the petition submitted to the superior judge and to be defined by the latter immediately before he proceeds with the investigation regarding the merits of the appeal proper, or as an incidental question to be decided when the judge pronounces his definitive sentence on the appeal proper.[86] This is not a rescissory action for the Code declares explicitly that acts of this kind are *ipso iure* null and void, not merely rescindable.[87] Ordinarily, the process should not proceed further until the condition of the cause has been restored to the state it possessed when the sentence was pronounced, i. e., before the *attentata* occurred.[88] Consequently, the appellate judge should declare by means of a decree that the *attentata* are null and void in

[85] Can. 1854, 1889, §1.

[86] Cf. Lega, *De Iudiciis*, I, n. 626; Reiffenstuel, lib. II, tit. XXVIII, n. 207.

[87] Can. 1855, §1.

[88] Lega, *De Iudiciis*, I, n. 561; Bouix, *De Iudiciis*, II, 289; Wernz-Vidal, *De Processibus*, n. 607.

accordance with the prescriptions of the Code regarding this procedure. The matter should be settled at once and there is no appeal admitted from this decree.[89]

After deciding the question of the *attentata,* the appellate judge is to examine the petition to ascertain whether or not the appeal has been thus far prosecuted according to the prescriptions of the law, that is, whether the party who filed the appeal was competent to do so, whether the appeal was interposed legitimately and against a sentence that permitted the exercise of this legal right, whether the formalities of the Code were complied with in all respects and whether the appeal was interposed and was being prosecuted before judges respectively competent to take cognizance of the cause. After this investigation has been completed and it has been found that some of the formalities have not been observed, the appeal is to be returned immediately to the appellant with a notation to that effect. It may then be returned by the appellant in its amended and corrected form, but within the prescribed time. If the investigation results in a favorable decision relative to the observance of all the required formalities, the judge will then proceed to examine the reasons and motives upon which the appeal has been based.[90] If the appeal rests on good grounds, the judge will admit it into his tribunal by the issuance of a decree in favor of the appellant. At the same time notice of the prosecution and admission of the appeal is to be communicated to the appellee.[91] This entire procedure parallels the proceedings of the previous instance.[92] The judicial petition here is similar in most respects to the introductory *libellus* or the original bill of complaint of the previous grade of judgment;[93] it undergoes almost a similar investigation at the hands of the appellate judge. Further, the appeal is admitted by the appellate tribunal and notice of this admission is sent to the appellee, the pro-

[89] Cf. can. 1679-1682; Roberti, *De Processibus,* II, n. 433; Noval, *De Processibus,* n. 604; cf. also can. 1854-1857; 1880, n. 7.

[90] Wernz-Vidal, *De Processibus,* n. 613.

[91] Wernz-Vidal, *De Processibus,* n. 613; Roberti, *De Processibus,* II, n. 479. Cf. also c. 70, X, *de appellationibus, recusationibus et relationibus,* II, 28; cc. 10, 44, *de electione et electi potestate,* I, 6 in VI°.

[92] Can. 1595.

[93] Can. 1706-1708.

cedure that is prescribed following the approval of the original bill of complaint in the lower court.[94] However, it may be remarked at this point that the comparison is not intended to prove that all the ordinances governing these various procedural steps required for the conduct of the first instance must absolutely be observed in the appellate grade of judgment. The purpose is merely to show how the proceedings of the court of second instance are similar in some respects to those of the prior instance and may be observed, *mutatis mutandis.*

The notification relative to the approval and admission of the appeal, that is sent to the appellee, is in the nature of a summons or citation.[95] At the same time, the judge of the appellate court should designate the time when the *litis contestatio,* or joinder of issue, will formally take place. The appellant likewise should be notified of this when he is informed that his appeal has been approved and admitted by the appellate judge.[96] This term may be prorogued by the judge with the consent of both parties. The defendant in the previous trial becomes the plaintiff in the appellate instance.

The appellant may renounce the second instance before any attempt has been made to prosecute the appeal. There are no required formalities for this proceeding. The mere neglect or refusal of the party concerned, to introduce the appeal into the superior instance, indicates his renunciation or desertion of the cause in question.[97] The matter thereby becomes a *res iudicata* and the sentence of the lower court is to be executed.[98] However, if the judicial petition had been sent to the appellate court, the appellant may not renounce or forswear the new instance without complying with the procedure prescribed by canons 1740 and 1741. The reason for this is apparent, for, with the transmission of the judicial petition and the copies of the impugned sentence and the *libellus appellatorius,* the approval and admission thereof by the appellate judge and the com-

[94] Can. 1711-1725.
[95] Can. 1711 ff.
[96] Roberti, *De Processibus,* II, n. 479.
[97] Can. 1886.
[98] Can. 1902, n. 2.

munication of this fact to the interested parties, the *litis contestatio* is practically formed and the instance or judgment of the cause proper begins.[99] Consequently, a mere desertion of the cause on the part of the appellant is contrary to the spirit of canon 1740 and should not be tolerated.[100] The formalities of the law as outlined in a previous chapter, concerning canon 1880, n. 9 should be observed. The consent of the appellee can scarcely be withheld since the sentence becomes a *res iudicata* by the desertion or the renunciation of the appeal by the aggrieved party.[101] While renunciation of an instance, validly made, ordinarily results in the immediate quashing of the instance itself, yet in this case, the appellate judge retains his jurisdiction over the cause, in order to define the amount of the costs or expenses which are to be paid by the appellant who renounced the instance.[102]

Official recognition and notation of all the foregoing acts should be made by the notary who will enter them on the record and minutes of the trial.[103]

## Article III. The Legal Term

**Canon 1883. Appellatio prosequenda est coram iudice *ad quem* dirigitur intra mensem ab eius interpositione, nisi iudex *a quo* longius tempus ad eam prosequendam parti praestituerit.**

### §1. *Tempus Utile Prorogabile*

The law prescribes that an appeal must be prosecuted before the judge *ad quem* within a month from the date on which it was interposed. This *term* is designated as legally peremptory but *prorogabilis* by Roberti [104] whereas Vidal[105] declares that it is *improro-*

[99] Wernz-Vidal, *De Processibus,* n. 613.
[100] Roberti, *De Processibus,* II, n. 479.
[101] Roberti, *De Processibus,* II, n. 316.
[102] Can. 1741; 1888; cf. Wernz-Vidal, *De Processibus,* n. 613, note 72.
[103] Can. 1585, §1; cf. Noval, *De Processibus,* n. 142; Roberti, *De Processibus,* I, nn. 116, 117.
[104] *De Processibus,* I, n. 180.
[105] Wernz-Vidal, *De Processibus,* n. 611.

*gabilis*, that is, that it cannot be prorogued or extended by the judge except in those cases expressly mentioned in the Code. The canon in question, however, contains no qualifying clause; it merely states that the judge *a quo* may extend the time if he sees fit to do so and circumstances demand this extension.

As is the case of canon 1881, the time allotted by the Code for the prosecution of the appeal is *tempus utile*, so that it only *runs* when the party concerned is free and able to act on his case.[106] It is subject to all the concessions allowed by the law for *tempus utile* and accordingly, if an appellant is prevented from acting during a notable part of any one day, that day is not counted in the general computation of the month.[107] The *tempus utile* is *in effect* when the appellant is notified by the judge *a quo* that his appeal has been received by the lower court. Since this notification will ordinarily not coincide with the beginning of a day and since the *terminus a quo* is assigned by the law itself, the first day, that is, the day on which the notice was received, is not counted. The month begins with the start of the following day. It is computed as it is in the calendar [108] and accordingly, the time allowed for the prosecution of the appeal ends with the expiration of the day of the same number in the following month.[109] The expression *"ejusdem numeri"* in this canon refers to the day on which the notice was received, not to the following day when the month begins to be computed;[110] e. g., if notice of the reception of the appeal is received from the judge *a quo* on the fourteenth day of February, that day is not counted in the month conceded by this canon for the prosecution of the appeal; the month starts with the beginning of the following day, that is, the fifteenth of February and concludes with the expiration of the fourteenth day of March.[111] If, however, the

[106] Can. 35.

[107] Michiels, *Normae Generales*, II, 161; Maroto, *Institutiones*, I, n. 260; cf. also commentary on canon 1881 in a previous chapter.

[108] Can. 34, §3, n. 1.

[109] Can. 34, §3, n. 3.

[110] Michiels, *Normae Generales*, II, 155; Maroto, *Institutiones*, I, n. 259; Matthaeus a Coronata, *Institutiones*, I, n. 55.

[111] Cocchi, *De Processibus*, n. 227. Roberti, *De Processibus*, II, n. 479, §2 seems to have made a miscalculation in this regard in the example he has given here to illustrate canon 34, §3, n. 3.

following month lacks a day of the same number, the month is concluded at the expiration of the last day of the month in question, that is, if notice of the approval of the appeal is received by the appellant on the thirtieth day of January, the month term of canon 1883 begins on the thirty-first and ends with the completion of the last day of February, the twenty-eighth, or in a leap year, the twenty-ninth.[112]

The *tempus utile* runs continuously in this sense, that it is not interrupted by the occurrence of a holiday or a day on which the court of appeal is not in session. Such days are included in the general computation. However, if the final day of the month term falls on one of these days, the term is prorogued or extended to the next immediate day on which the court is in session.[113]

The Code allows this term of one month to be extended and interrupted under certain conditions and when circumstances demand these exceptions. Canon 1883 states that the judge *a quo* can concede to the appellant a period of time longer than that allowed by law, in which to prosecute his appeal. He is empowered by this canon to do this when it appears to him that there is a just cause for his action. The appellant should be informed of his privilege in this regard so that he can request an extension of the time limit if necessary. This necessity may occur when the appellate tribunal is located at some distant point, e. g., the Rota, or when the difficulties of communication are such as to preclude the possibility of the canonical term being of any great benefit to the appellant. The extension of the term seems to be left solely to the judgment of the judge *a quo*. The wording of the canon indicates moreover that the privilege should be sought by the appellant at the beginning of the term. Certainly, it will be of no avail whatever to seek it after the lapse of the term itself, for the judge cannot extend what does not exist. The appellant should foresee all the possible difficulties that may be encountered in the prosecution of his appeal and request at the beginning an extension of the canonical term commensurate with the exigencies of time, place, etc.

[112] Can. 34, §3, n. 4. Cf. Michiels, *Normae Generales,* II, 155; Ojetti, *Commentarium,* I, 204; Maroto, *Institutiones,* I, n. 259, n. 2, B, c.

[113] Can. 1635; cf. Roberti, *De Processibus,* I, nn. 183, 185; II, n. 479; Noval, *De Processibus,* n. 230.

### §2. *The Legal Interruption of the Term*

**Canon 1884. §2. Quod si pars exemplar impugnatae sententiae intra utile tempus a tribunali *a quo* obtinere nequeat, interim termini non decurrunt et impedimentum significandum est iudici appellationis, qui iudicem *a quo* praecepto obstringat officio suo quamprimum satisfaciendi.**

This paragraph of canon 1884 permits a legal interruption in the term of one month allotted by the Code for the prosecution of an appeal. The first paragraph of the same canon requires that a copy of the impugned sentence be sent to the appellate judge together with the judicial petition and a copy of the *libellus appellatorius*. If this procedure is not observed, the appeal as such will be invalid and will not be admitted to the appellate court.[114] Accordingly, the judge *a quo* is held to give this copy when requested to do so by the appellant. If he refuses, the law states that the term does not run and that notice of the refusal or neglect of the judge *a quo* is to be sent to the superior judge. The latter is empowered to force the judge of the lower court, by precept, to perform his duty in this respect.[115] Evidences of this necessary cooperation between ecclesiastical courts are encountered in the Decretals,[116] the decrees of the Council of Trent [117] and the later instructions and constitutions of the Roman Congregations and Popes.[118] It is aptly demonstrated hereby what the mind of the Church is with regard to this feature of judicial procedure and the administration of justice. The judicial process must be carried out expeditiously, justly and with due regard to the observance of the formalities of correct judicial procedure, nor will interference, obstruction or opposition from any agency whatsoever be permitted or tolerated.

[114] Roberti, *De Processibus,* II, n. 479, §1; Cocchi, *De Processibus,* n. 227.

[115] Can. 1570, §2; 1710; 1625; cf. Roberti, *De Processibus,* I, nn. 90, 160, 286; Noval, *De Processibus,* nn. 104, 217, 218, 391; Blat, *De Processibus,* n. 414.

[116] Cc. 2, 18, 38, X, *de appellationibus, recusationibus et relationibus,* II, 28.

[117] Conc. Trident., sess. XXIV, *de ref.,* c. 20.

[118] S. C. Ep. et Reg., *decr.,* 16 Oct. 1600—*Fontes,* n. 1586; Bened. XIV, const. "*Ad Militantis,*" 30 March 1742, nn. 5, 44—*Fontes,* n. 326.

**Canon 1885. §2. Si (casus de quo in can. 1733) contigerit postquam fuerit appellatum, appellatio interposita eisdem denuntiatur, in quorum favorem a die denuntiationis denuo currere incipit tempus utile ad appellationem prosequendam.**

Another interruption permitted by the Code is mentioned in this canon. If, after the appeal has been interposed but before it has been prosecuted, the appellant should die, change his state of life, resign or in any other manner surrender the office by virtue of which he was acting in the cause in question,[119] the canonical term of one month is interrupted and does not begin to run until the notice of the interposition of the appeal has been communicated to the heirs or successors in office of the appellant.[120] This is the more liberal opinion for it makes provision for those extreme cases where an impediment, as mentioned above, would occur on one of the final days of the term. If the term were merely *suspended* until the interposition of the appeal was made known to the heirs of the successors in office of the appellant and then begin to *run* again, a very short space of time would be left to the new appellant in which to prosecute the appeal. If the term was only *suspended,* the days that had passed before the death, etc., of the appellant, would be counted in the general computation of the term; whereas, in the case of an *interruption* of the term, the days preceding it are not computed at all, and a new term of one month is granted to the heirs or successors in office of the appellant.[121]

The appellant is required to observe all the necessary formalities in the prosecution of his appeal; therefore, if his appeal is rejected by the appellate judge, he must submit it again in its corrected and amended form, within the legitimate, canonical term. Otherwise, he will lose his right to appeal and the sentence will become a *res*

119 Can. 1733, §1.

120 Vermeersch-Creusen, *Epitome,* III, n. 239, §3; Muniz, *Procedimientos Eclesiásticos,* III, n. 470; Roberti, *De Processibus,* II, n. 479; Blat, *De Processibus,* n. 415.

121 Cf. S. R. Rota in c. *Aegypti,* nullitatis matrim., 20 June 1922—*AAS.,* XIV (1922), 606.

*iudicata,*[122] for the law does not favor needless delay, negligence or crass ignorance in these cases.

### §3. *The Lapse of the Term*

**Canon 1886. Inutiliter elapsis fatalibus appellatoriis sive coram iudice *a quo,* sive coram iudice *ad quem,* deserta censetur appellatio.**

One of the *fatalia legis* of canon 1634, §1 is the month allowed by the Code for the prosecution of an appeal. Wherefore, if this term is permitted to pass without any attempt having been made to prosecute the appeal in the superior instance, the right of doing so is thereby forfeited. The process is extinguished by the negligence or inertia of the appellant and this is regarded as a tacit renunciation or desertion of the appeal.[123] When the appeal thus goes by default, the sentence becomes a *res iudicata* and the execution thereof follows as a matter of law and right,[124] the appellant being held liable for all costs incurred in the second as well as in the first instance.[125]

The *defensor vinculi* is similarly obliged by the tenor of canon 1883 to prosecute his appeal within the legal term. The word "appeal" includes the idea of prosecuting as well as interposing a complaint against an obnoxious sentence; consequently, the obligation of canon 1986 which requires the defender of the marriage bond to appeal *ex officio* from the first sentence declaring for the nullity of a marriage, extends to the prosecution of this appeal before the superior instance. He must introduce the cause into the appellate tribunal, where the *defensor vinculi* of the latter court takes over the defense of the marriage tie. He may be compelled to the performance of this act by the judge *a quo* who is empowered by this canon to act on the negligence of the defender. If this negligence is delib-

[122] Roberti, *De Processibus,* II, n. 479.

[123] Cf. can. 1738; cf. also commentary on this canon with respect to the interposition of an appeal, in a preceding chapter.

[124] Can. 1902, n. 2; 1917.

[125] Can. 1888; 1910, 1913, §2.

erate or criminal in intent, it may be denounced to the judge *a quo* who can punish the *defensor* and remove him from office.[126] If, however, it happens that the term has lapsed without any further action on the part of the defender of the bond, the sentence does not thereby become a *res iudicata,* for it is one of the class that is concerned with the state of a person. A cause of this type requires two conformable sentences to become a *quasi-res iudicata* and consequently, the lapse of the term in the case in question would have no practical effect on the sentence as such. Therefore, the defender of the bond may prosecute his appeal even after the lapse of the term of one month. This procedure would be entirely different, however, if the sentence appealed by the defender was the second conformable verdict decreeing the nullity of a marriage. In this case, if the defender within the month allowed by law for the prosecution of the appeal, had made no attempt whatever to introduce his appeal into the superior tribunal, the sentence after the expiration of the last day of the term would become for all practical purposes a *res iudicata* and the parties concerned would be free to contract new marriages. This is in accordance with the provision of canon 1987. The defender would lose his right to appeal as far as the present sentence was concerned, unless new and substantial evidence relative to the cause in question was uncovered.[127]

The process is also extinguished if, in the absence of a legitimate impediment, no processual act was performed or placed in the appellate court within the space of one year from the time that the appeal was admitted by the superior judge.[128] This abatement of the instance is not a penalty for lack of action but rather a measure for the public good which demands the speedy termination of lawsuits and trials, consonant with the right administration of justice.[129] Accordingly, an appeal is regarded by the Code as having been tacitly deserted or abandoned when no effort has been made in the course of a year to continue the actual conduct of it through the appellate

[126] Cf. can. 1935, §1; 1635, §3.

[127] Cf. can. 1987, 1903, 1971; Roberti in *Apollinaris,* II (1929), 517.

[128] Cf. Roberti, *De Processibus,* I, nn. 188, 189; II, n. 314; Noval, *De Processibus,* n. 424; canon 1736.

[129] Cf. can. 1620; Noval, *De Processibus,* nn. 205, 206; Vermeersch-Creusen, *Epitome,* III, nn. 62, 154; Roberti, *De Processibus,* II, n. 313.

instance. The consequence of this annulment of the appellate instance is that the sentence becomes a *res iudicata* and the responsible party or parties are liable for all costs incurred.[180]

[180] Can. 1902, n. 2; 1910, 1913, §2; cf. also can. 1737, 1888.

# CHAPTER XI

# THE APPELLATE PROCESS

THE trial of the appealed cause for all practical purposes begins when the judge of the superior tribunal informs the appellant and the appellee that the appeal has been approved and admitted. The notification, in the case of the appellee, may be compared to the citation or summons of the first instance.[1] It should include the term assigned for the *litis contestatio*, the joinder of issue.

## ARTICLE I. THE "LITIS CONTESTATIO"

**Canon 1891. §1. In gradu appellationis non potest admitti nova petendi causa, ne per modum quidem utilis *cumulationis;* ideoque litis contestatio in eo tantum versari potest ut prior sententia vel confirmetur, vel reformetur sive ex toto sive ex parte.**

This joinder of issue did not appear to be necessary before the Code since the first instance had already taken cognizance of the object of the controversy and the scope of the appeal was limited by the *libellus appellatorius*. An historical survey of the evolution of the *litis contestatio* supplies the information that generally speaking, it was regarded as a necessary element of judicial procedure. It is only in recent times that the importance of the *litis contestatio* has been diminished, particularly through the influence of civil codes of law that stressed rather the necessity of the citation; this latter proceeding seems to have developed as a necessary element in solemn judicial procedure in the same ratio as the formal importance of

[1] Can. 1711 ff.; cf. Roberti, *De Processibus*, II, n. 479.

the *litis contestatio* proper was lessened.[2] The Code defines the *litis contestio* as the formal contradiction made by the defendant to the petition of the plaintiff with the intention of prosecuting the case before a judge.[3] The elements of this definition are to be found essentially in the statement of the object of the trial, or in the determination of the terms of the controversy, or if it be necessary, in the decisive definition of the points at issue made by both parties at the demand of the judge or of either party in the face of difficulties or doubtful claims, occurring respectively in the defendant's answer to the citation or in the plaintiff's *libellus.*[4] While the *litis contestatio* has lost some of its solemnity and importance, it is still a necessary element in judicial proceedings, and as such, it is required and prescribed for the appellate instance.[5]

In the case of an appeal, the *litis contestatio* is concerned only with the sentence of the inferior court, whether it should be wholly or in part reformed or confirmed; [6] and the appellate process extends only to that part of the sentence appealed. Since the matter of the judgment has been determined by the *litis contestatio,* no counter-pleas or new petitions may be admitted into the appellate instance; the same restriction holds for the substitution of a new action or a new cause. The appellant is not permitted to vindicate

[2] Cf. cc. 58, 70, X, *de appellationibus, recusationibus et relationibus,* II, 28; c. 2, *de appellationibus,* II, 12 *in Clem;* c. 2, *de verborum significatione,* V, 11 *in Clem;* cf. Wernz-Vidal, *De Processibus,* n. 397; Roberti, *De Processibus,* I, nn. 299, 300; Noval, *De Processibus,* nn. 409-412.

[3] Can. 1726.

[4] Cf. can. 1706, 1708, 1711, 1715, 1727, 1728; Roberti, *De Processibus,* I, n. 301; Noval, *De Processibus,* nn. 412, 413.

[5] Roberti, *De Processibus,* I, n. 301, §3; Noval, *De Processibus,* n. 655; *Lex Propria,* can. 23, §1; *Reg. Serv. in iud. apud S. R. Rotae Trib.,* §12, n. 2. Wernz (cf. Wernz, *Jus Decretalium,* V, n. 457; Wernz-Vidal, *De Processibus,* n. 399) did not regard the *litis contestatio* as necessary in the appellate instance, because, although it is a new grade of judgment, yet the cause is one and the same; the *litis contestatio* was not extinguished by the sentence of the judge of the lower court. However, the sense of canon 1891, §1, seems to militate against this opinion; the view held by Noval, Roberti, Cocchi (*De Processibus,* n. 229) and Blat (*De Processibus,* n. 421) is preferable in the light of the present legislation on the matter.

[6] Can. 1891, §1; Roberti, *De Processibus,* II, n. 480; Noval, *De Processibus,* n. 655: "1. Utrum sententia, lata in prima instantia, sit confirmanda an vero reformanda; 2. quatenus reformanda, utrum ex toto an tantum ex parte; 3. quatenus ex parte, in quo reformanda sit."

any new right or title of law, nor change his original plea. Similarly, he may not add another title to that on which he based his plea in the first instance; [7] e. g., a plaintiff who sues for a *separatio mensae, tori et habitationis* on the ground of adultery, cannot in the appellate instance base his plea on cruelty instead of adultery; nor may he add the ground of cruelty to that of adultery in prosecuting his appeal. The judge of the appellate instance should reject *ex officio* any attempt to have a new *causa petendi* admitted, for he would be incompetent *ratione gradus* to take cognizance of a cause that had not been judged in an original instance.[8] The grades of tribunals have been established for the public good and ordinarily a cause must be tried first in the lowest instance or grade of judgment. This prohibition, however, is not absolute.[9]

New arguments may be submitted later to sustain an appeal that might otherwise be rejected, as long as they do not constitute a *nova causa petendi*.[10] Similarly, accessory clauses to the principal petition do not comprise a new petition and the judge is allowed by law to admit these if it seems fitting for him to do so. Such clauses may have for their object, the expenses of the trial or suit [11] or they may be concerned with possessory actions. The possessor of property belonging to another ceases to be in good faith after the joinder of issue has taken place; if he is condemned to restore the property, he is held to make restitution in addition of all the fruits, interest or profits drawn from that property after the *litis contestatio* began. Likewise, he is held for any loss or injury that may have happened either to the property or to the defendant himself. But since the *litis contestatio* exists only until the sentence is pronounced on a cause, what becomes of the profits or interest that accrue after the sentence has been pronounced and appealed? Accessory clauses may be added to the principal petition in the appellate instance for the

[7] Roberti, *De Processibus*, II, n. 480; Noval, *De Processibus*, n. 655; Wernz-Vidal, *De Processibus*, n. 613; Cocchi, *De Processibus*, n. 229; Vermeersch-Creusen, *Epitome*, III, n. 240; *Reg. Serv. in iud. apud S. R. Rotae Trib.*, §230, n. 1.

[8] Can. 1570, 1572.

[9] Can. 1569; Roberti, *De Processibus*, II, n. 480; Noval, *De Processibus*, n. 655; Lega, *De Iudiciis*, I, n. 650.

[10] Wernz-Vidal, *De Processibus*, n. 613.

[11] Cf. *Reg. Serv. in iud. apud S. R. Rotae Trib.*, §230, n. 3.

purpose of obtaining the restoration of the accumulated profits or indemnification for losses suffered since the sentence was rendered in the previous instance. Nor will such accessory clauses constitute new causes.[12]

## Article II. The "Litis Instantia" or Proceedings Proper

The *litis contestatio* or joinder of issue marks the beginning of the appellate process. The *litis instantia* or the judicial examination designates the proceedings proper which begin with the joinder of issue and end with the pronouncement of the final verdict in the case.[13] In the superior court, an appeal is ordinarily conducted through the same stages of the *litis instantia, mutatis mutandis,* that marked its progress through the lower instance. The more salient features of this process will be indicated in the ensuing titles.

### §1. *The Quashing of the "Litis Instantia"*

The examination of the appealed cause may be suppressed temporarily or permanently. The *litis instantia* is temporarily abated by any legally recognized interruption. This may occur if one of the contending parties dies, changes his state in life or resigns or otherwise gives up the office by reason of which he was involved in the suit.[14] The instance may likewise be interrupted by the death, resignation, etc., of the proctor, attorney, defensor vinculi, etc.[15] During the interruption, the process cannot be continued and any acts performed during this period, are null and void.[16] However, the issue is still *in pleading* and the instance cannot be entirely extinguished or permanently suppressed. The interruption ceases and the examination of the cause is resumed when it is taken up by the heirs or successors in office of the previous litigant or when new officials, proctors, defender of the bond, etc., have been appointed

[12] Can. 1731, §3; 1689, Roberti, *De Processibus,* I, n. 305; Noval, *De Processibus,* nn. 346, 418.

[13] Can. 1732.

[14] Can. 1733.

[15] Can. 1735.

[16] Roberti, *De Processibus,* II, n. 309.

by the proper authority. The client himself may also decide to handle his own cause in the appellate instance, upon the loss of his proctor.[17]

The instance may be permanently abrogated by abatement or by renunciation. The former condition occurs when, notwithstanding the fact that no legal impediment or obstacle can be alleged as an excuse, one year has passed from the time that the appeal was admitted into the superior instance, during which period of time, no procedural act was performed by either of the litigants or by their representatives, or by the judge.[18] Abatement of the appellate instance by this neglect or indifference, holds for all classes of litigants and their attorneys, proctors or agents, according to the provisions of the Code.[19] Likewise, the instance may be permanently quashed through the renunciation of it by the *actor* or plaintiff in accordance with the prescriptions of the Code.[20] The plaintiff may renounce the instance in any stage of the judgment and forswear the acts of the process wholly or in part. In either case, the renunciation must be done formally in writing, proper signed, communicated to and accepted by the opponent tacitly or otherwise, and admitted by the judge.[21] Valid renunciation has the same effects as abatement; the instance as far as the *acta processus* are concerned, is formally declared extinguished by a decree of the judge. This decree does not nullify the action proper, which may be brought to trial at some other time. The decree establishes also the costs incurred and names the parties responsible for the renunciation of the instance and as such, held to the payment of all expenses in the matter.[22] By the force of this decree quashing the renounced or abated

[17] Can. 1735; cf. also commentary on canon 1885 in a previous chapter; Roberti, *De Processibus,* II, nn. 308-311; 479, n. 2; Noval, *De Processibus,* n. 419 ff.; Blat, *De Processibus,* n. 231; Cocchi, *De Processibus,* n. 124; Wernz-Vidal, *De Processibus,* n. 410.

[18] Can. 1736.

[19] Can. 1737-1738; Noval, *De Processibus,* n. 424; Wernz-Vidal, *De Processibus,* n. 413; Roberti, *De Processibus,* II, n. 313 ff.

[20] Can. 1740, §1.

[21] Can. 1740, §2.

[22] Can. 1739, 1741; cf. Roberti, *De Processibus,* II, n. 316; Wernz-Vidal, *De Processibus,* n. 415; Noval, *De Processibus,* n. 428; Vermeersch-Creusen, *Epitome,* III, n. 155; Blat, *De Processibus,* n. 238 ff.

instance, the sentence of the lower court becomes a *res iudicata* and is to be summarily executed.[23]

### §2. *The Presentation of Evidence in the Appellate Instance*

**Canon 1891. §2. Sed novis exhibitis documentis et novis probationibus poterit causa instrui, servatis regulis traditis in can. 1786, 1861.**

The correction or revision of an unjust sentence is the primary purpose of an appeal. For the fulfillment of this aim, it is required that the appellate judge submit the cause to a new examination in order that he may ascertain on what premises the unjust sentence may rest. This investigation extends to all the evidence produced in the previous instance, the testimony, proofs, documents, all must be scrutinized by the judge; for, in the appellate instance, all continue to hold the same value and have a kindred bearing on the cause as in the first instance.[24] Moreover, either of the interested parties may introduce into the appellate instance, new proofs, documents, evidence or testimony for the purpose of strengthening the cause and of affording the judge the opportunity of adjudicating the matter with greater care and precision. The ancient juristic principle, "non deducta deducam, non probata probabo," holds likewise in the appellate instance.[25]

Canon 1891, §2, however, prescribes certain limitations in this regard in order to render the danger of perjured testimony or fraudulent documents as remote as possible.[26] The Code is somewhat more stringent on this point than the former discipline and accordingly falls in line with modern civil statutes that restrict the examination in the appellate instance to the acts and evidence offered in the pre-

[23] Can. 1902, 1917, 1918, ff.

[24] Roberti, *De Processibus*, II, n. 482.

[25] Roberti. *De Processibus*, II, n. 482. Cf. also Lega, *De Iudiciis*, I, n. 650, §2; c. 4, X, *de appellationibus, recusationibus et relationibus*, II, 28; c. 10, X, *de fide instrumentorum*, II, 22; the introduction of new proofs in the case of appeals from interlocutory sentences was prohibited by c. 5, *de appellationibus*, II, 12 *in Clem*.

[26] Cf. c. 2, *de test*., II, 8 *in Clem*.—"cum non minus in appellationibus quam in principali causa subornatio sit timenda."

vious grade of judgment. This procedure of itself guarantees a complete *instructio causae* in the first instance, shortens the appellate trial and removes the danger of perjury and fraud in connection with the appeal.[27]

The distinction is drawn in this canon between causes that of their nature may become finally and decisively judged and causes that never become *res iudicatae,* that is, causes that affect the personal state of the litigants, as matrimonial, clerical, religious and in some instance, criminal causes.[28] The hearing of new witnesses and the admission of new evidence is regulated by enactments and provisions in the Code relative to other procedural points.[29] The Code ordains that new proofs may not be admitted in the appellate instance to substantiate causes that *per se* can become *res iudicatae.* This is a general prohibition enacted to prevent any undue protraction or extension of the appellate instance. However, it is not absolute, admitting exceptions in certain well defined cases. New documents that bear directly on the cause proper and that have just been discovered or received, may be introduced into the appellate instance. In this class of documents may be placed all those which for some good reason were not taken cognizance of during the previous instance. This would hold if the proper party possessed the documents but was unable to produce or exhibit them at the opportune time.[30] In addition to the admission of new documents, new witnesses may likewise be introduced into the appellate instance, witnesses who were prevented from testifying at the previous trial due to some physical indisposition or to some other excusing cause.[31] For the lawful admission of new documents or new witnesses in this class of causes, the Code for evident reasons requires a *very grave* cause. It is left to the prudence of the judge to determine whether or not the reason for admission is sufficiently grave. Moreover, the new evidence must be important enough to warrant its admittance.

[27] Noval, *De Processibus,* n. 656.

[28] Roberti, *De Processibus,* II, n. 511; Noval, *De Processibus,* n. 675; cf. can. 1903.

[29] Can. 1786, 1861.

[30] Roberti, *De Processibus,* II, n. 438; Wernz-Vidal, *De Processibus,* n. 478.

[31] Can. 1755, 1756; Augustine, *A Commentary,* VII, 202 ff.; Roberti, *De Processibus,* II, n. 336 ff.; can. 1757 ff.

The judge should not allow the introduction of useless, futile or inane testimony.[32] If he decided to permit the new documents and new witnesses to have a part in the trial, it is encumbent upon him to take such measures as he may deem necessary to insure and guarantee the right conduct of the process. The introduction of fraudulent documents or perjured testimony on the part of intimidated or corrupt witnesses, may be attempted at this stage of the appellate process as a final desperate effort to bolster up an otherwise weak case. Consequently every precaution must be taken to prevent the admission of documents or witnesses of this calibre.[33]

With regard to causes that never become *res iudicatae,* new proofs or documents and similarly, new witnesses may be admitted in the appellate instance. The very nature of causes of this type demands that the restrictions and limitations be not so severe or stringent as in the previous case, for here, the question is concerned with the personal state of the litigant, his freedom of action, the exercise of his natural rights, etc. Consequently, a *grave* cause only is required,[34] whereas in the previous case, a *very grave* reason was necessary for the proper admission of such testimony. The gravity of the cause willl be determined by the nature of the case and consequently, it may be noted that any reasonably grave cause will suffice to move the judge to admit new evidence into the trial being conducted before him, so long as this evidence or testimony is not useless or futile and has a direct bearing on the cause proper.[35] Furthermore, the judge must take all necessary precautions to prevent the admission of fraudulent documents and corrupt witnesses who might give perjured testimony.

[32] Wernz-Vidal, *De Processibus,* n. 580.

[33] Wernz-Vidal, *De Processibus,* n. 478; Roberti, *De Processibus,* II, n. 350; Noval, *De Processibus,* n. 507; Blat, *De Processibus,* n. 295.

[34] Can. 1786.

[35] Roberti, *De Processibus,* II, n. 438; Wernz-Vidal, *De Processibus,* n. 580. In causes of this character, when the question involved is concerned with the marriage bond, the *defensor vinculi* enjoys special privileges and faculties (can. 1969, n. 3, n. 4) and the judge is obliged to recognize these rights, particularly that of proposing new proofs and testimony and of producing new witnesses. Cf. Roberti, *De Processibus,* II, n. 438; Noval, *De Processibus,* n. 846; Cocchi, *De Processibus,* n. 292; Blat, *De Processibus,* n. 523; Wernz-Vidal, *Ius Matrimoniale,* n. 636.

The correct legal procedure should be followed in producing new documents or introducing new witnesses into the appellate instance in either of the foregoing cases. The party who desires the admission of new evidence of this kind should embody this in a petition which should determine the character of the evidence, explain the reason why the documents or witnesses were not produced in the previous instance and why they should be admitted into the present grade of judgment and conclude with a plea for the acceptance of this new evidence. It should then be submitted to the judge who will take it under advisement and admit it if it seems prudent for him to do so. He should notify in the meanwhile the other party to the case of the reception of the petition; the *defensor vinculi* and the *promotor iustitiae* are to be heard relative to the admission of the new evidence if either is interested in the case. If the judge admits the evidence, he should issue a formal decree to that effect, which will be noted by the actuary in the minutes of the trial.[36] The judge shall allow the other party a certain period of time in which to propose, if possible, contrary proofs in his own defense. This is an important consideration and if it be neglected or refused to the other litigant, the judgment is thereby nullified.[37] After the decree of admittance has been issued by the judge, the trial proceeds according to the accepted norms.

### §3. *Incidental Causes in the Appellate Instance*

All exceptions and incidental causes which could be proposed in the court of first instance, may likewise be submitted to the judge of the appellate tribunal.[38] One or two features may be indicated here with reference to incidental causes occurring in the course of the appellate process. These will seldom occur for the *instantia* of the appellate judgment centers rather about the *periodus probationis*.

[36] Noval, *De Processibus*, n. 507.

[37] Can. 1861, §2; cf. Wernz-Vidal, *De Processibus*, n. 580; Cocchi, *De Processibus*, n. 211; Roberti, *De Processibus*, II, nn. 438, 482; Blat, *De Processibus*, n. 387; *Lex Propria*, can. 27, §3; *Reg. Serv. in iud. apud S. R. Rotae Trib.*, §52.

[38] Roberti, *De Processibus*, II, nn. 482, 483; can. 1628, 1629 ff.; 1837 ff.

## A. *Contempt of Court*

Contumacy or contempt of court is one of the incidental questions common to all trials and it may perchance come up during the appellate instance as well as in the original grade of judgment. However, as an incidental question, it does not happen as often in the appellate process, for the peculiar nature of the *litis contestatio* and the manner in which the trial is conducted before the appellate tribunal is such that the occasion is not offered usually for the filing of contempt proceedings. It may be remarked also that while contumacy in the appellate instance is governed by the regular enactments and prescriptions of the Code,[39] there are certain points peculiar to the nature of the process in question that may be noted. If the appellant himself is guilty of contempt, he thereby loses all right to prosecute his appeal before the appellate tribunal.[40] The appellee may then seek to be freed from the claims of the appellant and discharged from the jurisdiction of the court; [41] in which case, the sentence pronounced by the previous court becomes a *res iudicata,*[42] for the appellant is considered to have renounced or deserted his appeal. However, the application of the appellee may not be received if the judge orders the *defensor vinculi* or the *promotor iustitiae* to resume the conduct of the appellant's cause in the interests of the common good.[43]

If, on the other hand, the appellee has been guilty of contempt, all the exceptions proposed by him in the first instance, all the proofs and evidence likewise produced in the first trial, maintain their full force in the appellate instance, for the *litis contestatio* has already taken place.[44] The judge, however, is not permitted to supply other proofs unless the public good is in some manner involved in the case.[45] As far as the defense of the appellee's case is concerned, he is to rely on the justice of the court as provided by the

[39] Can. 1842 ff.
[40] Can. 1850, §1.
[41] Can. 1850, §3.
[42] Can. 1902; cf. Roberti, *De Processibus,* II, nn. 411, 483.
[43] Can. 1850, §2.
[44] Can. 1844, §2.
[45] Can. 1619, §1, §2.

Code.[46] The appellant, on the other hand, must continue to press his appeal and demonstrate satisfactorily his contention that the sentence in question was unjust and should be reformed.[47]

If the plaintiff and the appellant had both appealed from the sentence and if one of them be found guilty of contempt, the other is permitted to prosecute his appeal in order to get a revision of the sentence for his own benefit. This prosecution and subsequent revision or confirmation will be limited to those parts of the sentence which were appealed.[48] The party who is judged to be contumacious by the court is held liable for all costs incurred in the appellate instance.[49]

## B. *The Intervention of a Third Party*

Another incidental cause that may be admitted into the appellate grade of judgment is that concerned with the *intervention* of a third party. This is not to be confused with that extraordinary remedy of legal redress, the *opposition* of a third party, *oppositio tertii.*[50] This particular remedy as well as the *intervention* of a third person [51] has been established for the protection of the rights of a third person in view of the legal principles *"cum res inter alios iudicatae nullium aliis praeiudicium faciant,"* [52] *"res inter alios iudicatae neque emolumentum adferre his qui iudicio non interfuerent, neque praeiudicium solent irrogare"* [53] found in Roman Law and *"cum res inter alios acta non noceat regulariter aliis juxta constitutiones canonicas et civiles"* [54] and *"cum regulariter aliis non noceat res inter alios iudicata"* [55] of the Decretals. While the object and motive of each mode of defense are more or less similar, each is governed by different norms. The question of intervention is more directly concerned

[46] Can. 1867; cf. *Reg. Serv. in iud. apud S. R. Rotae Trib.*, §26, n. 6.
[47] Can. 1844; Roberti, *De Processibus*, II, n. 405.
[48] Roberti, *De Processibus*, II, n. 483.
[49] Can. 1851, §1.
[50] Can. 1898-1901.
[51] Can. 1852, 1853.
[52] *Dig.*, 44, 2, 1.
[53] *Cod.*, 7, 56, 2.
[54] C. 17, X, *de sententia et re iudicata*, II, 27.
[55] C. 25, X, *de sententia et re iudicata*, II, 27.

with the subject under consideration and will be considered exclusively.

Intervention may be effected in any grade of judgment, original or appellate, but only during the course of the trial proper and before the *conclusio in causa* itself.[56] If the third party has not intervened in the first instance and the sentence in its effects restricts the lawful exercise of his rights, he may, if the sentence has been appealed by either of the litigants, intervene during the appellate instance to protect his interests. If the sentence has not actually been appealed, he may oppose the execution of the verdict by directing a judicial petition to the judge who pronounced the sentence and requesting that the sentence be reformed or revised either by that particular magistrate or by a superior judge.[57] If the former method is requested, the judge himself will settle the opposition according to the norms laid down in the Code for incidental causees; [58] if the latter, the third party's appeal will be regulated by the enactments governing the interposition and prosecution of an appeal.[59] When a third party ascertains that a cause in litigation affects his interests or foresees that the sentence to be pronounced on the cause in question will injure or unduly restrict the exercise of his rights, *intervention* properly so-called is to be preferred to *opposition* to the execution of the sentence, for the former grants the person the same privileges of law as the latter and at the same time saves time and expense. The Code amply provides for the admission of a third party into any instance of a cause for the purpose of protecting his interests and accordingly regulates the procedure to be followed in such cases.[60] The intervention of a third party is held to

[56] Can. 1852.

[57] Can. 1898, 1899.

[58] Can. 1838-1841.

[59] Can. 1879-1891. It is not within the confines of this dissertation to discuss other judicial remedies, whether ordinary or extraordinary. Cf. for a complete treatment of the *oppositio tertii*, Wernz-Vidal, *De Processibus*, n. 624 ff.; Noval, *De Processibus*, n. 665; Roberti, *De Processibus*, II, n. 501; Blat, *De Processibus*, n. 429; Vermeersch-Creusen, *Epitome*, III, n. 243; Augustine, *A Commentary*, VII, 333; Cocchi, *De Processibus*, n. 236; Muniz, *Procedimientos Eclesiásticos*, III, n. 508.

[60] Can. 1852, 1853.

be *voluntary* when he himself seeks to participate in the process; it is regarded as *necessary* when he is forced by the judge *ex officio* or at the insistence of either party to enter the litigation. The person who seeks to intervene in the cause may do so as a principal or as an accessory according as he opposes both contending parties or assists one litigant in the suit against the other.[61] With regard to appeals, what is termed the necessary intervention of a third party, as distinct from voluntary intervention, is not allowed in the appellate instance if it is sought by one or both of the litigants; for in this case, the intervening party really becomes a litigant in the judgment and no one may be unwillingly deprived of the first instance or first grade of judgment.[62] On the other hand, a third person may be requested *ex officio* by the judge to take part in the cause, not as a party or litigant strictly so-called, but in order to complete the instance or enable the judge to conduct a more thorough investigation into the merits of the cause or the claims of the contesting parties.[63] This mode of intervention is usually required only in causes that are concerned with the public welfare.

Any person may intervene as a principal during the appellate instance of a trial in order to protect his interests or to vindicate his rights in some respect. While the Code prohibits the introduction of any new petition into the appellate instance as a general rule,[64] for the reason that the judge would be incompetent, *ratione gradus*, to take cognizance of it, yet it will allow this intervention under certain conditions in order to expedite the trial itself and to prevent future processes, particularly the interference or opposition of a third person, *oppositio tertii*. Intervention in a cause as a principal is effected by submitting a judicial petition to the appellate judge before the *conclusio in causa*, which will determine the complaint against both parties and the right of the petitioner to guard his interests in the matter, demonstrating at the same time the manner in which his interests will be affected by the forthcoming sentence. The petition will conclude with a plea that the judge permit the third party to in-

[61] Roberti, *De Processibus*, II, n. 415; Noval, *De Processibus*, n. 598.

[62] Roberti, *De Processibus*, II, n. 423.

[63] Wernz-Vidal, *De Processibus*, n. 567; Roberti, *De Processibus*, II, n. 428.

[64] Can. 1891, §1.

tervene in the cause as a principal.[65] Intervention as an accessory is obtained likewise by addressing a petition to the judge while the cause is pending in the appellate instance. The petition must similarly show that the intervening party has some rights to protect or interests to guard and that this may be obtained by joining with one litigant against the other. By intervention in a cause as an accessory, the third party does not act or stand on his own rights; he rather acts with or through the party with whom he associates himself.[66]

In both cases of intervention, the other party or parties should be notified by the judge of the filing of the petition. The former then are entitled to oppose such interference, and if the right to intervene is not sufficiently vindicated particularly in the face of such opposition, the question is decided according to the norms enacted for the solution of incidental questions.[67] When the intervention of the third person has been recognized and permitted by the judge, the former becomes, if he intervened as a principal, strictly speaking, a party to the suit with all the attendant rights and duties. In both cases of intervention, principal and accessory, the third party must accept the cause as it is when he enters it, and accordingly, he is bound to conform to and observe all the acts and decrees that have been respectively performed or issued.[68] New petitions may be advanced and new proofs produced, but they must be adequately substantiated and presented within the term allowed by the judge. The admission of these petitions just as the petition for permission to intervene in the appellate instance, is to be passed on by the judge and the action of the latter in this regard is to be included by the notary in the minutes of the trial.

If the principal process is abated or extinguished for some reason or other, the cause of the intervening party, whether principal or accessory, is similarly affected. If the original litigants effect a compromise or either one renounces the appellate instance, the third party may continue to prosecute the cause by himself if he

[65] Can. 1852, §2; Roberti, *De Processibus*, II, n. 417; Wernz-Vidal, *De Processibus*, n. 564.

[66] Wernz-Vidal, *De Processibus*, n. 562, note 2.

[67] Cf. can. 1837 ff.

[68] Can. 1852, §3; 1628, §1; 1764, §4; 1786, etc.

has entered it as a principal; [69] if the third party has intervened merely as an accessory, a compromise or the renunciation of the appellate process extinguishes it for him also.[70] In pronouncing his sentence, the judge will declare the amount of expenses to be borne by the intervening party as well as by the original litigants.[71]

### §4. *The "Discussio Causae" in the Appellate Instance*

If any additional acts have been performed during the probative period of the appellate process, viz., the intervention of a third party, the admission of new evidence or witnesses, etc., they must be published in accordance with the enactments of the Code as contained in canon 1858 and 1859.[72] Thereupon, the Code ordains that the judge, by a formal decree, declare the cause to be completed.[73] This *conclusio in causa* is merely the formal declaration that the evidence bearing on the cause in question has been exhausted and that new evidence may no longer be received, except under extraordinary circumstances. The *conclusio in causa* is then followed by the defense or the discussion of the cause. The procedure as outlined in the Code is to be observed in this regard.[74] The *discussio causae* is a new juridical development and is based on the practise of the Rota. It cannot be found in the Decretals nor in any subsequent legislation until the promulgation of the *Lex Propria* in 1908.[75] The discussion comprises the deductions and conclusions that are drawn by the parties or their advocates from the evidence that has been presented in support of the original complaint. It is a necessary element in all causes that affect the public welfare. It enables the judge or judges as the case may be, to become familiar with the claims and

[69] Roberti, *De Processibus,* II, n. 418.
[70] Roberti, *De Processibus,* II, n. 421.
[71] Can. 1910 ff.
[72] Roberti, *De Processibus,* II, n. 435; Noval, *De Processibus,* n. 606; Wernz-Vidal, *De Processibus,* n. 576; Blat, *De Processibus,* n. 384.
[73] Can. 1860; cf. Roberti, *De Processibus,* II, n. 436; Noval, *De Processibus,* n. 610; Wernz-Vidal, *De Processibus,* n. 579; Blat, *De Processibus,* n. 386.
[74] Can. 1862 ff.; cf. Roberti, *De Processibus,* II, n. 439; Noval, *De Processibus,* n. 612; Wernz-Vidal, *De Processibus,* n. 581; Blat, *De Processibus,* n. 388.
[75] *AAS.,* I (1909), 20.

allegations as well as the denials and complaints of each party; it is a most important feature from the standpoint of the *defensor vinculi* for it is at this period of the trial more than at another time that he formally exercises his ministry of defending and protecting the integrity of the matrimonial bond.[76] The *promotor iustitiae* likewise engages in the discussion with the advocate of his opponent in criminal trials[77] or in other causes concerned with the public welfare. The *discussio* in itself is probably the most important feature of the appellate grade of judgment particularly if no new evidence or witnesses have been introduced. The object of subjecting the sentence of the lower court to another examination is for the purpose of ascertaining the alleged unjust features of it. To discover these vitiating elements, the discussion must touch upon every point and act in the preceding trial. Consequently, it should be conducted zealously and faithfully by those who take part in it. The cause must undergo a rigorous and severe investigation to the end that the demands of justice be satisfied and observed. It would not be consonant with right reason and sound judgment for the appellate judge or judges, the *defensor vinculi*, the *promotor iustitiae,* or other court officials to place such confidence in the judgment of the previous tribunal that as a result the cause would be given only a cursory and superficial examination in the appellate instance. The common good, the public welfare and the natural, inalienable rights of an individual are at stake and there can be no compromise with injustice. The demands of justice are firm, inflexible, inexorable!

## Article III. The Sentence and Subsequent Appeal

### §1. *The Appeal from a Sentence Pronounced on Ordinary Appellate Causes*

When the *discussio causae* has taken place, the appellate instance reaches its termination through the sentence of the appellate tribunal. The judge or judges are to render their verdict in accordance with the provisions of the Code which defines the nature and

[76] Can. 1968, 1969.

[77] Can. 1587, §2; 1655, §1.

contents of the sentence and the procedure to be followed in drawing up and publishing it.[78] The primary duty of the appellate judge is to confirm or reform by a new sentence, the verdict rendered by the lower court and appealed to his tribunal; this he is to do after he has taken full cognizance of the cause and subjected it to a mature and rigid investigation. However, no ordinance in the Code prevents him from rejecting facts or evidence that were admitted to the previous grade of judgment or from admitting what the lower court rejected. He may also recognize and receive exceptions proposed to but rejected or neglected by the court of first instance.[79] His judgment will likewise be pronounced on the merits of any interlocutory sentence that has been appealed in conjunction with the definitive sentence. If the appeal has been interposed against a particular point of a final sentence, the judge should consider only that part appealed and questions implicitly contained therein when he renders his verdict on the cause. When the tribunal has taken all these elements into consideration, it must pronounce a sentence on the merits of the appeal. The cause is not to be returned to the lower court with a request that that tribunal alter its sentence, if such be the case. The appeal must be finally and decisively settled by the appellate court. Consequently, the superior judge will consider whether or not the sentence of the lower court was justly pronounced in view of the complaint made and the evidence, witnesses, documents, etc., produced in support of that complaint. If he regards it as just, he will confirm it; if unjust, he will revise or reform it, wholly or in part depending on whether or not the appeal was interposed against the entire sentence or merely a portion of it.[80] Similarly, he may submit a new sentence based entirely on his own findings in the case, in favor of the appellant or of the appellee even in the event that the latter had not interposed an appeal.[81]

The sentence is then to be published as the Code directs.[82] Although the judge may use any of the methods of publication allowed

[78] Can. 1868 ff. Cf. Noval, *De Processibus,* n. 618 ff.; Roberti, *De Processibus,* II, n. 443 ff.; Wernz-Vidal, *De Processibus,* n. 587 ff.

[79] Roberti, *De Processibus,* II, n. 485.

[80] Noval, *De Processibus,* n. 655.

[81] Wernz-Vidal, *De Processibus,* n. 613.

[82] Can. 1876, 1877.

by the law, he will naturally employ that means which is most agreeable and convenient to the contesting parties. A copy of the sentence is then to be sent to the judge of the lower court, the Ordinary of the place where the cause was first tried,[83] who will proceed to execute it if it has confirmed his own verdict or that of his *Officialis* for with this confirmation, the sentence becomes a *res iudicata* under ordinary circumstances.[84] If the cause and sentence affect the state of a person, the inferior judge will take this circumstance into consideration and regulate his actions accordingly.[85] If the judge of first instance refuses to execute the sentence, the interested party has the right to demand that the sentence be put into effect by the appellate judge.[86] The judge of first instance or of the appellate tribunal, as the case may be, is to observe the prescriptions of the Code relative to the execution of a sentence.[87]

If on the other hand, the appellate tribunal has revoked or reformed the sentence pronounced by the lower court, the Code permits a further appeal on the matter. This appeal is subject to all the foregoing prescriptions, provisions and restrictions that have been discussed in the course of this work. If the appeal has been heard by the ordinary tribunal of second instance, the Sacred Roman Rota is competent to take cognizance of the appeal in the third instance; [88] if the Rota has heard the appeal as a court of second instance and in the event that the sentence of the inferior court has not been confirmed,[89] the third instance will be held again before the Rota [90] but the trial will be held before another and distinct

[83] Can. 198; Roberti, *De Processibus,* II, n. 485; Wernz-Vidal, *De Processibus,* n. 613; Noval, *De Processibus,* n. 707.

[84] Can. 1920, §1; 1902, n. 1. If the sentence thus receeived by the Ordinary of the original process from the appellate court has confirmed his own sentence of nullity with regard to a marriage, he should, if no further appeal has been taken from the sentence, order a note to this effect to be made in the baptismal and matrimonial registers where the baptism and marriage respectively where the baptism and marriage respectively took place. Can. 1988.

[85] Can. 1903; Roberti, *De Processibus,* II, nn. 511, 512.

[86] Can. 1920, §2.

[87] Can. 1917 ff.

[88] Cf. can. 1594, 1599, §1, n. 2; *Lex Propria,* can. 14, §3.

[89] Can. 1599, §1, n. 1; *Lex Propria,* can. 14, §2.

[90] Can. 1599, §1, n. 2; *Lex Propria,* can. 14, §3.

*turnus.*[91] Appeals are interposed before the Rota, subject first to the prescriptions of the Code[92] and secondly, to the particular rules and norms contained in the "*Lex Propria*" and the "*Regulae Servandae in iudiciis apud S. R. Rotae Tribunal*" which are not contrary to the provisions of the Code.[93]

## §2. *The Appeal from a Sentence Pronounced on a Matrimonial Cause in the Second Instance*

### A. *The Solemn Process*

In accordance with what has been stated previously, a sentence rendered in a solemn matrimonial trial never becomes a *res iudicata.*[94] Consequently after two conformable sentences declaring for the validity or for the nullity of a marriage as the case may be, the sentence can be appealed by either of the parties or the *defensor vinculi* provided new arguments or authentic documents of a weighty nature are produced in support of the complaint or contention of the appellant.[95] For similar reasons, the cause may be reopened at a later date despite the fact that a sentence of nullity has been passed on the cause in question on two, three or more occasions or that an appeal was not interposed against the second or any subsequent sentence or that the parties concerned have each contracted new marriages.[96] The new arguments by force of which the cause is reopened, must be of a serious and important character and of sufficient value to urge in all probability the reversal of the sentence.[97] More latitude is permitted with regard to the new arguments that are offered; reasons that were proposed in the preceding instance

[91] *Lex Propria,* can. 11, 12, §2; 33, §2; *Reg. Serv. in iud. apud S. R. Rotae Trib.,* §211, n. 1.

[92] Can. 1555, §2.

[93] Roberti, *De Processibus,* I, n. 136; Cocchi, *De Processibus,* n. 32; Vermeersch-Creusen, *Epitome,* III, n. 49; cf. can. 6, §1.

[94] Can. 1903, 1989.

[95] Can. 1903, 1989; cf. also can. 1786, 1861.

[96] Cappello, *De Sacramentis,* III, n. 887; Noval, *De Processibus,* n. 871; Augustine, *A Commentary,* V, 433; Vlaming, *Praelectiones,* II, n. 802; Chelodi, *Ius Matrimoniale,* n. 179.

[97] Cf. S. R. Rota in c. *Diocesis Z.,* nullitatis matrim., 19 May 1921—*AAS.,* XIII (1921), 547.

but the real value of which was not recognizeed or which were not thoroughly and exhaustively presented might be offered again in an effort to reopen the cause.

The role played by the *defensor vinculi* in the second instance is similar with regard to his various obligations and rights to that occupied in the previous grade of judgment. Relative to appeals, the *defensor vinculi* of the appellate tribunal, who is a separate and distinct person from that of the first court, must appeal under the same circumstances mentioned in canon 1986 from a sentence declaring the nullity of a marriage if the first verdict had decreed its validity. If the second sentence confirms the first in favoring the nullity of the marriage, the *defensor vinculi* can appeal if in conscience he believes that an appeal should be made. If in the judgment of the *defensor vinculi* of the appellate court, an appeal should be interposed against the second conformable sentence of nullity, it is his duty to make that appeal. Under no circumstances may he shift the obligation of appealing to the defender of the bond in the lower court on the plea that the cause originated in the court of the latter and consequently it is his duty to see the cause through to a successful finish. Such procedure is absolutely against the spirit and letter of the Code. A defender of the marriage bond is an integral part of each tribunal [98] and it is his duty to represent the Church in the defense of the matrimonial bond from the time a matrimonial cause enters the court with which he is connected until it leaves either by way of an appeal which he must make if it is to be interposed at all or by the lapse of the ten day term allowed for an appeal.

The *defensor* is not obliged to appeal from a second sentence confirming the first sentence of nullity of a marriage if he is satisfied with the character and weight of the proofs, evidence and testimony offered in support of the original complaint. The defender of the bond should not make it a practise to appeal under such circumstances merely as a matter of routine procedure. A man of sound practical judgment and well versed in the principles of canonical jurisprudence should be able to differentiate at once between a sentence that is based on substantial and convincing evidence and one that is only probably endowed with these qualities. While it is true

[98] Cf. can. 1586; *Lex Propria,* can. 4.

that the *defensor vinculi* is the defender and champion of the integrity of the marriage bond, it is also evident that the individual use of certain natural, inalienable rights is at stake. Certainly the exercise of such rights should not be restricted by nor depend on the vagrant whim of an ultra-scrupulous *defensor vinculi.* If the defender has interposed no appeal against the second sentence of nullity, the parties interested in the cause are permitted to contract new marriages after the ten days allowed for an appeal have elapsed and no appeal has been filed against the sentence.[99] This twofold conformable sentence of nullity that permits the interested parties to enter new unions if no appeal has been made, presupposes that the sentences were given on the same point contained in the original complaint. Two sentences cannot be said to be conformable if each declared the marriage null for different reasons or on different points.[100] Even if the *defensor vinculi* did not enter an appeal against the second sentence of nullity, either party may interpose an appeal within the prescribed time and if it is admitted, it will have a suspensive effect, thereby preventing the other party from contracting a new marriage until the cause is once more judged.[101] Payen [102] summarizes the question of appeals relative to matrimonial causes in excellent fashion and it was thought advisable to reproduce his analysis at this juncture.

[99] Can. 1987; cf. Noval, *De Processibus*, n. 869; Payen, *De Matrimonio*, III, n. 2715; Cappello, *De Sacramentis*, III, n. 887; Blat, *De Processibus*, n. 547; Chelodi, *Ius Matrimoniale*, n. 179; Vlaming, *Praelectiones*, II, n. 802.

[100] Cappello, "Quaestiones de Matrimonio: Utrum conformes ad normam can. 1903 et 1987 dicendae sint duae sententiae de nullitate matrimonii latae, si eiusdem nullitas declarata fuerit ex diverso capite."—*Periodica*, XX (1931), 20*-28*.

[101] Blat, *De Processibus*, n. 547. On the other hand, Payen (*De Matrimonio*, III, n. 2714) declares that an appeal from the second sentence of nullity, unless interposed by the *defensor vinculi*, would not *seem* to prevent the other party from contracting a new marriage. This opinion hardly seems tenable in view of the general legislation on appeals and the fact that causes of this type never become *res iudicatae.* Certainly if the party against whom the sentence of nullity was rendered had sufficient reason to appeal, his appeal would suspend the effect of the verdict of nullity and prevent the other party from entering a new union. This is merely theoretical, however, for if there were any cause for an appeal at all, the *defensor vinculi* would interpose the complaint.

[102] *De Matrimonio*, III, n. 2714, 2715.

## § 1. *De Iure Partium*

2714. *Appellatio ab alterutra sententia.*—In causis nullitatis, aut prima vel ulterior sententia fuit pro *valore* matrimonii, aut contra fuit pro ejus *nullitate.* Ab alterutra sententia pars quae gravatam se putat potest appellare.

(1) *A sententia pro valore.*—Pars quae petebat declarationem *nullitatis* et *victa est,* potest appellare: §1 semper a *prima* sententia; §2 semper a *secunda* sententia; §3 imo, "si nova argumenta praesto sint" (can. 1989), a *qualibet* sententia: nam sententiae in causis matrimonialibus numquam transeunt in rem iudicatam.

(2) *A sententia pro nullitate.*—Decreta matrimonii *nullitate,* pars *contra* quam pronuntiata est, potest appellare: §1 semper a *prima* sententia; §2 semper a *secunda* sententia, . . .[103] §3 etiam ab *ulteriore* sententia, si iam praesto sint nova argumenta, quae matrimonii valorem *certum* aut *vere probabilem* efficiant (can. 1989, 1903).

## §2. *Iura et Officia Defensoris Vinculi*

2715. *Tria distinguenda.*—Defensor vinculi *modo* nequit, *modo* debet ex officio, *modo* potest appellare.

(1) *Nequit.*—Appellare nequit:

§1. A PRIMA SENTENTIA quae fuerit pro *valore:* nam ejus non est matrimonii valorem impugnare.

§2. A TERTIA SENTENTIA, quae primam et secundam pro *nullitate* confirmaverit, et contra quam nullum novum argumentum aut novum documentum praesto sit (can. 1989, 1903).

(2) *Debet.*—Ex eo duplici principio proficiscendum est quod *defensor vinculi* tenetur, pro viribus, matrimonii valorem tueri, quodque, ante secundam sententiam quae matrimonii nullitatem confirmaverit, nullum ius conjugibus est novas nuptias contrahendi. Hoc posito, defensor vinculi *appellare debet:*

§1. SEMPER A PRIMA SENTENTIA quae fuerit pro nullitate;

§2. SEMPER A SECUNDA SENTENTIA, quae, *difformis* a prima sententia, pronuntiaverit esse nullum matrimonium, cujus valor fuerat in prima instantia decretus;

§3. QUANDOQUE A SECUNDA SENTENTIA, quae, *congruens* cum

[103] "Licet appellatio, nisi a defensore vinculi facta fuerit, *videatur* non obstare quominus ad novas nuptias transeat pars quae duplicem sententiam conformem nullitatis obtinuit (can. 1987)"; this particular opinion is disputed. Reference was made to it in the preceding footnote.

> prima, declaraverit matrimonii nullitatem, id est quando, pro sua conscientia, credit esse appellandum (can. 1987).
>
> Tantum est officium appellandi a *prima* sententia pro nullitate, ut defensor vinculi sit, auctoritate iudicis ad appellandum compellendus, si, intra legitimum tempus, neglexerit officium suum implere (can. 1986).
>
> (3) *Potest.*—Appellare potest:
>
> §1. A SECUNDA SENTENTIA, si prior fuerit pro nullitate et posterior pro valore;
>
> §2. RURSUS A SECUNDA SENTENTIA, si primam quae nullitatem declaravit, confirmaverit, salva quandoque, ut diximus, appellandi obligatione;
>
> §3. ETIAM A TERTIA SENTENIA, si, a tribus sententiis, duae fuerint pro nullitate et una pro valore;
>
> §4. DENIQUE A QUALIBET SENTENTIA, si, decreta matrimonii nullitate, ante mortem alterutrius conjugis, nova reperiantur argumenta vel documenta quae probent matrimonii valorem (can. 1989, 1903).
>
> Ideo enim sententiae in causis nullitatis, numquam transeunt in rem iudicatam, quia matrimonium est intrinsice, imo, si fuerit inter baptizatos consummatum, extrinsice indissolubile (can. 1118). Falsa igitur sententia fovet peccatum, sive veros conjuges separando, sive fictos inter se conjungendo.

The *defensor vinculi* or either party to the suit is required to observe all the prescriptions of the general law relative to appeals when interposing complaints of this kind. Appeals from the ordinary court of second instance are to be placed before the Rota and appeals from the second instance in the Rota are prosecuted before another and distinct *turnus* of the same tribunal, as stated in a previous article.

### B. *The Documentary Process*

Canon 1992 obliges the judge of the appellate tribunal to examine the "documentary case" brought before his court by the appeal of the *defensor vinculi* of the first instance. With the intervention of the *defensor vinculi* of the court of appeal, the judge is to proceed along the same lines and to subject the documents to the same thorough investigation that took place before the inferior judge; after which, he shall decide through the medium of a judicial sentence whether the sentence of nullity pronounced by the judge of the prior instance is to be confirmed or whether the case remains doubtful and as such, is to be submitted to a normal, solemn, matrimonial trial. In the event of the latter decision, the judge will return all the documents with his sentence to the lower court; if, however, the sentence of the appellate judge confirms the first sentence of nullity, the question arises relative to a further appeal on the part of the *defensor vincula,* if in his judgment, there still remains an element of doubt concerning the existence of the impediment or the grant of a dispensation therefrom. May the *defensor vinculi* appeal from this second conformable sentence of nullity rendered in a documentary process? Certainly he would not be obliged to appeal if his conscience was satisfied with the judgment rendered. Authors, with the exception of Payen,[104] are silent on the matter. Payen seems to provide for a further appeal for he declares that in the event that the first sentence of nullity is confirmed by the appellate court, the Ordinary of the lower tribunal shall inform the parties of their right and freedom to contract new marriages *after the lapse of the ten day term* allowed for the interposition of an appeal.[105] This expression indicates that the defender of the bond may appeal again. Moreover, when the duty of the *defensor vinculi* is taken into consideration, it would seem in fact that he would be obliged in conscience to appeal if any doubt remained as to the nullity of the marriage in question. He must use every legal weapon at his disposal to defend the integrity of the matrimonial bond and in this case, his only alternative is to appeal. Nor may the objection be raised that he has no right to appeal because the party against whom the verdict was rendered is deprived of his right in the matter, since the non-confirmation of the first sentence of nullity ends the process and results in the submission of the case to the formality of a solemn trial. But the aggrieved party is not deprived of his right entirely for the case

[104] *De Matrimonio,* III, n. 2725, §2.

[105] Payen, *De Matrimonio,* III, n. 2725, §2—"Munus Ordinarii.—Postquam certior factus fuerit de decreto iudicis secundae instantiae, loci Ordinarius *aliter et aliter* se gerit, prout sententia confirmata est an contra reformata. *Si confirmata fuerit,* monet partes ius eis esse, saltem decem diebus elapsis, novas nuptias contrahendi." Payen maintains that the documentary process is administrative in nature and consequently his terminology is somewhat confused.

is to be tried again by the solemn process and he may appeal from the sentence rendered therein if he does not think it just. The exercise of his right to appeal is not restricted wholly; it is merely deferred until a formal sentence is passed on the cause in question. There seems to be no substantial argument or reason against allowing the *defensor vinculi* to appeal from a second conformable sentence of nullity pronounced in a documentary process as long as he entertains a prudent doubt on the matter in question.

### §3. *The Determination of Costs*

The definitive sentence rendered by the judge of the appellate instance should contain a statement regarding the expenses of the trial,[106] in accordance with the prescriptions of the Code on the matter.[107] The Code declares in canon 1913, §1 that no appeal as such from a sentence condemning a party to pay the costs of a trial may be made separately or distinctly from the principal appeal. An appeal from a definitive sentence includes an appeal from the judgment of the court relative to the payment of costs. The Code makes no explicit declaration relative to the party who is to bear the expenses incurred in an appellate instance. Authors, however, generally agree that the appellant is to pay the costs of the appellate and the original instance if the sentence which he has appealed has been confirmed; the party against whose interests two conformable sentences have been pronounced is held liable for the expenses incurred in all instances or grades of judgment. If a sentence is appealed and reformed, the appellee is to bear the costs of both instances unless he appeals from the second sentence; in which case, the sentence rendered by the court of third instance will determine the party who is to pay the costs of all three instances. If the appealed sentence is only partially confirmed and in part reformed, the expenses of both instances will ordinarily be shared by the appellant and the appellee according to the discretion of the judge.

When there are several plaintiffs or several defendants engaged

[106] Can. 1873, §1, n. 4; *Reg. Serv. in iud. apud S. R. Rotae Trib.*, §184; cf. Roberti, *De Processibus*, II, n. 485.

[107] Can. 1908, 1914 ff.

in litigation before the court and but one of the parties appeals, the appeal benefits the other parties jointly united in the cause with the appellant if the litigious object is indivisible or the obligation binds *in solidum*. In this case, if the sentence appealed is confirmed, the appellant alone must stand for the costs of the appellate trial; he is also to pay his share of the expenses incurred in the first process.[108]

The determination by the judge of all court costs will be regulated by the provisions of the Code.[109] The rules herein contained apply likewise in all criminal causes except when the guilty party is deprived of his benefice and the fruits thereof by the sentence rendered on his case and consequently does not possess sufficient means to defray the court costs.[110] If the judge of the appellate court has confirmed the sentence of the lower tribunal, he shall order the notary to return the acts of the case to the original court where they will be preserved as the Code prescribes.[111] The same procedure should be followed if, in the event that the sentence of the appellate court reverses or reforms the verdict of the lower tribunal, no further appeal is made; likewise, if the cause once introduced into the court of appeal is abandoned,[112] abated by non-prosecution [113] or formally renounced.[114]

In transmitting the *acta*, the notary should use the necessary precautions to guarantee the safe delivery of the acts, documents, etc.[115] If an appeal has been interposed against the sentence rendered by

[108] Can. 1888; cf. Roberti, *De Processibus*, II, nn. 474, §1; 532; Wernz-Vidal, *De Processibus*, n. 608; Noval, *De Processibus*, n. 652.

[109] Can. 1908-1916; cf. *Reg. Serv. in iud. apud S. R. Rotae Trib.*, §184 ff.; §226 ff. Cf. Roberti, *De Processibus*, II, n. 532; Wernz-Vidal, *De Processibus*, n. 647.

[110] *Reg. Serv. in iud. apud S. R. Rotae Trib.*, §185, n. 5; S. R. Rota in c. *Limburgen*, 13 Feb. 1915—*AAS.*, VII (1915), 223; cf. also can. 1914-1916, Roberti, *De Processibus*, II, n. 541 and Noval, *De Processibus*, n. 694, for gratuitous services in this matter, permitted by the Code.

[111] Can. 1645, 379; cf. Wernz-Vidal, *De Processibus*, n. 613; Roberti, *De Processibus*, I, n. 190.

[112] Can. 1886.

[113] Can. 1736.

[114] Can. 1740.

[115] Can. 1719; cf. Roberti, *De Processibus*, I, n. 294; Wernz-Vidal, *De Processibus*, n. 389 and commentary on canon 1890 above.

the appellate court, the notary shall forward the *acta causae* to the court of third instance in accordance with the prescriptions of the Code [116] and the practise of the Sacred Roman Rota.[117]

[116] Can. 1890; 1719; 1871, §2; 1642-1644.

[117] *Lex Proprio*, can. 19, 25 ff.; *Reg. Serv. in iud. apud S. R. Rotae Trib.*, §1, §2, §13, §43 ff.

# BIBLIOGRAPHY

## Sources

*Acta Apostolicae Sedis* (*AAS.*), Romae, 1909—
*Acta Sanctae Sedis* (*ASS.*), 41 vols., Romae, 1865-1908.
*Bullarii Romani Continuatio Summorum Pontificum*, 19 vols., Prati, 1765-1883.
*Canones et Decreta Concilii Tridentini*, 19th ed., Taurini, 1913.
*Codex Juris Canonici Pii X Pontificis Maximi iussu digestus Benedicti Papae XV auctoritate promulgatur*, Romae, 1918.
*Codicis Juris Canonici Fontes*, 5 vols., Romae, 1923-1930.
*Collectanea Sacrae Congregationis de Propaganda Fide*, 2 vols., Romae, 1907.
*Collectio Lacensis, Acta et Decreta Sacrorum Conciliorum Recentiorum*, 7 vols., Friburgi Br., 1870-1890.
*Concilii Plenarii Baltimorensis III, Acta et Decreta*, Baltimorensi, 1884.
*Corpus Juris Canonici*, ed. Richter-Friedberg, 2 vols., Lipsiae, 1922.
*Corpus Juris Civilis: Institutiones*, recognovit P. Krueger; *Digesta*, recognovit Th. Mommsen, retractavit P. Krueger, vol. I, Berolini, 1928; *Codex Justinianus*, recognovit et retractavit P. Krueger, vol. II, Berolini, 1929; *Novellae*, recognovit R. Schoell, opus Schaelli morte interceptum absolvit G. Kroll, vol. III, Berolini, 1928.
*Corpus Scriptorum Ecclesiasticorum Latinorum*, 65 vols., Vindobonae, 1866.
Hardouin, *Conciliorum Collectio Regia Maxima*, 12 vols., Parisiis, 1715.
*Lex Propria S. Romanae Rotae et Signaturae Apostolicae*, Romae, 1908.
Mansi, *Sacrorum Conciliorum Nova et Amplissima Collectio*, 53 vols., Paris—Arnhem—Leipzig, 1901-1927.
Migne, *Patrologia Graeca*, 161 vols., Parisiis, 1858-1864.
Migne, *Patrologia Latina*, 221 vols., Parisiis, 1847-1870.
*Regulae Servandae in iudiciis apud S. Romanae Rotae Tribunal*, Romae, 1910.
*Regulae Servandae in iudiciis apud Supremum Signaturae Apostolicae Tribunal*, Romae, 1912.
*Sanctae Romanae Rotae Decisiones seu Sententiae*, 14 vols., Romae, 1912-1930.
*Theodosiani Libri XVI cum Constitutionibus Sirmondianis*, ed. Th. Mommsen, Berolini, 1905.
*Thesaurus Resolutionum Sacrae Congregationis Concilii*, 167 vols., Romae, 1718-1908.

## Works of Reference

Andre, M., *Droit Canon*, 2 vols., Paris, 1844.
Ayrinhac, Henry A., *General Legislation in the New Code of Canon Law*, New York, 1923.
Ayrinhac, Henry A., *Penal Legislation in the New Code of Canon Law*, New York, 1920.
Badii, C., *Institutiones Juris Canonici*, 2 vols., Florentiae, 121.
Baart, Peter A., *The Roman Court*, 4th ed., New York, 1899.
Baart, Peter A., *Legal Formulary*, 2d ed., New York, 1898.

(Bachofen), Charles Augustine, *A Commentary on the New Code of Canon Law*, 8 vols., St. Louis, 1918-1922.
Barbosa, Augustinus, *Collectanea in Jus Pontificium Universum*, Lugduni, 1646.
Bareille, Georges, *Code de Droit Canonique*, Arras, 1929.
Benedictus XIV, *De Synodo Diocesana*, 2 vols., Romae, 1806.
Berardi, Carolus, *Gratiani Canones Genuini ab Apocryphis Discreti, Corrupti ad emandationem Codicum Fidem Exacti, Difficiliores Commoda interpretatione illustrati*, 4 vols., Venetiis, 1777.
Blat, Albertus, *Commentarium Textus Codicis Canonici*, 6 vols., Romae, 1921-1927.
Bouix, D., *De Iudiciis Ecclesiasticis*, 3d ed., 2 vols., Parisiis, 1883.
Bouuaert, F. C.-Simenon, G., *Manuale Juris Canonici*, 2d ed., Bandae et Leodii, 1926.
Buckland, W. W., *A Text Book of Roman Law*, Cambridge, 1921.
Burke, Thomas J., *Competence in Ecclesiastical Tribunals*, Washington, 1922.
Cance, Adrien, *Le Code de Droit Canonique*, 3 vols., Paris, 1929.
Cappello, Felix M., *De Curia Romana*, 2 vols., Romae, 1911.
Cappello, Felix M., *Tractatus Canonico-Moralis de Sacramentis*, 3 vols., Romae, 1926-1928.
Cappello, Felix M., *Tractatus Canonico-Moralis de Censuris*, 2d ed., Taurini, 1925.
Cappello, Felix M., *Summa Juris Publici Ecclesiastici*, Romae, 1928.
*Catholic Encyclopedia, The*, 16 vols., New York, 1912.
Cavagnis, Felix, *Institutiones Juris Publici Ecclesiastici*, 3 vols., Romae, 1896.
Cerato, Prosdocimus, *Censurae Vigentes ipso facto a Codice Juris Canonici Excerptae*, Patavii, 1918.
Cerato, Prosdocimus, *Matrimonium a Codice Juris Canonici integra Desumptum*, 4th ed., Patavii, 1927.
Cerchiari, Emmanuel, *Capellani Papae et Apostolicae Sedis Auditores Causarum Sacri Palatii Apostolici seu Sacra Romana Rota*, 4 vols., Romae, 1921.
Chelodi, Joannis, *Jus de Personis*, 2d ed., Tridenti, 1927.
Chelodi, Joannis, *Jus Matrimoniale*, 3d ed., Tridenti, 1921.
Chelodi, Joannis, *Jus Poenale*, Tridenti, 1920.
Cicognani, Hamletus, *Commentarium ad Librum I Codicis*, 2 vols., Romae, 1925.
Cocchi, Guidus, *Commentarium in Codicem Juris Canonici ad usum Scholarum*, 8 vols., Taurinorum Augustae, 1925-1927.
Coronata, Matthaeus a, *Institutiones Juris Canonici*, 2 vols., Taurini, 1928.
Costa, Amilio, *Profilo Storico del Processo Civile Romano*, Romae, 1918.
D'Angelo, Sosio, *La Curia Diocesana*, 2 vols., Romae, 1922-1928.
De Angelis, Philippus, *Praelectiones Juris Canonici*, 3 vols., Romae, 1878.
De Becker, Julius, *De Sponsalibus et Matrimonio Praelectiones Canonicae*, 2d ed., Lovanii, 1903.
De Luca, Joannis, *Theatrum Veritatis et Justitiae*, 16 vols., Coloniae Agrippinae, 1706.
De Luca, Marianus, *Praelectiones Juris Canonici*, 3 vols., Romae, 1897.
De Meester, A., *Juris Canonici Compendium*, 3 vols., Brugis, 1921-1928.
De Smet, Aloysius, *Tractatus Theologico-Canonicus de Sponsalibus et Matrimonio*, 4th ed., Brugis, 1927.

Devoti, Joannis, *Jus Canonicum Universum*, 3 vols., Romae, 1837.
Droste, F.-Messmer, S., *Canonical Procedure in Disciplinary and Criminal Causes of Clerics*, New York, 1887.
Dugan, Henry F., *The Judiciary Department of the Diocesan Curia*, Washington, 1925.
Eichmann, Eduard, *Das Prozessrecht des Codex Juris Canonici*, Paderborn, 1921.
Esmein, A.-Génestal, R., *Le Mariage en Droit Canonique*, Paris, 1929.
Fagnanus, Prosperus, *Commentaria in V Libros Decretalium*, Venetiis, 1696.
Farrugia, Nicholaus, *De Matrimonio et Causis Matrimonialibus*, Romae, 1924.
Febronius, Justin, *De Statu Ecclesiae et Legitima Potestate Romani Pontificis*, Bullioni, 1764.
Ferraris, Lucius, *Bibliotheca Prompta Canonica*, 8 vols., Romae, 1885.
Ferreres, Joannis, *Institutiones Canonicae*, 2 vols., Barcinone, 1920.
Fourneret, Pierre, *Le Mariage Chrétien*, Paris, 1925.
Gasparri, Petrus, *Tractatus Canonicus de Matrimonio*, 3d ed., 2 vols., Parisiis, 1904.
Giraldi, Ubaldus, *Expositio Juris Pontificii*, 2 vols., Romae, 1829.
Girard, Paul F., *Manuel Élémentaire de Droit Romain*, 7th ed., Paris, 1924.
Gougnard, A., *Tractatus de Matrimonio*, 7th ed., Mechliniae, 1931.
Grandclaude, E., *Jus Canonicum juxta Ordinem Decretalium*, 3 vols., Parisiis, 1882.
Haring, Johann B., *Grundzüge des Katholischen Kirchenrechts*, 2 vols., Graz, 1924.
Heiner, F.-Wynen, A., *De Processu Criminali Ecclesiastico, Romae*, 1912.
Hinschius, Paul, *System des Katholischen Kirchenrechts*, 6 vols., Berlin, 1869-1895.
Hostiensis (Henricus de Segusia), *Summa Aurea*, Lugduni, 1568.
Hunter, W., *Introduction to Roman Law*, London, 1880.
Hyland, Francis, *Excommunication*, Washington, 1928.
Kay, Thomas, *Competence in Matrimonial Procedure*, Washington, 1929.
Kearney, Raymond, *The Principles of Delegation*, Washington, 1929.
Kenrick, Francis P., *The Primacy of the Apostolic See*, 5th ed., Baltimore, 1855.
Korr, Wilhelm, *Die Appellation an Die Sacra Romana Rota nach geltendem Kanonischem Recht*, Bonn-Köln, 1927.
Lanier, C. Henri, *Guide Pratique de la Procédure Matrimoniale en Droit Canonique*, Paris, 1927.
Leage, R. W., *Roman Private Law*, London, 1924.
Lega, Michael, *De Iudiciis Ecclesiasticis*, 2 vols., Romae, 1896.
Leitner, Martinus, *De Curia Romana*, Romae, 1909.
Leurenius, Petrus, *Forum Ecclesiasticum de Universo Iure Canonico*, 5 vols., Venetiis, 1729.
Lijdsman, Bernardus, *Introductio in Jus Canonicum*, 2 vols., Hilversum in Hollandia, 1924.
Maroto, Philippus, *Institutiones Juris Canonici*, 2 vols., Romae, 1921.
Martin, Michael, *The Roman Curia*, New York, 1913.
Michiels, Gommarus, *Normae Generales Juris Canonici*, 2 vols., Lublin, 1929.
Mommsen, T., *Le Droit Public Romain*, 8 vols., Paris, 1889-1895.
Mommsen, T., *Le Droit Pénal Romain*, 3 vols., Paris, 1907.
Monin, Arturus, *De Curia Romana*, Lovanii, 1912.

Mothon, Joseph, *Institutiones Canoniques,* 3 vols., Paris, 1922.
Muniz, T., *Procedimientos Eclesiásticos,* 3 vols., Seville, 1930.
Noval, Josephus, *De Judiciis,* Romae, 1920.
Ojetti, B., *De Romana Curia,* Romae, 1910.
Ojetti, B., *Commentarium in Codicem Juris Canonici,* 2 vols., Romae, 1928.
O'Neill, William H., *Papal Rescripts of Favor,* Washington, 1930.
Ottaviani, A., *Institutiones Juris Publici Ecclesiastici,* 2 vols., Romae, 1925.
Pallotini, S., *Collectio Omnium Conclusionum et Resolutionum Sacrae Congregationis Sacri Concilii Tridentini*—1564-1860, 17 vols., Romae, 1868-1893.
Payen, G., *De Matrimonio in Missionibus,* 3 vols., Zi-ka-wei, 1928-1929.
Perathoner, Anton, *Das Kirchliche Gesetzbuch,* 3d ed., Brixen, 1923.
Péries, G., *La Procédure Canonique Moderne dans les Causes Disciplinaires et Criminelles,* Paris, 1898.
Péries, G., *Code de Procédure Canonique dans les Causes Matrimoniales,* Paris, 1894.
Pierantonelli, Pacificus, *Ordo Judiciarius in praxim Traductus,* Romae, 1904.
Pierantonelli, Pacificus, *Praxis Fori Ecclesiastici ad Praesentem Ecclesiae Conditionem Accommodata,* Romae, 1883.
Pirhing, Enricus, *Jus Canonicum in V Libros Decretalium,* 4 vols., Dilingae, 1674-1678.
Prümmer, Dominicus, *Manuale Juris Canonici,* 3d ed., Friburgi Brisgoviae, 1922.
Radin, Max, *Handbook of Roman Law,* St. Paul, 1927.
Reiffenstuel, Anacletus, *Jus Canonicum Universum,* 4 vols., Venetiis, 1735.
Rivet, L., *Institutiones Juris Ecclesiastici Privati,* 2 vols., Romae, 1914.
Roberti, Franciscus, *De Processibus,* 2 vols., Romae, 1926.
Roby, Henry J., *Roman Private Law,* 2 vols., Cambridge, 1902.
Santi, F.-Leitner, M., *Praelectiones Juris Canonici,* 5 vols., Romae, 1904.
Scaccia, Sigismundus, *Tractatus de Appellationibus, Coloniae,* 1717.
Schmalzgrueber, F., *Jus Ecclesiasticum Universum,* 12 vols., Romae, 1845.
Schneider, Egon, *Die Römische Rota nach geltendem Recht auf geschichtlicher Grundlage,* Paderborn, 1914.
Sebastianelli, G., *Praelectiones Juris Canonici,* 2 vols., Romae, 1906.
Sherman, C. P., *Roman Law in the Modern World,* 3 vols., New York, 1924.
Sipos, Stephenus, *Enchiridion Juris Canonici,* Pecs, 1926.
Smith, S. B., *Elements of Ecclesiastical Law,* 2 vols., New York, 1883.
Smith, S. B., *New Procedure in Disciplinary and Criminal Causes of Ecclesiastics in the United States,* New York, 1898.
Sole, Jacobus, *De Delictis et Poenis,* Romae, 1920.
Sohm, R.-Ledie, J., *Institutes of Roman Law,* Oxford, 1892.
Strachan-Davidson, J. L., *Problems of the Roman Criminal Law,* 2 vols., Oxford, 1912.
Tanquerey, A., *Synopsis Theologiae Dogmaticae,* 19 ed., Romae, 1922.
Thomassinus, L., *Vetus et Nova Ecclesiae Disciplina,* 3 vols., Parisiis, 1688.
Van Espen, Z. B., *Jus Ecclesiasticum Universum,* 5 vols., Venetiis, 1769.
Vecchiotti, Septimus, *Institutiones Canonicae,* 3 vols., Taurinorum Augustae, 1886.
Vermeersch, A.-Creusen, J., *Epitome Juris Canonici,* 3 vols., Romae, 1928.
Vidal, P., *Institutiones Juris Civilis Romani,* Prati, 1915.

Vlaming, Th. M., *Praelectiones Juris Matrimonii ad Normam Codicis Juris Canonici,* 3d ed., 2 vols., Bossum in Hollandia, 1919-1921.
Wernz, Franciscus, *Jus Decretalium,* 6 vols., Romae, 1906-1913.
Wernz, F.-Vidal, P., *Jus Canonicum,* 3 vols., Romae, 1927-1928.
Woywod, Stanislaus, *A Practical Commentary on the New Code of Canon Law,* 2 vols., New York, 1925.
Zaccaria, F. A., *Anti-Febronius,* 6 vols., Lovanii, 1829.

PERIODICALS

*Analecta Ecclesiastica,* Romae, 1893-1911.
*Analecta Juris Pontificii,* Romae, 1855-1868; Parisiis, 1869-1890.
*Apollinaris, Commentarium Juridico-Canonicum,* Romae, 1928—
*Archiv für Katholisches Kirchenrecht,* Mainz, 1857—
*Dublin Review, The,* London, 1836—
*Ephemerides Theologicae Lovanienses,* Lovanii, 1924—
*Irish Ecclesiastical Record, The,* Dublin, 1864—
*Jus Pontificium,* Romae, 1921—
*Monitore Ecclesiastico,* Il, Romae, 1888—
*Periodica de Re Morali, Canonica, Liturgica,* Romae et Brugis, 1912—
*Theologisch-praktische Quartalschrift,* Linz, 1832—

UNIVERSITAS CATHOLICA AMERICAE

WASHINGTONII, D. C.

FACULTAS JURIS CANONICI

1932

No. 79

DEUS LUX MEA

---

# TITULI

QUOS

AD DOCTORATUS GRADUM

IN

# JURE CANONICO

APUD UNIVERSITATEM CATHOLICAM AMERICAE

CONSEQUENDUM

PUBLICE PROPUGNABIT

**THOMAS ARTHURUS CONNOLLY**

SACERDOS ARCHIDIOECESIS

SANCTI FRANCISCI

JURIS CANONICI LICENTIATUS

HORA XI A.M., DIE XIX MAII MCMXXXII

# TITULI

## IN IURE CANONICO

| | | |
|---|---|---|
| I. | De Dissertatione. | |
| II. | De Historia Iuris Canonici. | |
| III. | Canones 1-7 | De Ambitu Codicis. |
| IV. | Canones 8-24 | De Legibus Ecclesiasticis. |
| V. | Canones 25-30 | De Consuetudine. |
| VI. | Canones 31-35 | De Temporis Supputatione. |
| VII. | Canones 36-62 | De Rescriptis. |
| VIII. | Canones 63-79 | De Privilegiis. |
| IX. | Canones 80-86 | De Dispensationibus. |
| X. | Cannoes 87-107 | Generales Notiones de Personis. |
| XI. | Canones 111-117 | De Clericorum Adscriptione Alicui Dioecesi. |
| XII. | Canones 118-123 | De Iuribus et Privilegiis Clericorum |
| XIII. | Canones 124-144 | De Obligationibus Clericorum. |
| XIV. | Canones 145-195 | De Officiis Ecclesiasticis. |
| XV. | Canones 196-210 | De Potestate Ordinaria et Delegata. |
| XVI. | Canones 487-498 | De Notione Religionis, et de Erectione et Suppressione Religionis, Provinciae, Domus. |
| XVII. | Canones 499-537 | De Religionum Regimine. |
| XVIII. | Canones 538-586 | De Admissione in Religionem. |
| XIX. | Canones 673-681 | De Societatibus sive Virorum sive Mulierum in Communi Viventium sine Votis. |
| XX. | Canones 1012-1018 | De Matrimonio in Genere. |
| XXI. | Canones 1019-1034 | De Iis quae Matrimonii Celebrationi Praemitti debent. |
| XXII. | Canones 1035-1057 | De Impedimentis in Genere. |
| XXIII. | Canones 1058-1066 | De Impedimentis Impedientibus. |
| XXIV. | Canones 1067-1080 | De Impedimentis Dirimentibus. |
| XXV. | Canones 1081-1093 | De Consensu Matrimoniali. |
| XXVI. | Canones 1552-1568 | De Notione Iudicii et de Foro Competenti. |
| XXVII. | Canones 1569-1607 | De Variis Tribunalium Gradibus et Speciebus. |
| XXVIII. | Canones 1608-1645 | De Disciplina in Tribunalibus Servanda. |
| XXIX. | Canones 1646-1666 | De Partibus in Causa. |
| XXX. | Canones 1667-1705 | De Actionibus et Exceptionibus. |
| XXXI. | Canones 1706-1725 | De Causae Introductione. |
| XXXII. | Canones 1726-1746 | De Litis Contestatione, de Litis Instantia, et de Interrogationibus Partibus in Iudicio Faciendis. |
| XXXIII. | Canones 1747-1836 | De Probationibus. |
| XXXIV. | Canones 1837-1857 | De Causis Incidentibus. |

| | | |
|---|---|---|
| XXXV. | Canones 1858-1877 | De Processus Publicatione, de Conclusione in Causa, de Causae Discussione, et de Sententia. |
| XXXVI. | Canones 1879-1891 | De Appellatione. |
| XXXVII. | Canones 1902-1907 | De Re Iudicata et de Restitutione in Integrum. |
| XXXVIII. | Canones 1960-1992 | De Causis Matrimonialibus. |
| XXXIX. | Canones 2195-2198 | De Natura Delicti eiusque Divisione. |
| XL. | Canones 2199-2211 | De Imputabilitate Delicti, de Causis illam Aggravantibus vel Minuentibus, et de Iuridicis Delicti Effectibus. |
| XLI. | Canones 2212-2213 | De Conatu Delicti. |
| XLII. | Canones 2214-2240 | De Poenis in Genere. |
| XLIII. | Canones 2241-2285 | De Poenis Medicinalibus seu de Censuris. |
| XLIV. | Canones 2286-2305 | De Poenis Vindicativis. |
| XLV. | Canones 2306-2313 | De Remediis Poenalibus et Poenitentiis. |

ROMAN LAW

XLVI. The Periods of Roman Law.
XLVII. The Sources of Roman Law.
XLVIII. Personality.
XLIX. Slavery.
L. Citizenship.
LI. Patria Potestas.
LII. Personae in Manu.
LIII. Tutela et Cura.
LIV. Personae in Mancipio.
LV. Ownership.

AMERICAN CHURCH CIVIL LAW

LVI. Tax Exemption.
LVII. Trusts.
LVIII. Marriage.
LIX. Christian Burial.
LX. Wills.

Vidit Facultas:

VALENTINUS T. SCHAAF, O.F.M., J.C.D., Vice-Decanus.
LUDOVICUS H. MOTRY, S.T.D., J.C.D., a Secretis.
FRANCISCUS J. LARDONE, S.T.D., J.U.D.

Vidit Rector Magnificus Universitatis:

JACOBUS HUGO RYAN, S.T.D., PH.D., LL.D., LITT.D.

## BIOGRAPHICAL SKETCH

THOMAS ARTHUR CONNOLLY was born on October 5, 1899, in San Francisco. He received his elementary education in the schools of that city and in September, 1915, he entered Saint Patrick's Seminary, Menlo Park, California. He was ordained to the Holy Priesthood on June 11, 1926, and was engaged in parochial work during the subsequent four years at Sausalito, California. In September of 1930, he enrolled in the School of Canon Law at the Catholic University of America, in Washington, D. C., where in 1931 he received the degree of Licentiate of Canon Law.

# CANON LAW STUDIES

1. Freriks, Rev. Celestine A., C.PP.S., J.C.D., Religious Congregations in Their External Relations, 121 pp., 1916.
2. Galliher, Rev. Daniel M., O.P., J.C.D., Canonical Elections, 117 pp., 1917.
3. Borkowski, Rev. Aurelius L., O.F.M., De Confraternitatibus Ecclesiasticis, 136 pp., 1918.
4. Castillo, Rev. Cayo, J.C.D., Disertacion Historico-canonica sobre la Potestad del Cabildo en Sede Vacante o Impedida del Vicario Capitular, 99 pp., 1919 (1918).
5. Kubelbeck, Rev. William J., S.T.B., J.C.D., The Sacred Penitentiaria and Its Relations to Faculties of Ordinaries and Priests, 129 pp., 1918.
6. Petrovits, Rev. Joseph J. C., S.T.D., J.C.D., The New Church Law on Matrimony, X-461 pp., 1919.
7. Hickey, Rev. John J., S.T.B., J.C.D., Irregularities and Simple Impediments in the New Code of Canon Law, 100 pp., 1920.
8. Klekotka, Rev. Peter J., S.T.B., J.C.D., Diocesan Consultors, 179 pp., 1920.
9. Wannenmacher, Rev. Francis, J.C.D., The Evidence in Ecclesiastical Procedure Affecting the Marriage Bond, 1920. (Not Printed.)
10. Golden, Rev. Henry Francis, J.C.D., Parochial Benefices in the New Code, IV-119 pp., 1921. (Printed 1925.)
11. Koudelka, Rev. Charles J., J.C.D., Pastors, Their Rights and Duties According to the New Code of Canon Law, 211 pp., 1921.
12. Melo, Rev. Antonius, O.F.M., J.C.D., De Exemptione Regularium, X-188 pp., 1921.
13. Schaaf, Rev. Valentine Theodore, O.F.M., S.T.B., J.C.D., The Cloister, X-180 pp., 1921.
14. Burke, Rev. Thomas Joseph, S.T.B., J.C.D., Competence in Ecclesiastical Tribunals, IV-117 pp., 1922.
15. Leech, Rev. George Leo, J.C.D., A Comparative Study of the Constitution "Apostolicae Sedis" and the "Codex Juris Canonici," 179 pp., 1922.
16. Motry, Rev. Hubert Louis, S.T.D., J.C.D., Diocesan Faculties according to the Code of Canon Law, II-167 pp., 1922.
17. Murphy, Rev. George Lawrence, J.C.D., Delinquencies and Penalties in the Administration and the Reception of the Sacraments, IV-121 pp., 1923.
18. O'Reilly, Rev. John Anthony, S.T.B., J.C.D., Ecclesiastical Sepulture in the New Code of Canon Law, II-129 pp., 1923.
19. Michalicka, Rev. Wenceslas Cyrill, O.S.B., J.C.D., Judicial Procedure in Dismissal of Clerical Exempt Religious, 107 pp., 1923.
20. Dargin, Rev. Edward Vincent, S.T.B., J.C.D., Reserved Cases According to the Code of Canon Law, IV-103 pp., 1924.
21. Godfrey, Rev. John A., S.T.B., J.C.D., The Right of Patronage According to the Code of Canon Law, 153 pp., 1924.
22. Hagedorn, Rev. Francis Edward, J.C.D., General Legislation on Indulgences, II-154 pp., 1924.

23. King, Rev. James Ignatius, J.C.D., The Administration of the Sacraments to Dying Non-Catholics, V-141 pp., 1924.
24. Winslow, Rev. Francis Joseph, A.F.M., J.C.D., Vicars and Prefects Apostolic, IV-149 pp., 1924.
25. Correa, Rev. Jose Servelion, S.T.L., J.C.D., La Potestad Legislativa de la Iglesia Católica, IV-127 pp., 1925.
26. Dugan, Rev. Henry Francis, M.A., J.C.D., The Judiciary Department of the Diocesan Curia, 87 pp., 1925.
27. Keller, Rev. Charles Frederick, S.T.B., J.C.D., Mass Stipends, 167 pp., 1925.
28. Paschang, Rev. John Linus, J.C.D., The Sacramentals According to the Code of Canon Law, 129 pp., 1925.
29. Piontek, Rev. Cyrillus, O.F.M., S.T.B., J.C.D., De Indulto Exclaustrationis necnon Saecularizationis, XIII-289 pp., 1925.
30. Kearney, Rev. Richard Joseph, S.T.B., J.C.D., Sponsors at Baptism According to the Code of Canon Law, IV-127 pp., 1925.
31. Bartlett, Rev. Chester Joseph, A.M., LL.B., J.C.D., The Tenure of Parochial Property in the United States of America, V-108 pp., 1926.
32. Kilker, Rev. Adrian Jerome, J.C.D., Extreme Unction, V-425 pp., 1926.
33. McCormick, Rev. Robert Emmett, J.C.D., Confessors of Religious, VIII-266 pp., 1926.
34. Miller, Rev. Newton Thomas, J.C.D., Founded Masses According to the Code of Canon Law, VII-93 pp., 1926.
35. Roelker, Rev. Edward G., S.T.D., J.C.D., Principles of Privilege According to the Code of Canon Law, XI-166 pp., 1926.
36. Bakalarczyk, Rev. Richardus, M.I.C., J.U.D., De Novitiatu, VIII-208 pp., 1927.
37. Pizzuti, Rev. Lawrence, O.F.M., J.U.L., De Parochis Religiosis, 1927. (Not Printed.)
38. Bliley, Rev. Nicholas Martin, O.S.B., J.C.D., Altars According to the Code of Canon Law, XIX-132 pp., 1927.
39. Brown, Brendan Francis, A.B., LL.M., J.U.D., The Canonical Juristic Personality with Special Reference to its Status in the United States of America, V-212 pp., 1927.
40. Cavanaugh, Rev. William Thomas. C.P., J.U.D., The Reservation of the Blessed Sacrament, VIII-101 pp., 1927.
41. Doheny, Rev. William J., C.S.C., A.B., J.U.D., Church Property: Modes of Acquisition, X-118 pp., 1927.
42. Feldhaus, Rev. Aloysius H., C.PP.S., J.C.D., Oratories, IX-141 pp., 1927.
43. Kelly, Rev. James Patrick, A.B., J.C.D., The Jurisdiction of the Simple Confessor, X-208 pp., 1927.
44. Neuberger, Rev. Nicholas J., J.C.D., Canon 6 or the Relation of the Codex Juris Canonici to the Preceding Legislation, V-95 pp., 1927.
45. O'Keeffe, Rev. Gerald Michael, J.C.D., Matrimonial Dispensations, Powers of Bishops, Priests, and Confessors, VIII-232 pp., 1927.
46. Quigley, Rev. Joseph, A.M., A.B., J.C.D., Condemned Societies, 139 pp., 1927.
47. Zaplotnik, Rev. Ioannes Leo, J.C.D., De Vicariis Foraneis, X-142 pp., 1927.

48. DUSKIE, REV. JOHN ALOYSIUS, A.B., J.C.D., The Canonical Status of the Orientals in the United States, VIII-196 pp., 1928.
49. HYLAND, REV. FRANCIS EDWARD, J.C.D., Excommunication, Its Nature, Historical Development and Effects, VIII-181 pp., 1928.
50. REINMANN, REV. GERALD JOSEPH, O.M.C., J.C.D., The Third Order Secular of Saint Francis, 201 pp., 1928.
51. SCHENK, REV. FRANCIS J., J.C.D., The Matrimonial Impediments of Mixed Religion and Disparity of Cult, XVI-318 pp., 1929.
52. COADY, REV. JOHN JOSEPH, S.T.D., J.U.D., A.M., The Appointment of Pastors, VIII-150 pp., 1929.
53. KAY, REV. THOMAS HENRY, J.C.D., Competence in Matrimonial Procedure, VIII-164 pp., 1929.
54. TURNER, REV. SIDNEY JOSEPH, C.P., J.U.D., The Vow of Poverty, XLIX-217 pp., 1929.
55. KEARNEY, REV. RAYMOND A., A.B., S.T.D., J.C.D., The Principles of Delegation, VII-149 pp., 1929.
56. CONRAN, REV. EDWARD JAMES, A.B., J.C.D., The Interdict, V-163 pp., 1930.
57. O'NEIL, REV. WILLIAM H., J.C.D., Papal Rescripts of Favor, VII-218 pp.,
58. BASTNAGEL, REV. CLEMENT VINCENT, J.U.D., The Appointment of Parochial Adjutants and Assistants, XV-257 pp., 1930.
59. FERRY, REV. WILLIAM A., A.B., J.C.D., Stole Fees, X-107 pp., 1930.
60. COSTELLO, REV. JOHN MICHAEL, A.B., J.C.D., Domicile and Quasi-Domicile, VII-201 pp., 1930.
61. KREMER, REV. MICHAEL NICHOLAS, A.B., S.T.B., J.C.D., Church Support in the United States, VI-136 pp., 1930.
62. ANGULO, REV. LUIS, C.M., J.C.D., Legislación de la Iglesia sobre la intención en la aplicación de la Santa Misa, VII-104 pp., 1931.
63. FREY, REV. WOLFGANG NORBERT, O.S.B., A.B., J.C.D., The Act of Religious Profession, VIII-174 pp., 1931.
64. ROBERTS, REV. JAMES BRENDAN, A.B., J.C.D., The Banns of Marriage, XIV-140 pp., 1931.
65. RYDER, REV. RAYMOND ALOYSIUS, A.B., J.C.D., Simony, IX-151 pp., 1931.
66. CAMPAGNA, REV. ANGELO, PH.D., J.U.D., Il Vicario Generale del Vescovo, VII-205 pp., 1931.
67. COX, REV. JOSEPH GODFREY, A.B., J.C.D., The Administration of Seminaries, VI-124 pp., 1931.
68. GREGORY, REV. DONALD J., J.U.D., The Pauline Privilege, XV-165 pp., 1931.
60. DONOHUE, REV. JOHN F., J.C.D., The Impediment of Crime, VIII-110 pp., 1931.
70. DOOLEY, REV. EUGENE A., O.M.I., J.C.D., Church Law on Sacred Relics, IX-143 pp., 1931.
71. ORTH, REV. CLEMENT RAYMOND, O.M.C., J.C.D., The Approbation of Religious Institutes, 171 pp., 1931.
72. PERNICONE, REV. JOSEPH M., A.B., J.C.D., The Ecclesiastical Prohibition of Books, XII-267 pp., 1932.
73. CLINTON, REV. CONNELL, A.B., J.C.L., The Paschal Precept, 1932.
74. DONNELLY, REV. FRANCIS B., A.M., S.T.L., J.C.L., The Diocesan Synod, 1932

75. TORRENTE, REV. CAMILO, C.M.F., J.C.L., Las Processiones Sagradas, 1932.
76. MURPHY, REV. EDWIN J., C.PP.S., J.C.L., Suspension Ex Informata Conscientia, 1932.
77. MACKENZIE, REV. ERIC F., A.M., S.T.L., J.C.L., The Delict of Heresy in its Commission, Penalization, Absolution, 1932.
78. LYONS, REV. AVITUS E., S.T.B., J.C.L., The Collegiate Tribunal of First Instance, 1932.
79. CONNOLLY, REV. THOMAS A., J.C.L., Appeals, 1932.
80. SANGMEISTER, REV. JOSEPH V., A.B., J.C.L., Force and Fear as Precluding Matrimonial Consent, 1932.
81. JAEGER, REV. LEO A., A.B., J.C.L., The Administration of Vacant and Quasi-Vacant Episcopal Sees in the United States, 1932.
82. RIMLINGER, REV. HERBERT T., J.C.L., Error Invalidating Matrimonial Consent, 1932.
83. BARRETT, REV. JOHN D. M., S.S., J.C.L., Comparative Study of the Third Plenary Council and the Code, 1932.

www.ingramcontent.com/pod-product-compliance
Lightning Source LLC
LaVergne TN
LVHW050243080826
844660LV00012B/590

* 9 7 8 0 8 1 3 2 2 2 6 8 4 *